The Indy 500

PRAISE FOR THE INDY 500
A Year-Long Quest to Win the Greatest Spectacle in Racing

"Every year a select group of race drivers focus on a single day. It has been true over a hundred years. They and their teams go to the crucible of speed, the Indianapolis 500 Mile Race. They bet their skills and that of each team member in search of the pinnacle of motor racing. It is a long and dangerous road, and *The Indy 500: A Year-Long Quest to Win the Greatest Spectacle in Racing* tells the story well. A great work about a singular event, the largest single day sporting event in the world—the Indianapolis 500 Mile Race."

~ **Paul Page,** award-winning journalist and broadcaster, long-time "Voice of the 500," and member of both the Indianapolis Motor Speedway and Indiana Broadcaster Halls of Fame

"As someone who's truly fallen in love with the Month of May, *The Indy 500: A Year-Long Quest to Win the Greatest Spectacle in Racing* captures exactly what makes this event so special. Take a journey through the preparation, the drama, and the heart of the Indianapolis 500—showing why it is, and will always be, The Greatest Spectacle in Racing."

~ **Georgia Henneberry**, NBC pitlane reporter and host of Roku Channel's *Recharge*

"The Indianapolis 500 is a month-long annual tradition for my family. *The Indy 500: A Year-Long Quest to Win the Greatest Spectacle in Racing* encapsulates what it is like to be there and gives a behind-the-scenes look at the build-up to, and running of, the largest single-day sporting event in the world. From first-timers to fifty-year ticket holders, readers get an inside view of the drama and excitement that keeps us coming back yearly for more."

~ **Chad Ballagh**, race fan and Indianapolis Motor Speedway season ticket holder

"As the son of a race car driver who competed with racers named Unser, Andretti, and Johncock, the Indy 500 was an annual holiday for our family. *The Indy 500: A Year-Long Quest to Win the Greatest Spectacle in Racing* captures the energy and passion of the greatest spectacle in racing. The author takes readers behind the pit wall, into the owner's box, nestled into the driver's seat, and delivers one an all-access tour of the experience that is the Indianapolis 500. A must read for race fans and casual observers alike!"

~ **Clint Daly**, sportswriter & host of the *Daly Dose Sports Podcast*

"As a child growing up in the 1970s around the drivers and teams of Formula 1, I was always intrigued by the mystery and glamor of American oval racing and the Indy 500 as one of the 'Big Three' races every driver wanted to win. In 2005 I finally attended the Indy 500 as an F1 writer and was immersed into the Indianapolis spirit, the unique sea of 400,000 fans alone worth the trip. My lasting impression was summed up in one word: History! There is no other race in the world like it—a Parthenon to racing. *The Indy 500: A Year-Long Quest to Win the Greatest Spectacle in Racing* is an inspirational book about 'The Race' and its considerable challenge to cars and drivers."

~ **Nicholas Frankl**, three-time Olympian, entrepreneur, and motorsports pundit

"Racing is life. Anything before or after is just waiting."

Steve McQueen, in the movie, *Le Mans*

THE INDY 500

A YEAR-LONG QUEST TO WIN THE GREATEST SPECTACLE IN RACING

RAY HARTJEN

NEW YORK

LONDON • NASHVILLE • MELBOURNE • VANCOUVER

THE INDY 500

A Year-Long Quest to Win the Greatest Spectacle in Racing

© 2025 Ray Hartjen

All rights reserved. No portion of this book may be reproduced, stored in a retrieval system, or transmitted in any form or by any means—electronic, mechanical, photocopy, recording, scanning, or other—except for brief quotations in critical reviews or articles, without the prior written permission of the publisher.

Published in New York, New York, by Morgan James Publishing. Morgan James is a trademark of Morgan James, LLC. www.MorganJamesPublishing.com

Proudly distributed by Publishers Group West®

Morgan James BOGO™

A **FREE** ebook edition is available for you or a friend with the purchase of this print book.

CLEARLY SIGN YOUR NAME ABOVE

Instructions to claim your free ebook edition:
1. Visit MorganJamesBOGO.com
2. Sign your name CLEARLY in the space above
3. Complete the form and submit a photo of this entire page
4. You or your friend can download the ebook to your preferred device

ISBN 9781636985817 paperback
ISBN 9781636985824 ebook
Library of Congress Control Number: 2024947345

Cover Design by:
Ale Urquide

Interior Design by:
Chris Treccani
www.3dogcreative.net

Morgan James is a proud partner of Habitat for Humanity Peninsula and Greater Williamsburg. Partners in building since 2006.

Get involved today! Visit: www.morgan-james-publishing.com/giving-back

CONTENTS

Acknowledgments — xi
Preface — xiii

Sunday, May 28, 2023 | The 107th Indianapolis 500 — 1
Monday, May 29, 2023 | Victory Gala — 8
Tuesday, May 30, 2023 | The Indianapolis Motor Speedway — 11
Wednesday, May 31, 2023 | The Captain — 18
Wednesday, June 7, 2023 | Silly Season — 22
Friday, August 11, 2023 | Alex Palou Stirs Silly Season Yet Again — 25
Tuesday, August 22, 2023 | Foyt & Penske Form Technical Alliance — 29
Wednesday, August 23, 2023 | Ericsson Leaves Ganassi for Andretti — 34
Tuesday, September 5, 2023 | Meyer Shank Expands IndyCar Program — 40
Thursday, September 7, 2023 | Arrow McLaren Signs Malukas to Finalize Driver Lineup — 43
Monday, September 18, 2023 | Ganassi Confirms 2024 Driver Lineup — 47
Friday, September 29, 2023 | McLaren Racing Sues Palou — 53
Wednesday, October 11, 2023 | Rookie Orientation Program — 55
Thursday, October 12, 2023 | Rookie Orientation Program & Hybrid Assist Testing — 58
Wednesday, October 25, 2023 | Rasmussen Joins Ed Carpenter Racing — 62
Thursday, November 2, 2023 | Grosjean Joins Canapino at Juncos Hollinger Racing — 65
Monday, November 27, 2023 | Palou Admits Breach of Contract — 68
Thursday, December 7, 2023 | Hybrid Power Unit Delayed—Yet Again — 70
Friday, December 15, 2023 | The Borg-Warner Trophy Adds a New Face — 73

Tuesday, January 9, 2024 | Foyt Finalizes Lineup by Confirming Ferrucci	76
Monday, January 22, 2024 | Preseason Testing at Homestead	80
Tuesday, January 23, 2024 | An Entry to End the Andretti Curse?	84
Thursday, February 1, 2024 | Dreyer & Reinbold Confirm Hunter-Reay & Daly	89
Thursday, February 15, 2024 | Sato to Return with Rahal Letterman Lanigan	92
Tuesday, February 26, 2024 | New Suspension Uprights Mandated	95
March 5, 2024 | Coyne Rounds Out the Season's Field	98
March 10, 2024 | Newgarden, Team Penske Dominate at St. Pete	100
Tuesday, April 9, 2024 | Coyne Adds Katherine Legge to Push Entries to Thirty-Four	104
Wednesday, April 10, 2024 | Open Testing at IMS	109
Sunday, April 21, 2024 | Dixie Triumphs on the Streets of Long Beach	116
Friday, April 26, 2024 | Scandal Blazes Through the IndyCar Paddock	119
Sunday, April 28, 2024 | McLaughlin Rebounds with a Decisive Victory	123
Monday, April 29, 2024 | Arrow McLaren Moves on from Malukas	125
Monday, May 6, 2024 | Pourchaire Completes IndyCar Oval Test	128
Tuesday, May 7, 2024 | Penske Suspends Four	130
Saturday, May 11, 2024 | Palou Roars into May	132
Monday, May 13, 2024 | Silence before the Storm	134
Tuesday, May 14, 2024 | Déjà vu All Over Again	140
Wednesday, May 15, 2024 | Rain, Rain, Go Away	145
Thursday, May 16, 2024 | The Weather Cooperates . . . Mostly	152
Friday, May 17, 2024 | Fast Friday	159
Saturday, May 18, 2024 | Go Fast Day	171
Sunday, May 19, 2024 | Dreams and Despair	193
Monday, May 20, 2024 | Race Setups	207
Tuesday, May 21, 2024 | Got Milk?	214
Friday, May 24, 2024 | Carb Day	216
Saturday, May 25, 2024 | Eyes on the Sky	228
Sunday, May 26, 2024 | Race Day	231
Monday, May 27, 2024 | Victory Celebration	263
Acknowledgments	*267*
About the Author	*269*

ACKNOWLEDGMENTS

To my loving and supportive wife, Lori; our two wonderful children, Olivia and Raymond; my extended family; and my network of friends who somehow, for whatever reason, get me.

And a very special acknowledgment to the 801 men and women who have raced in the Indianapolis 500, the legions of racing team members who supported them, and the generations of fans who have made their annual treks to the Indianapolis Motor Speedway, making the Indianapolis 500 "The Greatest Spectacle in Racing."

PREFACE

As a child, I was a sports fan. It didn't matter the season or the sport. They all fascinated me.

Every morning, I pored over the sports section of the daily newspaper, reading every article and every box score. Not just the articles and box scores of my favorite teams, mind you. Rather, every sport, every team, every article, and every box score.

I recall memorizing *Street & Smith's* National Football League season preview magazine ahead of the 1970 season. While I didn't set out to do so, after having repeatedly read the magazine cover to cover, I memorized the rosters of every team. One of my grandfathers didn't believe my mother when she told him, so he opened the magazine to a random page and asked me about Gene Washington of the San Francisco 49ers. I quickly answered back with his number, position, height, weight, years pro, and college alma mater.

Having passed the quiz, Gramps surrendered and closed the magazine. Afterward, I'm certain he spoke to my mom about maybe getting me outside more.

In reading the sports section, I was most familiar with the "big four"—football, basketball, baseball, and hockey. But, if it was covered, I read about it, and that included the occasional mention of auto racing.

It was sometime during the 1971–72 school year when one of my teachers passed around an edition of the Scholastic America catalogs from which we could purchase books to be delivered to the school. Those thin little papers contained countless golden nuggets for a child's imagination, and out of this catalog, I discovered a real gem titled, *The Indy 500: Thirty Days in May*, written by Hal Higdon.

That book chronicled the 1970 Indianapolis 500, from April 30, the day before the Indianapolis Motor Speedway opened for practice, until the last lap of "The Greatest Spectacle in Racing" on May 30. That book ignited my passion for the sport of auto racing and, very much in particular, the Indianapolis 500.

I read that book over and over and over again. Seriously, I probably read that book two to three times a year for a decade. After that first reading, I would ride my bicycle, pretending to be my heroes, like Al Unser, AJ Foyt, Johnny Rutherford, Mario Andretti, Dan Gurney, and others.

After subsequent readings, though, I imagined myself as a flashy young racer, competing against all those heroes of mine, and winning more often than not. For a year, I had a perfect replica, at least in my imagination, of the Indianapolis Motor Speedway too, in which to further cement my status as an Indy legend.

For my fifth-grade year, 1974–75, my father, a career military officer, was stationed in Ft. Leavenworth, Kansas. We lived on post, in a rectangular courtyard with a handful or two of other military families. A rectangle! Kind of like the Indianapolis Motor Speedway.

Inspired by Higdon's storytelling, I rode countless laps around my "track," the sidewalk circling our courtyard. There were some minor complications to deal with, what with other kids in the neighborhood, but that just meant more overtaking possibilities. The biggest obstacle was the driveway that entered our shared courtyard, resulting in having to navigate two curbs in the short chute between Turns Three and Four of my Speedway replica.

Back in the 1970s, race drivers were very much like astronauts, and racing captivated the public's attention, not just for the spectacle, but for the sport's inherent danger. Crashes were frequent and often spectacular. Too many times, those accidents were tragic, resulting in serious injuries and fatalities.

It was not uncommon for drivers to suffer horrendous injuries, yet it did little to deter them. One memory from Higdon's book is the story of

Mel Kenyon, who many consider the greatest midget car racer ever. In a 1965 accident, Kenyon suffered burns to his hands, losing much of the fingers on his left hand. Going into surgery, he told the doctor to shape them so he could hold a steering wheel. Later, Kenyon raced in the Indy 500 eight times, recording four top-five finishes.

Fatalities were less common than serious injury, but still far too commonplace. Racers didn't get too close to other drivers in the paddock, unlike drivers today. They didn't want to lose friends when the almost inevitable happened.

For me, everything added up to an absolute fixation on "The Race." Year after year, I was captivated by the race teams' initial efforts to build speed to qualify for the race. Then, once qualified, their meticulous preparation to set up the car to cover the entire 500-mile distance. Finally, on race day, the three-plus hour drama of the 200 laps and all the individual stories created up and down the grid left me literally counting the days to next year's race.

I got my first in-person taste of the Speedway in May 1978. My father had been stationed at the since-closed Fort Benjamin Harrison in Indianapolis, and our family had relocated there. On the opening day of practice, we were listening to live updates from the Speedway on the radio while working in the garage and the yard. Around mid-afternoon, my father looked at me and said, "You want to go to the track?"

I think I jumped into the car without even saying, "Yes!"

I vividly remember Gordon Johncock's Atlas Van Lines Wildcat sitting on Pit Lane. The first car I saw scream down the track escapes me, but I knew if I wasn't hooked previously, I was then. Complete sensory overload—sight, smell, and sound, of course, but I swear, when a race car is at speed, you can *feel* it too.

That year, I forced my parents to take me to qualifications so we could watch in person as the drivers looked to go over 200 miles per hour and establish new track records. Tom Sneva delivered too. Driving for Roger Penske, Sneva raised the bar on both one- and four-lap track records, becoming the first driver in history to complete all four qualifying laps over 200 miles per hour.

We didn't attend the race that year, but as a local, I was glued to the radio broadcast as Al Unser won his third 500. The next year, 1979, our family repeated our practice and qualifying attendance, and we added on the race, sitting outside of Turn Four. Rick Mears won that day, the first of four race victories for him, and the first Indy 500 for me.

I've held tickets for the 500 for nearly forty years now, and I've sat pretty much everywhere. For the past decade or so, I've settled in the Paddock Penthouse, Section 23, Rows BB and CC, seats 13 and 14. If you find yourself in the area on the last Sunday in May, please wave and shout out a "hi!"

I've wanted to follow Higdon's lead and write about a single year's running of the 500 for several years now. Finally, I figured if not the 108th running of the Indianapolis 500 scheduled for May 26, 2024, then when?

I hope you enjoy *The Indy 500: A Diary of the Greatest Spectacle in Racing*. And, if you're not a race fan, I hope this makes you curious enough to attend the Indy 500 at least once. Admittedly, it's not for everyone. But it is for me.

And, if you're a child reading this book, maybe through a Scholastic America program (if it's still a thing), it's my hope and wish that you become as enamored with the race as I was when I first thumbed through Higdon's book!

SUNDAY, MAY 28, 2023

The 107th Indianapolis 500

Josef Newgarden sat in his race car, stopped at the south end of the pits at the Indianapolis Motor Speedway (IMS). The red flag had been thrown for the third time in twelve laps, pausing the 107th running of the Indianapolis 500 with just two laps remaining around the storied 2.5-mile racetrack.

Just a few moments earlier, Newgarden had led the field out of Turn Four to resume the race after it had been paused to clean up the debris of a five-car accident. Following behind in his slipstream, the wake of air left behind Newgarden's leading car, defending champion Marcus Ericsson and third-place runner Santino Ferrucci had gotten a strong jump on him, Ericsson overtaking Newgarden on his left and Ferrucci pulling alongside him on the right.

Just as Ferrucci seemed destined to relegate Newgarden to third, yellow lights illuminated along the side of the track, signaling caution and for drivers to slow down and maintain their positions. Behind the three leaders, another crash had occurred, sending damaged cars into each other and the concrete retaining walls surrounding the racing surface along the frontstretch.

Newgarden had been fortunate with the timing of the yellow flag. Ferrucci had not quite completed the overtake, allowing Newgarden to keep his second-place position on the track. However, at the time, he didn't know it.

Ferrucci, thinking he had not only overtaken Newgarden but also Ericsson, pulled next to Ericsson as they went through the short chute between Turns Three and Four at the end of the lap, seemingly forcing the issue for the top position in the field. Ferrucci thought better of his contesting the order, and ducked in behind Ericsson as they, along with the rest of the field, slowly navigated through the crash debris littering the racing surface, threading between wrecked race cars and safety personnel on both sides.

As they crossed the yard-wide strip of bricks that marks the IMS's start/finish line, only three laps remained in the event long billed as The Greatest Spectacle in Racing. Almost everyone thought the race to be essentially over, with the remaining laps to be completed at the reduced speeds under the yellow flag.

Race officials, however, had another idea. Nobody wants a race to end anticlimactically, under caution, without the drivers racing for position. That goes for any race, much less the biggest and most eagerly awaited race on the calendar, an internationally televised event that has captured the attention—and imagination—of people for over one hundred years.

On lap 198, race officials made their decision to red flag the race once again, and drivers were made aware over their in-helmet radios to come into the pits and stop their cars, in the order they ran, at the far south end. Getting to that position, they passed the start/finish line in the pits, signaling the end of that lap and the beginning of the next.

With the engines turned off, the cars sat on Pit Lane. Just two laps remained.

Newgarden sat third in line, behind both Ericsson and Ferrucci, worried that he may have lost his best opportunity to win the 500. In his eleven previous appearances in the race, the two-time IndyCar Series champion, awarded for the best overall results over the entire season, had managed a best finish of just third, achieved in 2016.

While crews attended to drivers involved in the crash, removed the battered and broken machines, and cleared the racing surface of any debris, race officials quickly looked at data, including frame-by-frame analysis of various video feeds, to determine the exact order of cars at the precise moment the caution lights illuminated.

A great deal of attention focused on the chaos that erupted in the middle and tail end of the field, where the accident had occurred during the mad dash down the front straightaway. However, they also looked at the front of the field, where the video showed Ericsson clearly in front, as well as Newgarden just inches ahead of Ferrucci.

Newgarden's Chevrolet-powered car was pushed up to second, ahead of Ferrucci and behind only Ericsson for the coming restart. Oddly, it was the exact place in the queue Newgarden wanted.

In this era of IndyCar racing, aerodynamics plays an enormous role in how cars perform on superspeedways like Indianapolis. Trailing cars face much less air resistance than the leader, whose car is tasked with punching a hole through the air. If the trailing car is close enough, there's a pocket of only slightly turbulent air, almost like a vacuum at over 200 miles per hour, where the driver faces much less air resistance pushing against the car.

Closely following behind a car on either of the Speedway's two five-eighths-of-a-mile-long straightaways allows for a significant advantage. First, the trailing car can keep pace by using less of the throttle, and, therefore, less fuel. More importantly, when the time comes for an overtake, the driver, tucked nicely into the aerodynamic slipstream, can rapidly close the distance to the car ahead, then quickly move to either side, the edge of that slipstream momentarily wrapping around the rear of the car and essentially pushing the car forward for a critical second or two. Usually, that's enough for the overtake.

Of course, following closely behind a car comes with disadvantages too. When the leading car pushes air up and out to the sides, it removes much of the airflow from the car trailing behind. On the straightaways, that's an advantage for the trailing car. However, on the Speedway's four quarter-mile-long turns, it means less air flows over the trailing car's body, including the critical front and rear wings of the race car. Those wings are much like the wings of an airplane but are inverted. Instead of creating lift, an IndyCar's wings are designed to push the car down on the track, providing it enough grip to maneuver the ninety-degree turns at speeds well over 200 miles an hour.

Thus, the key for drivers is to be close enough to the leading car going through the turns but not too close to lose the grip and traction. Ideally, the trailing car builds momentum going into either Turns Two or Four, allowing them to gain on the leading car down the long straightaways, leaving enough time and space at the end of the straight to duck out and make the overtake. It's easier said than done, particularly when the leading car isn't inclined to allow the overtake. Getting the job done requires equal parts proper car setup, driver skill, and driver experience.

Newgarden sat on pit road knowing he had all three. Ericsson, just in front of him, also knew he had all three.

Their experience included thousands of laps around the Speedway, both in practice and Indianapolis 500 races. However, their experience did not include anything like what they were about to undergo.

Ordinarily, in a restart from a red-flag situation, including the two previous restarts in this race, the race cars follow the pace car out of the pits, where they then run at least one yellow flag lap to allow the drivers an opportunity to get their tires warm.

When tires are at their peak operating temperature, they afford their optimal traction, and traction equates to safety. However, when pushing race speeds on relatively cool tires, there is substantially less traction, and the element of danger rises exponentially.

Because race officials waited for one complete lap to run under caution before red-flagging the race, only two laps remained. If officials were to get the green-flag finish to the race they and spectators alike coveted, they would need to throw the green flag before the completion of lap 199.

That's not what Ericsson wanted. If the race finished under yellow-flag conditions, in the position the cars held currently, he would win his second consecutive Indianapolis 500, complete with an additional $420,000 in prize money from BorgWarner.

Of course, a green-flag finish was exactly what Newgarden and Ferrucci wanted.

After a brief delay to clear the track, race officials gave the order for the teams to restart their cars. Soon thereafter, the pace car led the field out of the pits to resume lap 199 under caution.

Ericsson, being the leader, held the responsibility of dictating the start, and he went slowly through the south end, through Turns One and

Two, and onto the backstretch, the field close behind him and the pace car speeding off into the distance.

Into the north end of the Speedway, Ericsson picked up his pace just a bit, but not a full-on restart. For that, he waited until the entrance to Turn Four, where he accelerated in earnest, with Newgarden and the pack responding in kind.

Exiting Turn Four and coming down the front stretch to take the white flag, the signal of the last lap of the race, Ericsson started serpentining, weaving his car left and right, the en vogue strategy of the last several years, to break up the draft behind him.

His weaving was not technically a violation of rules established to prevent the often dangerous practice of blocking. In blocking, the driver in front, following the action behind him in his rearview mirrors, moves reactively to prevent the car behind from overtaking. Rules allow a driver to make one reactive move, leaving the trailing driver the opportunity to counter the block and make an overtaking maneuver.

In Ericsson's case, as the leader, he was proactively making his moves, with Newgarden and the field reacting to the leader, following his moves. In many ways, it's a case of semantics, and old-timers continue to bristle at the practice.

Still, Ericsson weaved side to side, the pack following, until he moved to the far right to set himself up for entering Turn One, Newgarden behind. In the battle for third, Ferrucci held off a fast-charging Alex Palou, the fastest qualifier for the race.

Ericsson held the lead through Turn One, the short chute, and Turn Two. But Newgarden had a tremendous run on Ericsson, quickly closing the distance between them as they went through Turn Two.

Exiting Turn Two and entering the backstretch, Newgarden carried much more momentum between the two cars. Ericsson, in a continued effort to break the slipstream, the "tow" in the vernacular of racers and fans, moved to his left to weave along the straightaway.

Newgarden followed Ericsson to his left, then almost instantly changed his mind, as it was clear he could carry his advantage in momentum to pull alongside Ericsson and, further down the backstretch, easily past Ericsson before entering Turn Three.

Ericsson, on the inside, was helpless to fight off Newgarden. Instead, he surrendered the lead and followed Newgarden into Turn Three, where he, in turn, benefited from the draft in the short chute between Turns Three and Four.

Now, Ericsson had the momentum advantage, closing on Newgarden through Turn Four before blasting onto the frontstretch in a final dash to reach the checkered flag first.

Newgarden, taking a page out of the serpentining playbook, aggressively weaved his car exiting Turn Four, diving dangerously below the white line separating the racing surface and that of the Pit Lane entry, Ericsson hot on his tail.

Ericsson kept closing as Newgarden again weaved right then back again to his left. But, covering a distance greater than a football field every second, Newgarden streaked over the finish line first, just 0.0974 seconds in front of Ericsson, the fourth-closest finish in Indianapolis 500 history.

In the end, the gap between the two cars was slightly longer than a single car length!

As his competitors pulled into the pits on the cool-down lap, Newgarden continued on the racecourse to the yard of bricks denoting the start/finish line of the Indianapolis Motor Speedway, where he stopped in the middle of the track. He unfastened his safety harness, removed his steering wheel, and climbed out of his car, standing on the right sidepod and saluting the cheering fans.

Then he dashed to the wall and its chain-link catch fence and slid through a gap designed as an ingress/egress point for drivers and emergency personnel. Once there, he hopped a barrier and ran into the stands.

Always a fan favorite, Newgarden celebrated his crowning achievement with the fans who had supported him for so long.

Out of his car, a frustrated Ericsson was left to ponder what had happened. In a post-race interview, Ericsson said, "I just feel like it was an unfair and dangerous end to the race. I don't feel like it was enough laps to do what we did. We've never done a restart out of the pits."

While IndyCar had never restarted a race on the lap in which cars left the pits, the decision didn't run counter to any written rule. But, while the decision may have been allowed in the rulebook, there was no precedent for it, including the two previous restarts that had taken place earlier in the race.

The decision was essentially made when officials were one lap late in waving the red flag. However, that alone went against precedent. Just three years before, at the pandemic-delayed running of the 2020 Indianapolis 500, officials were content to let Takuma Sato run his final five laps under yellow to record his second 500 victory.

Regardless of whatever controversy surrounded the finish, Newgarden was a worthy winner. With car and driver finally gathered up and loaded onto the Speedway's raised Victory Lane platform, Newgarden celebrated with his wife, Ashley, and his team, wearing the winner's wreath and dousing himself with the traditional bottle of milk presented to the winner.

"We've had a tough go here the last three, four years, and we've had a lot of questions to answer every day, after every qualifying weekend," a tired but elated Newgarden said. "We've had to come out and put on a brave face. It's just not an easy place to succeed at.

"I don't necessarily subscribe to the fact that if you don't win the 500, your career is a failure. But I think a lot of people view this race and this championship with that lens. The 500 stands alone, and if you are not able to capture one, the career really is a failure."

MONDAY, MAY 29, 2023

Victory Gala

Monday, Memorial Day, the JW Marriott in downtown Indianapolis hosted the annual Indy 500 Victory Celebration, a formal event for racers, their teams, sponsors, automotive industry representatives, and, importantly, fans. The event was televised, both locally and streaming nationally on Peacock, and served as the culmination of more than two and a half weeks of activity at the speedway.

Race teams arrived at the Indianapolis Motor Speedway the second week of May, ahead of the GMR Grand Prix, the fifth round in the 2023 IndyCar Series schedule. That race was contested on Saturday, May 13 on the Speedway's 2.439-mile, fourteen-turn road course, where cars run the opposite direction down the famed front straight.

Immediately after that event, teams converted their cars from a road course setup, where drivers need to navigate both left and right turns, to a left turn-only oval setup for the 500-mile race. From there, they spent every waking moment searching for more speed, both in qualifying and race preparations. It had been a long, tiring three weeks for everyone involved. Yet only one team could counter the cumulative exhaustion with the euphoria of winning the biggest race in the world.

During the gala, drivers were brought up to the stage in their reverse order of finish, from thirty-third-place finisher Katherine Legge to winner Newgarden. Benjamin Pedersen, the driver of car No. 55 for AJ Foyt

Enterprises, was named the winner of the Indianapolis 500 Rookie of the Year award, based on being the highest classified rookie, both in having qualified eleventh and raced to a twenty-first-place finish. With the honor, Pedersen earned a $50,000 bonus prize.

The biggest prize, of course, went to Newgarden. To the victor goes the spoils, and for his winning drive the day before, Newgarden earned $3.666 million out of the record total purse of $17,021,500 for the entire thirty-three-car field. Ericsson, passed on the final lap, was awarded $1.043 million for his second-place finish.

The average payout for the field was a staggering $500,600, a record for the event. As typical, the race's total purse was determined through contingency and special awards from both IMS and IndyCar, the race's sanctioning organization. Drivers and teams who are season-long participants in the IndyCar Series earned higher shares of the purse.

The payouts for the 107th running of the Indianapolis 500 were:
1. Josef Newgarden, $3,666,000
2. Marcus Ericsson, $1,043,000
3. Santino Ferrucci, $481,800
4. Alex Palou, $801,500
5. Alexander Rossi, $574,000
6. Scott Dixon, $582,000
7. Takuma Sato, $217,300
8. Conor Daly, $512,000
9. Colton Herta, $506,500
10. Rinus VeeKay, $556,500
11. Ryan Hunter-Reay, $145,500
12. Callum Ilott, $495,500
13. Devlin DeFrancesco, $482,000
14. Scott McLaughlin, $485,000
15. Helio Castroneves, $481,500
16. Tony Kanaan, $105,000
17. Marco Andretti, $102,000
18. Jack Harvey, $472,000
19. Christian Lundgaard, $467,500
20. Ed Carpenter, $102,000

21. Benjamin Pedersen (R), $215,300
22. Graham Rahal, $565,500*
23. Will Power, $488,000
24. Pato O'Ward, $516,500
25. Simon Pagenaud, $465,500
26. Agustín Canapino (R), $156,300
27. Felix Rosenqvist, $278,300
28. Kyle Kirkwood, $465,500
29. David Malukas, $462,000
30. Romain Grosjean, $462,000
31. Sting Ray Robb (R), $463,000
32. RC Enerson (R), $103,000
33. Katherine Legge, $102,000

*Prize money divided between two teams: $460,000 to Rahal Letterman Lanigan Racing and $105,500 to Dreyer & Reinbold Racing/Cusick Motorsports.

At the end of the evening, drivers and teams made their way to Detroit, where the next round of the IndyCar Series season would get started in just four days—when the green flag would fly to open the first practice session ahead of the Chevrolet Detroit Grand Prix.

For others, though, attention had already turned to the Memorial Day weekend of 2024, and the 108th running of the Indianapolis 500.

TUESDAY, MAY 30, 2023

The Indianapolis Motor Speedway

Two days after hosting nearly 400,000 fans at the 107th running of The Greatest Spectacle in Racing, the Indianapolis Motor Speedway once again shined like a gem. The day before, a team of volunteers from the Solid Rock Baptist Church continued their yearly tradition of clearing the stands of refuse. Why volunteer? The recycling of the massive number of plastic bottles and aluminum cans pays for summer youth camps.

The famed Indianapolis Motor Speedway sits in Speedway, a tiny enclave of about 14,000 people completely engulfed by the sprawl of Indianapolis. The track lies about six miles west of downtown Indianapolis.

The Speedway itself—the track, not the city—was the brainchild of Indianapolis businessman Carl G. Fisher, a local bicycle enthusiast who began his entrepreneurial career by opening a bicycle shop with his brothers. In quick order, Fisher saw the opportunity to get involved in the emerging automobile industry in the United States.

In 1904, Fisher, along with his friend James A. Allison, bought an interest in the US patent to manufacture acetylene headlights, the automotive standard that served as a precursor to the development of electric lights. Almost immediately, their company, Prest-O-Lite, supplied nearly every headlight used by American automobile manufacturers, and the partners' wealth grew considerably; they sold the business in 2013 for $9 million, or the equivalent of over $275 million in 2024 dollars.

As a cyclist, Fisher had an interest in bicycle racing, and as cars were built, that passion for racing naturally grew to include automobiles. On a trip to France in 1905, Fisher determined Europe had an advantage in automobile design and manufacturing, and that an opportunity was there for the taking to help American manufacturers better test their products. It was then Fisher's vision of a speedway began to form.

At first, Fisher envisioned a long, three- to five-mile circular track, with a smooth, wide surface that would allow cars to be driven flat out to test their limits. A 1907 trip to London to view the banked Brooklands circuit only steeled his resolve. With a burgeoning automotive industry already rooted in Indiana, Fisher set out to realize his dream.

For a location, Fisher decided upon Pressley Farm, a level parcel of 328 acres just outside of Indianapolis. In December 1908, Fisher, joined by Allison, Arthur C. Newby, and Frank H. Wheeler, purchased the property for $72,000. Three months later, on March 20, 1909, the partners incorporated the Indianapolis Motor Speedway Company.

Construction of the racecourse started immediately, but very quickly, Fisher had to compromise his vision. To accommodate spectator grandstands, Fisher downscaled his plans from a circular track to a 2.5-mile oval track.

Dozens of buildings were constructed, along with grandstands capable of holding 12,000 spectators. The track itself was built with graded and packed soil covered by two inches of gravel, two inches of limestone covered with a solution of tar and oil called taroid, one to two inches of crushed stone chips also covered with taroid, and, finally, a layer of crushed stone.

Somewhat oddly, the first event at the Speedway wasn't an auto race. Rather, on June 5, 1909, before the oval track was completed, the Speedway hosted a helium balloon competition that drew a reported 40,000 spectators. Nine balloons participated in the race, with a balloon named *Universal City* winning the grand prize by staying afloat for more than a day and landing nearly 400 miles away in Alabama.

The first motor racing at the Speedway was a series of motorcycle races that took part on August 14, 1909. However, concerns over the suitability of the track surface for motorcycles saw the planned two-day event shortened to just a single day.

Cars took center stage at the Speedway for the first time on Thursday, August 19, 1909, when fifteen teams took to the track for practice, each car holding both a driver and a mechanic. It didn't take long, however, for the track surface to become a concern as ruts and holes formed in the turns, not to mention the dirt, tar, and oil that completely covered drivers and mechanics.

Working feverishly to ensure the show would go on, Speedway workers groomed the track, rolling it to smooth out bumps and fill holes, and covering it with even more oil. Then Fisher and company opened the gates to the queuing public, reported later to be between 15,000 and 20,000 spectators.

That first day of auto racing featured a 250-mile race, won by Bob Burman, who drove a Buick on his way to winning the Prest-O-Lite Trophy. Unfortunately, on lap fifty-eight, William Bourque, driving a Knox, suffered a mechanical failure that flipped his car end over end along the frontstretch before crashing into a fence post. Both Bourque and his mechanic, Harry Halcomb, died, the first of seventy-four fatalities attributed to events at the Speedway.

That first day of racing saw two land speed records established. But escalating concerns over safety prompted officials to consider canceling the final two days of events. Fisher, concerned his Speedway dreams might be vanquished before its first auto racing event concluded, promised the track would be repaired by the next day and convinced race officials the on-track activities should continue.

To Fisher's relief, Friday turned out to be a success. The Speedway attracted another 20,000 spectators, who took in a racing program that featured additional speed records and, most importantly, no major incidents.

However, the third and final day of the inaugural auto racing events, Saturday, August 21, proved to be disastrous. Thirty-five thousand spectators crammed into the facility to watch the final 300-mile race. Just over the halfway mark, though, Charlie Merz lost control of his car after suffering a right front tire failure, crashing through multiple fence posts and careening into the crowd. His riding mechanic, Claude Kellum, and two spectators were killed.

Moments after Merz's crash, Bruce Keen bounced over a pothole in the track and crashed heavily into a bridge support. Having seen enough, racing officials abruptly stopped the race. More damaging to Fisher and company, the American Automobile Association, the sanctioning body for the racing, imposed a boycott of the facility until significant improvements were made to the racing surface.

For the Indianapolis Motor Speedway Company, two potential remedies existed for upgrading the track's surface—bricks or concrete. However, with only a few miles of public road paved at the time, concrete posed an uncertain, and therefore risky, solution. Bricks, on the other hand, had lasted for millennia in cities around the world.

After traction tests proved bricks would hold up to the demands of car racing, the Speedway began the task of resurfacing its track. Five different manufacturers in Indiana supplied 3.2 million ten-pound brinks, each of which was laid by hand over two inches of sand. Once leveled, the gaps between the bricks were then filled with mortar. All that manual work was done in just sixty-three days.

At the same time the track was resurfaced, a thirty-three-inch-high concrete wall was built in front of the main straightaway grandstand and around the oval's four corners to better protect spectators. Commemorating the comprehensive makeover, the final brick of the track surface was made of gold and laid by Governor Thomas R. Marshall. With that, "The Brickyard" was born.

Drivers of cars and motorcycles returned to the Speedway in December 1909, convening for speed trials and putting the new track surface to the test. The surface responded well and proved to be a considerable improvement as cars blistered around the track, reaching speeds of well over one hundred miles an hour.

Competitive racing resumed in 1910, and over three holiday weekends—Memorial Day, Independence Day, and Labor Day—the Speedway hosted sixty-six auto races. Additionally, the Speedway hosted the National Aviation Meet, where Walter Brookins set a record by flying a plane to the dizzying height of 4,938 feet.

Fisher and company took a different approach in 1911 when they consolidated their efforts on just a single 500-mile race, hosted the day after Memorial Day, May 30. Forty cars competed, all but one configured with a driver and a riding mechanic.

Ray Harroun, the driver of the Marmon "Wasp," was the sole driver without a riding mechanic. Other competitors objected, complaining that driving solo was too dangerous, as Harroun couldn't be warned when cars approached from the rear. To satisfy competitors and officials, Harroun fashioned a mirror mounted on his car's bulkhead. It was the first rearview mirror on a car and remains a prime example of racing innovations making their way into production vehicles.

Harroun, of course, is remembered for much more than his invention of the rearview mirror. He won the inaugural Indianapolis 500, completing the distance at an average speed of 74.602 miles per hour in front of an estimated 80,000 spectators.

A Memorial Day tradition had begun.

Ownership of the Indianapolis Motor Speedway has changed hands over the years. After rebuking a generous offer from a real estate developer in 1926 for fear of what might come of the facility, Fisher and Allison sold the Speedway in 1927 to former auto racer and World War I flying ace, Edward V. Rickenbacker.

Rickenbacker ushered the Speedway through the turmoil of the Great Depression, with the 500 still attracting competitors and spectators despite a considerable drop in prize money. Racers being racers, those competitors pushed the limits of both man and machine.

Speeds grew to the extent that the track became increasingly dangerous— from 1931 to 1935, fifteen drivers and riding mechanics perished. To better accommodate the faster cars, parts of the racing surface were paved with tarmac, the inside retaining wall was removed in the four turns, and the outside wall was realigned to steepen its angle with the track in an attempt to keep cars from launching over it.

World War II shut down auto racing, and the Speedway fell into disrepair after four years of neglect. Local residents worked with the assumption the Speedway would be razed to make way for housing developments after the war.

Three-time 500 winner Wilbur Shaw had a different idea. Seeing the grave condition of the Speedway, he contacted Rickenbacker who told him the facility was for sale. Shaw, ever the racer, then set out to find a potential buyer who would reopen the Speedway as a racetrack and a public venue.

Fortunately for auto racing fans, Shaw connected with Anton "Tony" Hulman, a Terre Haute businessman who worked for his family's business, Hulman & Company, and whose biggest success had been making Clabber Girl baking powder a staple in kitchen pantries across America.

Hulman purchased the Indianapolis Motor Speedway on November 14, 1945, for what was reported by the *Indianapolis Star and News* to be a price of $750,000. Working through the winter and spring, major renovations were made in time for the Indianapolis 500 race to be resumed in May 1946.

Leveraging the success of each successive 500 and the event's soaring popularity, Hulman oversaw continued reinvestment into the facility, adding grandstands, suites, and a museum, all of which contributed to making the Speedway the premier racing facility in the world. An October 1961 project saw the last of the brick portions of the racing surface paved, except for a single yard of bricks at the start/finish line.

After Hulman died in 1977, his family continued to operate the Speedway, with Hulman's grandson, Tony George, taking the reins of president and CEO in 1989.

To characterize George's era at the helm of the Speedway as tumultuous would be an understatement. George brought the NASCAR stock car racing series to the Speedway, hosting the series for the first time in 1994. It was that same year that George's relationship with CART (Championship Auto Racing Teams), the sanctioning body of "Indy car" racing run by race team owners, became untenable.

CART was a series that ran races on a variety of racing courses, from superspeedway ovals like Indianapolis, to shorter ovals, natural terrain road circuits, and temporary street circuits. And its success was enormous.

George wanted the focus on open-wheel racing to be Indianapolis and oval racing. He also longed for more American drivers and American sponsorship. With those motivations, George created the Indy Racing League in 1996 to compete against CART, a move that is now known as "The Split."

The Split fractured the American racing scene, and the popularity of the sport and its events, including the Indianapolis 500, declined. The two series merged under the IndyCar banner in 2008, but the damage had been done. While the crown jewel of racing, the Indianapolis 500, continues to enjoy widespread public popularity, a great many of the country's races have yet to recover.

In 2020, George engineered the sale of the Indianapolis Motor Speedway, along with the IndyCar Series, to Penske Entertainment Corp., a subsidiary of the Penske Corporation, owned, by Roger Penske.

The sale to Penske was welcomed by race fans, for they knew that no better steward of The Greatest Spectacle in Racing could be found than the man who might be the event's biggest fan.

WEDNESDAY, MAY 31, 2023

The Captain

As teams finalized preparations for the IndyCar Series's next race in Detroit, Roger Penske was still basking in the glow of Newgarden's triumph at the Indy 500. But, true to his nature, Penske wasn't resting on his laurels. Rather, he was busily preparing for yet another of his business ventures—the Detroit Grand Prix.

The automobile capital of the United States, Detroit had a long and, truthfully, somewhat bumpy history as a race host. Back in the early days of automobile racing, the AAA sanctioned the Detroit 100 at the Michigan State Fairgrounds Speedway. Then, after a decades-long break, the city jumped into the deep end of global motorsport and hosted a round of the Formula One World Championship from 1982 to 1988 on a street circuit that included the picturesque Renaissance Center along the Detroit River.

After the 1988 Grand Prix, the FIA (Fédération Internationale de l'Automobile), the governing body of Formula One, decided the circuit's temporary paddock was substandard, and as no agreement could be made on new facilities, they took their racing elsewhere. The CART series filled the gap by contesting races on the downtown streets from 1989 to 1991.

Then, ahead of the 1992 edition, organizers moved the race to a temporary circuit constructed on Belle Isle, in the center of the river. The track was much smoother than the city streets but still very narrow, with limited opportunities for overtaking. Still, the race, despite the difficult access for spectators, enjoyed a period of success.

Harsh Michigan winters, however, transformed the track's smooth surface into a cascade of bumps, and with competitive racing lacking, attendance waned. After the 2001 race, CART dropped Detroit from its annual calendar.

That decision opened the door for Penske to save the race. Penske Entertainment Group became the promoter of the race and brought the IndyCar Series back to Belle Isle for 2007 and 2008. But then, as a worldwide recession severely damaged the US automotive industry and, subsequently, the Detroit-area economy, Penske canceled the 2009 race and put the Grand Prix on what was hoped to be a temporary hold.

Racing resumed in 2012, again on Belle Isle, and the race continued every year except for the pandemic-stricken 2020 season, contested from 2013 through 2021 as a doubleheader weekend, with a race on both Saturday and Sunday. After a single race in 2022, Penske Entertainment Group announced the race would return to the city's downtown streets for 2023. The race on a new downtown circuit had been highly anticipated, not only in the IndyCar paddock but in the Detroit-area community. For if there's one thing Penske, long nicknamed "The Captain," has long been known for, from the boardroom to the racetrack, it's winning.

Penske was born in 1937 in Shaker Heights, Ohio, near Cleveland, and his lifelong love affair with the Indianapolis Motor Speedway began when, as a fourteen-year-old, his father, Jay, drove him to Indianapolis to watch the 1951 500. Their seats for the race were horrible; Penske once told the *Indianapolis Star*, "You couldn't even see the cars going by." Still, the young man's fancy for racing was forever captured.

As a teenager, Penske bought older cars, fixed them up a bit, and sold them for a profit, running his emerging business out of the family home. After graduating from Shaker Heights High School, he attended Lehigh University, where he graduated in 1959.

Bitten by the racing bug, Penske first raced in hill-climbing events and then moved to racing Porsches on road circuits. Penske was a successful racer too—none other than *Sports Illustrated* named him Sports Car Club of America Driver of the Year in 1961.

In 1961 and 1962, Penske raced Formula One in one-off efforts for the United States Grand Prix at Watkins Glen, first for Cooper, finishing eighth in 1961, and then for Lotus, finishing ninth in 1962. For that 1961 race, Penske's Cooper was painted bright yellow for his sponsor, DuPont Anti-Freeze, and as such, it was one of the first cars in Formula One to have commercially branded sponsorship and livery.

Before he retired as a driver to focus on his business interests, Penske never raced at the Indianapolis Motor Speedway. However, his Speedway dreams were far from over. He formed Penske Racing, and the organization's first event was the 1966 24 Hours of Daytona sports car race. His three-driver team finished twelfth racing a Chevrolet Corvette Stingray.

But it was at Indy where the legend of The Captain grew.

Penske Racing entered Indy car racing in 1968, running a car driven by sports car ace Mark Donohue in two USAC-sanctioned road course races. The organization made its debut at the Indianapolis 500 in 1969, with Donohue finishing seventh and securing Rookie of the Year honors.

As it broke into the upper echelon of motorsports in the US, Penske Racing did more than just compete. It changed forever how teams approached racing. First and foremost, Penske Racing was a business, and like any of his business interests, The Captain wanted every detail optimized. Gone were the dirty garages of "grease monkey" lore. Penske believed you had to look good to race well, and that meant a shine to everything, from wheels and paint on the car to smiles at sponsor tents. The organization immediately raised the bar on car preparation, development, and, of course, presentation.

Already a stalwart in the paddock and garages, Penske Racing didn't take long to make its mark on the racetrack. In his second attempt at the Indy 500 in 1970, Donohue finished second at the Brickyard. One year later, he delivered the team's first Indy car victory at the Pocono 500.

In 1972, it all came together for Penske Racing at the Indianapolis 500, where Donohue drove to victory while setting a new average speed record of 162.962 mph. Over the next fifty-one years, appearances at Indy's Victory Lane, while not routine, certainly have been somewhat regular, with the team capturing nineteen total Indy 500 victories, more than any other racing team in the event's history. Included in those victories are all four 500 wins for Rick Mears and three of the four for Castroneves.

Penske Racing, now known as Team Penske, has long been the standard for teams competing in Indy car races, where it has captured nearly 300 poles for qualifying fastest, won more than 230 races, and secured seventeen season championships. In addition to the IndyCar Series, Team Penske competes in other series, including NASCAR, where it has won four driving titles and over 200 races. NASCAR driver Brad Keselowski delivered Penske's 500th victory as a team owner when he won the South Point 400 at Las Vegas Motor Speedway in September 2018.

Simply, Penske sets a high standard and then builds and directs his team to reach his lofty goals and ambitions. He's done it with racing teams, racing series, and racing venues, including the Indianapolis Motor Speedway. While he's always eying the Indy 500, the racing jewel that captured his imagination so many years ago, he's also eying the next racing weekend, where he's likely to have multiple cars competing at multiple tracks, including races, like at Detroit, that he also promotes.

WEDNESDAY, JUNE 7, 2023

Silly Season

It's called the "silly season," and it's the time of year when rumors and speculation run rampant about which drivers will be racing for which teams *next* year. Once silly season starts, it doesn't end until the last race seat has been filled. And as intriguing as silly season is, once it begins, it tends to be the top topic of conversation whenever two or more of the IndyCar community gather.

Silly season starts when the first seat becomes available, regardless of the cause. Causes range from driver retirements to injuries, expansion of a team's number of cars to a driver's contract expiring, incoming or outgoing sponsorship dollars to . . . well, almost anything else. When that first open seat comes available, who drives for whom becomes, in its own way, a high-stakes game of musical chairs, and no driver wants to be left standing with nowhere to sit when the music stops.

Silly season 2022 was one of the silliest of them all. On July 12, 2022, Chip Ganassi Racing issued a press release stating it was exercising its option on driver Alex Palou, the defending IndyCar champion, for the 2023 season.

Palou, however, had a very different thought.

Palou took to social media and tweeted, "I have recently learned from the media that this afternoon, without my approval, Chip Ganassi Racing issued a press release announcing that I would be driving with CGR in

2023. Even more surprising was that CGR's release included a 'quote' which did not come from me.

"I did not approve that press release, and I did not author or approve that quote. As I have recently informed CGR, for personal reasons, I do not intend to continue with the team after 2022."

Wait a second. What?

As if heads weren't already spinning in IndyCar circles, Arrow McLaren, just four hours after the CGR press release, distributed a release of its own, stating it had secured Palou's services for both the 2023 IndyCar Series campaign and as a test driver for its Formula One team as part of its Testing of Previous Cars (TPC) program.

Palou's approved quote read, "I'm extremely excited to join the driver roster for such an iconic team as McLaren. I'm excited to be able to show what I can do behind the wheel of a Formula One car and looking at what doors that may open. I want to thank everyone at Chip Ganassi Racing for everything they have done for me."

The apparent vacancy at one of the premier teams in IndyCar, in the car of the defending series champion no less, was an inflammatory catalyst to the silliest silly season in memory. Palou, Ganassi and McLaren only fanned the flames in the following weeks.

Just two weeks later, CGR filed a civil lawsuit against Palou in Marion County (Indiana) Superior Court. Keep in mind, the team filed a lawsuit against a driver who was still competing for the team with five more races to go in the season!

Eventually, a series of arbitration sessions were facilitated, and a seemingly uneasy truce was reached between the three parties: Palou, CGR, and McLaren. Palou would race for CGR in 2023, completing the terms of his contract. However, he would be allowed to pursue a Formula One testing program with McLaren, provided testing didn't interfere with his CGR IndyCar responsibilities. Finally, it was reported in the media that Palou's expiring contract would prevent him from negotiating a contract for 2024 and beyond until September 1, 2023.

"Palougate," and all its startling twists and turns over several weeks, was a sensational start to the 2022 IndyCar silly season. Silly season 2023 started much more sedately.

On Sunday, June 4, Conor Daly piloted his No. 20 BitNile Chevrolet to a fifteenth-place finish in Detroit, one week after he finished eighth at Indianapolis, his best finish of the 2023 campaign. Three days later, Ed Carpenter Racing parted ways with their thirty-one-year-old driver.

In ECR's press release, owner/driver Ed Carpenter commented, "This is the most difficult decision I have made as a team owner because I respect Conor and know what he means to IndyCar and its fans. Our team has not been performing at the level we are capable of this year, and despite making technical changes and investments in the offseason, 2023 has been extremely challenging. I have put a great deal of consideration into the current state of our team and realize it is my obligation to our employees, partners, and supporters to do whatever is necessary to elevate our team's competitiveness."

Replacing Daly for the remainder of the season, beginning at Road America in Elkhart Lake, Wisconsin, would be Ryan Hunter-Reay. Known as "Captain America," Hunter-Reay is a former winner of both the IndyCar season championship (2012) and the Indianapolis 500 (2014). Hunter-Reay had left the IndyCar grid after a long stint at Andretti Autosport and spent the entire 2022 season on the sidelines, notably helping Callum Ilott and Juncos Hollinger Racing prepare for the Indy 500. He returned to the cockpit for the 2023 Indy 500, finishing the race in eleventh place for Dreyer & Reinbold Racing.

Whether Hunter-Reay would be in the seat for Ed Carpenter Racing in 2024 would be later determined. Thus, the silly season began. The speculation of who would race for whom, and where, had just commenced.

FRIDAY, AUGUST 11, 2023

Alex Palou Stirs Silly Season Yet Again

The silly season is termed as such because the talk—so much of it unfounded speculation, innuendo, intentional misinformation, and good, old-fashioned gossip—is, in the end, just so . . . silly. On many levels, it's ridiculous to seasoned observers.

But, year after year, followers of any racing series just can't get enough of it.

Today, ahead of Saturday's second Grand Prix of Indianapolis on the Speedway's road course, silly season reappeared front and center and set the IndyCar Series paddock buzzing. Again, rather unbelievably, Palou was the catalyst. If last season's ruckus was unprecedented—what with a driver being sued by his team—this year now looked to be more so.

It started when the Associated Press broke a story in which it published the contents of a letter that Arrow McLaren boss Zak Brown circulated internally within the team. In the letter, Brown announced that Palou had "no intention of honoring his contract" with the team next season, despite multiple assurances from Palou and an advance on his 2024 salary.

Brown was also quoted as writing, "This is incredibly disappointing considering the commitment he has made to us both directly and publicly and our significant investment in him based on that commitment." Part of that investment had been Palou testing the McLaren Formula One car on both the track and in a simulator, as well as Palou serving as the team's reserve driver for the Miami Grand Prix held the first weekend of May.

The news broke on Friday, and Series observers were left scratching their heads. Certainly, it couldn't be true, right?

Saturday, Chip Ganassi stepped into the fray, issuing a statement that read, "Anyone that knows me knows that I don't make a habit of commenting about contract situations. Subsequently, I have been quiet since day one of this story but now I feel I must respond. I grew up respecting the McLaren Team and their success. The new management does not get my same respect.

"Alex Palou has been a part of our team and under contract since the 2021 season. It is the interference of that contract from McLaren that began this process and ironically, they are now playing the victim. Simply stated, the position of McLaren INDYCAR regarding our driver is inaccurate and wrong; he remains under contract with CGR."

Later, Palou's management team, Monaco Increase Management (MIM), the same agency that negotiated Palou's contract with McLaren last year, issued its own statement: "Monaco Increase Management is bitterly disappointed to learn about Alex Palou's decision to break an existing agreement with McLaren for 2024 and beyond. Together, we had built a relationship that we thought went beyond any contractual obligation and culminated in winning the 2021 IndyCar crown and tracing a path to F1 opportunities. Life goes on and we wish Alex all the best for his future achievements."

So, one of the most sought-after seats available in the IndyCar Series, Palou's No. 10 team at CGR, isn't available after all. Now that premier available seat resides over at Arrow McLaren. Or does it?

Again, as with all stories during silly season, time will eventually tell the full story.

That Palou is the source of bickering between rival teams isn't a surprise among the IndyCar paddock, for he is viewed as a generational talent behind the steering wheel of a racing car.

Twenty-six-year-old Álex Palou Montalbo was born in Sant Antoni de Vilamajor, Spain, near Barcelona, and he started racing karts when he was six. By 2014, Palou had graduated to open-wheel racing, where he competed in the Euroformula Open Championship with Campos Racing. In that first season, he won three races and finished third in the season championship.

From there, Palou steadily advanced his career, racing in various formulas in Europe and Japan. Despite his success, however, Palou couldn't see a direct line of sight to filling a seat in the Formula One series, his ambition since he started racing.

After a successful IndyCar test with Dale Coyne Racing in July 2019, Palou threw his hat into the IndyCar ring full-time for the 2020 season. Driving for the underdog DCR team during that tumultuous pandemic-affected season, Palou competed in fourteen races, secured one podium finish, and finished sixteenth in the championship standings. At his rookie appearance in the 2020 Indianapolis 500, Palou surprised observers by qualifying seventh fastest. However, he finished the race in the twenty-eighth position when, on lap 121, he lost control of his car in Turn One and crashed into the outside retaining wall.

Ahead of the 2021 season, Palou moved over to Chip Ganassi Racing, where he immediately made his mark. Palou won his maiden IndyCar race at the season's first event, on the road course at Barber Motorsports Park near Birmingham, Alabama. His second-place finish in the Indy 500 proved he was a bonafide contender for the season championship, which he sealed with two additional race victories and three other podium finishes.

The 2022 season saw Palou struggle to defend his championship. He finished on the podium six times but tasted victory only once, in the season finale at Laguna Seca. As a result, Palou slumped to fifth in the championship.

Thus far in 2023, Palou had won four of the season's first thirteen races, with four other podium finishes. Even on days where he hadn't had the best car setup, Palou had taken care of business—his worst finish of the season was two eighth-place results, and he was well on his way to his second IndyCar Series championship in three years.

Palou had been a protagonist at the Indianapolis Motor Speedway in all four of his appearances. He had qualified well at the Speedway, and, as a result, he had consistently run up front. Having finished second and fourth in the biggest race of the year, Palou was poised to break through for his first Indy 500 victory. Remaining at CGR, a team that routinely performs strongly at Indy, gave Palou the fighting chance every racer craves.

TUESDAY, AUGUST 22, 2023

Foyt & Penske Form Technical Alliance

On this day, AJ Foyt Racing and Team Penske announced a technical alliance that provided different benefits for each team. The two-car Foyt race team would immediately benefit from Team Penske's proven technical know-how. In turn, Team Penske would benefit over the mid- and long-term by having junior team members gain critical experience working in the IndyCar Series, as well as having a potential landing spot for up-and-coming driving talent ready to advance to Indy cars, but not yet ready to crack into Team Penske's star-studded driver lineup.

On the mechanical engineering front, Foyt would immediately put to use Team Penske dampers, along with technical support from engineering staff, to best incorporate into Foyt's chassis setups. That, alone, should go a long way to improving the consistent competitiveness of the Foyt team cars.

Ferrucci finished third for Foyt in the 2023 Indy 500 and looked a strong contender for the win from the moment practice commenced. However, Ferrucci's strong showing at Indianapolis was one of the few bright spots for the organization over the past fifteen years.

Through fourteen races thus far in the 2023 IndyCar Series season, Ferrucci's third place in the 500 was his only top-ten finish, and he had finished twentieth or worse nine times. His teammate, Pedersen, had fared even worse; his best finish had been fifteenth, with the remaining thirteen finishes being twentieth or worse, including four last-place finishes.

Takuma Sato produced the last win for Foyt, winning the Long Beach Grand Prix in 2013. Since then, there have been just three podium finishes for the team ahead of Ferrucci's run at Indy, with veteran Tony Kanaan delivering the last one in 2019. That season, Kanaan finished fifteenth overall in the season championship, the best finish for a Foyt driver since Vitor Meira finished twelfth in 2010.

The knock on AJ Foyt Racing has long been perceived to be the organization's inability to engineer a competitive car, and perhaps the biggest opportunity for development in the IndyCar Series lies in dampers. Unlike previous eras in the sport, all teams in the IndyCar Series use the same chassis, the Dallara DW12, and they've all used it since it was introduced in 2012. From an engine perspective, there are only two suppliers, Honda and Chevrolet.

Therefore, to gain a competitive advantage, there is precious little for race teams to differentiate themselves from others. One area, however, is dampers, otherwise known as shock absorbers. While they might seem relatively insignificant to the novice observer, dampers are critical to race car performance. It's particularly true throughout the season, as IndyCar competes on a variety of racetracks, from bumpy street circuits to the billiard-table-smooth Indianapolis Motor Speedway, and includes corners that are as slow as thirty miles per hour to Indy's 220-plus-mile-per-hour turns.

With very rare exceptions, Foyt Racing has struggled for years on every type of racing circuit. This new partnership had the potential to bring AJ Foyt Racing to the front end of the grid much quicker than it could have on its own.

AJ Foyt is a Brickyard legend. In fact, for decades, Foyt was very much *the* Brickyard legend.

Anthony Joseph Foyt Jr. was born on January 16, 1935, in Houston, Texas, to Emma Evelyn Monk Foyt and her auto mechanic and midget race car driver husband, Anthony "Tony" Foyt. When little AJ was just five years old, Tony built him a small racer powered by a lawnmower engine.

In just a few years' time, that little racer wasn't big enough for young AJ. When his folks returned from a night out after leaving then eleven-year-old AJ at home to fend for himself, they discovered a yard full of ruts, where the boy had run laps around the family home in his father's race car. They also found the charred remains of that race car's engine after a fire had to be extinguished by young AJ.

Foyt Sr. was undoubtedly upset. But he didn't have to guess where his son's direction in life would follow.

AJ later dropped out of high school to work as a mechanic and focus on racing. At eighteen, he began racing midget racers in a car owned and prepared by his father. However, AJ didn't exactly take the racing world by storm, at least initially. He didn't win his first feature race until three years later, in 1956, when he triumphed in a sprint car race at the Red River Fair in Fargo, North Dakota.

Foyt steadily climbed the racing ladder, making his debut at the Indianapolis Motor Speedway in 1958, where he finished sixteenth after spinning out on lap 148. Just two seasons later, though, Foyt was crowned the 1960 series champion, the first of his record seven national championships.

In 1961, Foyt won his first Indy 500 in an exciting duel with Eddie Sachs, decided only by late pit stops for both racers. The finish was the second closest in the forty-five-year history of the race. That same year, Foyt finished the season by successfully defending his national championship.

For the 1964 Indianapolis 500, after negotiations broke down with Ford to secure a ride in a rear-engine Lotus-Ford, Foyt stuck with his reliable front-engine roadster powered by an Offenhauser engine. The race got off to an inauspicious start when, on the second lap, Dave MacDonald lost control of his car exiting Turn Four and slid across the track before crashing heavily into the inside retaining wall, where his full fuel tanks exploded.

MacDonald's wrecked car then slid back across the track into incoming race traffic, collecting seven additional cars. Eddie Sachs attempted to pass the fiery accident on the right, up against the outside wall, but before he could get past, MacDonald's car slid up and into his way. With nowhere to go, Sachs crashed into McDonald, causing a secondary explosion of his own fuel tanks.

Sachs died instantly in the accident, and his car was covered in a tarp and taken to the garage area so his body could be removed. McDonald was taken to Methodist Hospital with seared lungs as a result of the fiery crash. He succumbed to acute pulmonary edema while the race was being run.

Foyt, benefiting from mechanical failures from three front runners, including the Lotus-Fords, won his second 500. He learned about the deaths of his two friends and fellow competitors when he was handed a newspaper while still in Victory Lane.

That 1964 Indy 500 was the final race won by a front-engine car. Foyt won the race again in 1967, his first 500 victory driving a rear-engine car, gingerly threading his way through a five-car crash in front of him on the main straightaway on his final lap. His victory made him the only driver to win the race in both a front- and rear-engine car. That victory also put Foyt in the prestigious three-winner club, joining Meyer, Shaw, and Mauri Rose.

After winning three Indy 500s in seven years, it took Foyt another ten years to capture his fourth race victory, which he did after outlasting Gordon Johncock in a riveting duel in the 1977 race. That victory made Foyt the first four-time winner of the 500 and cemented the status of "Super Tex" as a Brickyard legend.

It wasn't just at Indianapolis where Foyt excelled. During his storied career, Foyt won a record sixty-seven Indy car races and secured 120 podium finishes. He also won the 24 Hours of LeMans in his only attempt in 1967, as well as the 12 Hours of Sebring and 24 Hours of Daytona, making him the fourth-ever driver to win the world's three biggest endurance races.

Foyt also won NASCAR's Daytona 500 in 1972. Throughout his career, Foyt became the only driver to win the Indianapolis 500, the Daytona 500, the 24 Hours of Daytona, the 24 Hours of Le Mans, and the 12 Hours of Sebring. Simply, if it had an engine and went fast, Foyt raced it. And when he raced, he usually ran up front.

Foyt ran an incredible thirty-five consecutive Indianapolis 500s, and he recorded a top-ten finish in the Memorial Day classic in an amazing five different decades. In his career at the Brickyard, Foyt led thirty-nine different times over thirteen different races, both records. His other records at the Speedway include 4,909 racing laps covering 12,272.5 racing miles.

Foyt retired as a driver after the 1992 Indianapolis 500 and had since concentrated on his business interests, primarily AJ Foyt Enterprises, which, of course, fields cars in the IndyCar Series. It had been a long drought for Foyt at the Speedway—Kenny Bräck's 1992 Indy 500 victory was the team's sole victory in the 500. Still, every race day when Foyt walked down to his position on the team's stand along the Speedway's Pit Lane, he received the crowd's loudest ovation.

Foyt's technical partnership with Team Penske will likely improve the team's competitiveness over time. Whether it improves in time for the 108th running of the Indianapolis 500 will be determined where car performance has always been proven—on the racetrack.

WEDNESDAY, AUGUST 23, 2023

Ericsson Leaves Ganassi for Andretti

Thirty-two-year-old Marcus Ericsson won the Indianapolis 500 in 2022, in just his fourth attempt at the race. He nearly repeated that victory three months ago, narrowly missing out on defending his race win when he finished second to Newgarden. Today, he looked to take another step forward in his career by signing with Andretti Global to contest the 2024 IndyCar Series season.

After five seasons racing in Formula One for generally noncompetitive teams, Ericsson moved to the IndyCar Series ahead of the 2019 season, where he drove for what was then known as Arrow Schmidt Peterson Motorsports. His rookie season ended with rather modest results: one podium finish, a second-place at the second race of the Detroit doubleheader, three top-ten finishes, and a seventeenth-place position in the final season standings.

Looking for a deeper, more consistently competitive team, Ericsson joined Chip Ganassi Racing (CGR) ahead of the pandemic-affected 2020 season. Once the abbreviated season finally got underway, Ericsson showed what he could do, even on a team loaded with star drivers like Dixon and Palou. In fourteen races, he brought his car home in the top ten seven times, and if it wasn't for a disastrous thirty-second-place finish in the 2020 Indy 500, Ericsson would have finished much higher than his twelfth-place position in the championship standings.

In 2021, Ericsson finally broke through with his maiden IndyCar Series victory, winning the first race of the Detroit weekend and following it up with a victory in the inaugural race on the streets of Nashville. Ericsson had truly arrived on the scene of North American open-wheel racing.

He added two wins over the past two seasons, including that 2022 Indy 500 victory, which broke an unusually long ten-year CGR drought at the Speedway. He also displayed consistency in high-placed finishes, earning sixth-place finishes each of the past two seasons in the championship.

Ericsson, to his credit, wanted more. He believed he should be recognized as one of the leading drivers in the IndyCar Series, and nothing demonstrates the value of a racer to a team than how much he or she gets paid. And that topic, as it relates to Ericsson, brought light to the subject of "pay drivers."

Make no mistake about it, motorsports of any kind are expensive. The higher the class, the higher the cost. A well-known adage in auto racing goes like this: How fast do you want to go? How much do you want to spend?

Speed on the racetrack requires money. On average, it costs an IndyCar Series team $8–10 million to fund one car for an entire season. That's an expensive endeavor no matter how deep the pockets of a car owner.

In turn, teams look to sponsors to fund their cars, and cars are colorfully painted to show off brand logos. The brands benefit every time their cars are shown on television, particularly for building overall brand awareness. Of course, cars competing for the lead are shown on television more often, so sponsors clamor over one another to get associated with the teams they perceive to be the strongest.

Television is only part of a sponsorship arrangement, though—and maybe the smallest component. An enormous part of sponsorship returns involves on-site activations, both at the racetrack and at other events. Sponsors will set up elaborate hospitality tents and entertain their best customers and award-winning employees. And nothing makes a great impression like a guest appearance from a superstar driver!

One way teams attract sponsors is through drivers, many of whom have long-standing relationships with their financial backers. These drivers bring a budget to teams, hence the term "pay driver." They are, in a sense, paying for or buying a ride in the car.

Pay drivers are often derided by fans, who feel they take the place of more deserving drivers on the grid. In IndyCar, for example, there were only twenty-seven full-time cars entered in the 2023 season, and there were hundreds of drivers who would have loved an opportunity to be one of their drivers. The situation was even worse in Formula One, where there was currently only room for twenty drivers. Fans sometimes see pay drivers as having less merit than other racers who don't have strong financial backing. To be frank, many times, they are correct.

Pay driving is how the sport works, though, and nearly every driver has done it at one point in time. Just to start racing karts as a child takes a family with enough financial resources to make it a reality. They need a kart, a driver's uniform, and a helmet, as well as tools, spare parts, tires, fuel, and expenses to travel on weekends to races. In contrast, a child wanting to play basketball needs a pair of shoes. Many potential racing drivers never get an opportunity to get started.

As drivers make their way up the ranks, they and their families look for monetary or trade-in-kind sponsorships to ease the financial burden. In some instances, very promising drivers sign managerial contracts where their new manager pays for racing in return for a large percentage of future career earnings. The higher the driver goes in class, the more career earnings there will be.

Almost every great racer has been a pay driver at one time in their career. Ericsson has long been one, having a strong relationship with Swedish billionaire Finn Rausing, co-owner of the Tetra Laval packaging company and a man estimated by Forbes in 2019 to have a net worth of over $8 billion. Ericsson moved from Arrow Schmidt to Ganassi ahead of 2020 by bringing over the budget to run the car.

With his proven success, however, Ericsson had long wanted to join the upper echelon of drivers who get paid as opposed to a driver who pays. Now, Ericsson had been getting paid through his sponsorships and with percentages of race winnings, but he had been looking for a considerable bump in pay, one commensurate with his results.

Chip Ganassi, on the other hand, typically runs his four-car team with a combination of paid and pay drivers. The No. 9 and No. 10 cars are fully funded by sponsorships acquired, for the most part, by CGR, and those cars are solidly the domains of Dixon and Palou, both of whom are richly compensated, and deservedly so. Historically, CGR's other two cars require drivers to bring their own funding to cover a significant part of the total budget necessary to run the season. And at CGR, those two distinctive realities rarely intersect.

Ericsson had been vocal over the summer; he was keen to change his relationship, and rumors flew through the paddock at almost every race in 2023. Ganassi, for his part, tried to work something out, traveling to Europe to meet with Ericsson's backers to determine if some hybrid relationship could be developed. In the end, however, it couldn't.

Ericsson would now move on to Andretti for the 2024 season and would surely receive a significant pay increase. Remaining to be seen was if he would enjoy a continuation of his recent success. At CGR, Ericsson achieved his results despite not qualifying particularly well for races. For several seasons now, Andretti had shown periodic pace in qualifying but had generally failed to transition that one-lap qualifying pace into race wins. Ericsson and Andretti would be counting on combining strong qualifying performances with a knack for consistently bringing the car to a high finish to compete for race victories and championships.

Ericsson would be a strong addition to an Andretti lineup that included young drivers Colton Herta and Kyle Kirkwood. Left to be determined was whether Andretti would continue with a fourth full-time entry in the IndyCar Series.

Twenty-three-year-old Herta was a veteran above his years, having made his IndyCar Series debut at the season finale in 2018, where he placed twentieth on the road course at Sonoma. The solid weekend performance, along with a runner-up finish to Pato O'Ward in the Indy Lights series, earned him a full-time ride with Harding Steinbrenner Racing for 2019, a team affiliated with Andretti.

Herta, the son of former CART and IndyCar racer Bryan Herta, got his start in karting at age ten and quickly succeeded at every level of racing. Thus, it was no real surprise to see him stand atop the podium at just the second race of his rookie season, winning on the natural terrain road course at the Circuit of The Americas in Austin. Herta book-ended his season with another victory in the finale and finished an impressive seventh in the driver's championship.

Since his rookie season, Herta added another five victories to his resume, and his success at such a young age had him in the conversation to join the ranks of Formula One. Somewhat controversially, though, Herta hadn't qualified for the FIA's Super License required to compete—the easiest way to do so would be to win the IndyCar Series season championship.

The past season and a half had been a bit of a struggle for Herta; he won only once in 2022, albeit in spectacular fashion in treacherous, mixed-weather conditions on the road course at Indy. Thus far in the 2023 season, Herta, like the entire Andretti team, had searched for consistency, plagued with up-and-down performances. His highest finish was third, on the street course in Toronto, but he had suffered seven finishes outside of the top ten.

Herta had also struggled in his five previous attempts on the oval at Indianapolis. He finished thirty-third and last in his debut in 2019, and his best finish was eighth, the very next year. He was also remembered for a spectacular crash during the final practice session ahead of the 2022 race.

With the clock ticking down on the Carb Day practice, Herta lost control of his car in the middle of Turn One. After almost catching it, the rear end spun out for good and he walloped the outside wall with the right rear. The impact lifted the nose of the car, and at speed, when air got under the car, it flipped over. Herta, upside down, slid through the short chute and came to a stop in Turn Two.

Herta was uninjured, but the same could not be said of his destroyed car. Having to start in an untested backup car, Herta struggled in the race before finally dropping out with a mechanical issue after 129 laps, credited with thirtieth place.

Kirkwood was another promising young racer on the Andretti roster. The twenty-four-year-old Florida native was in his second year in the IndyCar Series after making his debut the season before for AJ Foyt Racing.

In his first year at Andretti, he rewarded the team with its only victories thus far in 2023, winning on the street courses at Long Beach and

Nashville. He, too, had struggled with consistency and, like Herta, had seven finishes outside of the top ten. One of those, of course, was the Indy 500, where he failed to finish after his own spectacular upside-down crash.

With Ericsson, Herta, and Kirkwood confirmed for 2024, a question remained about who, if anyone, would fill the seat of a fourth car that had been traditionally run out of the Andretti stable. Current drivers Romain Grosjean and Devlin DeFrancesco remained possibilities, but rumors around the paddock made it seem unlikely either would return. Grosjean, a former Formula One driver, had shown flashes of brilliance, particularly in qualifying, in his almost two years at Andretti, but he had also rubbed his teammates and car owner the wrong way on several occasions. DeFrancesco had regularly languished deep in the field in his two seasons with the team.

The knock on the Andretti team has been its inability to consistently execute, both in car setup and on Pit Lane during races. Part of that had been attributed to stretching talent across a broad spectrum of racing programs at Andretti Global. In addition to the IndyCar Series, the team prepared and raced cars in the INDY NXT, Formula E, and Extreme E series, and partnered with joint entries in IMSA and the Australian Supercars Championship. As if that was not enough, the team was also attempting to enter the rarified air of Formula One.

Addition through subtraction might be the best option for Andretti regarding its IndyCar programs. Allocating resources to just three cars instead of four might provide the answer for better on-track results. In the very recent past, Andretti was viewed as one of the "Big Three," alongside Penske and Ganassi. Now, it's arguably behind Arrow McLaren, on the outside looking in at the top teams of IndyCar.

TUESDAY, SEPTEMBER 5, 2023

Meyer Shank Expands IndyCar Program

Meyer Shank Racing, led by co-owner Michael Shank, had a long history of successfully competing in sportscar racing before testing the IndyCar waters with a one-off effort with Jack Harvey in the 2017 Indy 500. Since then, the team slowly grew into full-time participants.

Over several seasons, the team participated part-time, as a one-car entry, gradually building the organizational infrastructure to allow it to compete and grow. In 2021, the team entered a second car for the first time, a special one-off entry for Helio Castroneves in the Indy 500. Remarkably, Castroneves raced that entry to his fourth 500 victory and the team's maiden IndyCar win.

The team expanded to two full-time entries the past two seasons, but consistent success had been difficult to achieve. In thirty-three races with two cars, they had produced just eleven top-ten finishes, with the best being Simon Pagenaud's second-place finish in the first race on the Indianapolis road course in the 2023 season.

Aiming to compete at the top of the IndyCar Series, Meyer Shank announced an expansion of its program heading into next season. Felix Rosenqvist would join the organization next year on a multi-year contract to join rookie Tom Blomqvist, who signed with the team late in August. They will be allied with a third team entry at the Indianapolis 500, to be driven by Castroneves, who became a minority owner in Meyer Shank racing last month.

Rosenqvist had spent his previous five seasons racing for Ganassi and Arrow McLaren and had shown flashes of promise, including a fourth-place finish in his first-ever IndyCar race. Driving for Chip Ganassi that rookie season, Rosenqvist finished sixth in the season championship after producing ten top-ten finishes.

In his second year, Rosenqvist won the fourth race of the season. But, since then, further wins had proven elusive, and inconsistency had marked his performances. Quite often, Rosenqvist could be found at the front end of races, competing for high finishes. Yet, at other times, a variety of factors conspired to relegate him to the back of the field. In just the 2023 season alone, driving for Arrow McLaren, Rosenqvist's eight top-ten finishes had been tarnished by six finishes of twentieth or worse.

Rosenqvist looks to rebound with Meyer Shank, where he will be the lead driver for the team in 2024, teaming with Blomqvist, who comes from a primarily sportscar-racing background. For the past two seasons, Blomqvist raced for Meyer Shank in its sportscar program, and he had twice piloted the team's winning car at the Rolex 24 Hours at Daytona.

Today's announcement leaves Pagenaud out of both the Meyer Shank Racing team and the IndyCar Series, at least for the time being. Pagenaud is a thirty-nine-year-old Frenchman who had been at the top of the sport for years, winning fifteen IndyCar races over a fourteen-year career, including the 2019 Indianapolis 500. He's also an IndyCar Series season champion, having secured the 2016 title.

In July 2023, while practicing for the race at Mid-Ohio Sports Car Course, Pagenaud's No. 60 car suffered a brake failure going into the course's high-speed Turn Four, one of the most treacherous portions of track on the entire IndyCar schedule. Turn Four is the start of the "esses," and follows a long straightaway, and when Pagenaud went to apply the brakes, he found no response.

His car shot off track and flew airborne over the grass before landing on its right side in a sandy gravel pit. From there, the car violently barrel rolled several times before hitting a tire retaining wall and coming to a rest upside down. Incredibly, Pagenaud was on the radio in seconds, telling the team he was okay and that he had experienced a brake failure.

Pagenaud may have felt okay in the moment, but he wasn't, as he had suffered a concussion. He hadn't been back in the race car since, and the team had used three replacement drivers, including Blomqvist, in his absence.

Pagenaud was injured in an accident that wasn't his doing, as a brake manufacturing error had led to the mechanical failure. As of yet, though, his ability to return to car racing is unknown, and Meyer Shank had to make a difficult decision in moving forward.

As unfair as it might be for Pagenaud, Meyer Shank moved on and will be looking to take a much-needed step up in performance with Rosenqvist. In the meantime, Pagenaud worked on his full recovery and sought an opportunity to finish out his illustrious career with a more appropriate ending.

THURSDAY, SEPTEMBER 7, 2023

Arrow McLaren Signs Malukas to Finalize Driver Lineup

Having lost Palou from its driver lineup for 2024, Arrow McLaren completed its full-time roster by signing David Malukas to a multi-year contract. A twenty-one-year-old from Chicago, Malukas was a two-year veteran of the IndyCar Series, having raced the past two seasons for Dale Coyne Racing with HMD Motorsports. Next season, he would join a stout lineup of returning stars, Pato O'Ward and Alexander Rossi.

In his two seasons in the IndyCar Series, Malukas had shown considerable promise. Driving for the underdog Coyne team, along with substantial financial backing from his father's HMD Motorsports organization, Malukas had raced to two podium finishes—both on the oval at the World Wide Technology Raceway—and seven other top-ten finishes in thirty-three races ahead of the 2023 season finale.

At his two appearances in the Indy 500, Malukas had also accounted for himself well. In 2022, he qualified thirteenth and finished sixteenth, the highest-placed rookie in the final classification. This past May, after a consistent run in the mid-field, a crash on lap 160 took him out of the race and placed him twenty-ninth.

After enduring a frustrating stretch in 2023 with the Coyne team, Malukas was looking for a larger organization to take the next step forward with his career. In Arrow McLaren, he found it.

For years, the top three teams in IndyCar racing have been Team Penske, Chip Ganassi Racing, and Andretti Global. In the past couple of seasons, Arrow McLaren had performed well and was now included at the pinnacle as one of the sport's best teams. A persuasive argument could be made that Arrow McLaren had passed Andretti to be one of the top three teams.

And while Arrow McLaren may have missed out on the talents of Palou, they are far from suffering from a driver perspective. Both O'Ward and Rossi are proven race winners.

O'Ward was a twenty-four-year-old Mexican who attended high school in San Antonio, Texas. Like many young racers today, he got his start in karting, where O'Ward started when he was just six. From there, he rapidly advanced through various open-wheel formulas and was even part of the Red Bull Driver Academy on the global Formula One stage.

In 2017 and 2018, O'Ward won consecutive championships, first in sports cars, then in Indy Lights, the feeder series into IndyCar. At the finale of the 2018 IndyCar season, O'Ward made his Series debut. Driving for Harding, he demonstrated his enormous potential with a ninth-place finish.

Sponsorship issues resulted in O'Ward driving only part-time in 2019 for the Carlin team. In his first race, he posted an eighth-place finish on the Circuit of The Americas road course outside of Austin. However, because of conflicts with his Red Bull obligations, O'Ward competed in only six other races. Moreover, he suffered through a horrible debut at the Indianapolis Motor Speedway, where both he and his Carlin teammate, Max Chilton, along with two-time Formula One World Champion Fernando Alonso in a Carlin-prepared entry for McLaren, failed to qualify for the 500.

For 2020, McLaren partnered with Arrow Schmidt Peterson Motorsports to form the team that existed today. Recognizing raw talent when they saw it, the team snapped up the young O'Ward as one of its full-time drivers.

In the pandemic-affected 2020 season, O'Ward recorded three second-place finishes, a third, and five other top-ten finishes in fourteen races to finish fourth in the championship. Included in that was a sixth-place finish in the Indy 500, where he earned Rookie of the Year honors.

Finally, in 2021, O'Ward won his first two IndyCar races en route to a third-place finish in the championship standings. He followed that campaign with another two victories in 2022.

The 2023 season had been a solid one thus far for O'Ward, despite the lack of race victories. In sixteen races leading up to the 2023 season finale, he had earned four second-place and three third-place finishes, and sat fourth in the championship standings.

After his inauspicious debut at Indianapolis, O'Ward had been a force to reckon with at the 500. In three subsequent races after his rookie appearance, O'Ward battled for the lead, and in the last two years, he had looked a likely winner. In 2022, he was unable to make a daring overtake of Ericsson in Turn One on the final lap and finished second. In the 2023 Indy 500, intent on not letting the 500 get away from him once again, he lost control of his car in Turn Three trying to pass Ericsson for second place on lap 193, crashing out of the race and finishing twenty-fourth.

O'Ward's teammate at Arrow McLaren this past season had been Alexander Rossi. No matter what Rossi should go on and accomplish in an already illustrious racing career—he has eight IndyCar victories to his credit—he will always be remembered as the rookie winner of the 100th Indianapolis 500 in 2016. And what an improbable win it was.

Driving for Andretti, Rossi qualified tenth for the 2016 Indy 500 and ran most of the race steadily in the top half of the field, but not spectacularly up front, fighting for the lead. With more than thirty laps left in the race, Rossi's team took a gamble and coached Rossi into saving fuel. It was a simple win-or-lose strategy. If the race ran under green flag conditions to the very end, all of the leading cars would have to pit. If Rossi could stretch his fuel to the end, he'd be at the front.

As the leading cars in front of him pitted, Rossi inherited the lead on lap 197. He slowed down to stretch out his fuel as his rivals raced to catch up with him. On the final lap, Rossi literally coasted over the finish line, just over four seconds ahead of a hard-charging Carlos Muñoz.

Not wanting race observers to think he could only compete and win on a strategic call, Rossi had shown over the years that he had more than considerable pace at the Speedway. In eight total appearances in the 500, he had posted six top-ten finishes, including second place in a thrilling duel with Pagenaud in the 2019 race.

Rossi moved over to Arrow McLaren this season after his last three seasons at Andretti were plagued with diminishing team performance and inter-team conflicts on track, a period that produced just one win. The 2023 season had produced ten top-ten finishes thus far, but still, that first victory for his new team had proven elusive.

Arrow McLaren may have missed out on Palou, but its cupboard was far from empty. O'Ward and Rossi had the talent and experience to put up a strong, competitive front, and Malukas had shown promising potential. As the 2023 season came to a close and preparations begin for 2024, the papaya-colored cars of Arrow McLaren looked to be strong contenders for race wins, including at the biggest race of all.

MONDAY, SEPTEMBER 18, 2023

Ganassi Confirms 2024 Driver Lineup

Chip Ganassi Racing had long been one of the powerhouse teams in the IndyCar Series. Since its formation in 1990, the team had won fifteen combined CART and IndyCar season championships and 135 races, including five Indy 500 victories.

It was not just with Indy cars that Ganassi Racing excelled. The organization had won numerous races in series as divergent as NASCAR stock cars to sports cars to electric cars. Ganassi Racing was a winning organization that was quite familiar with celebrating race wins and championships.

Before becoming a successful racing team owner, Ganassi began his motorsports career as a promising driver. While in high school in 1977, he attended a driving school, and from there, his racing career took off. Upon graduating from Duquesne with a degree in finance in 1982, Ganassi started competing in the CART series. In five races that season, his best finish was eleventh.

For the 1983 season, Ganassi found himself driving for legendary Indy car owner Pat Patrick. His first race for the team was the Indianapolis 500, and he finished eighth as a rookie. Later in the season, Ganassi scored two podium finishes, both third places. Finishing ninth in the season championship, he was named the series' Most Improved Driver.

In 1984, Ganassi returned to Patrick Racing to run the entire campaign. At Indianapolis, a blown engine relegated him to a twenty-eighth-place finish. He rebounded with four strong finishes, the last of which was a career-high second-place finish at Cleveland. Then, at the next race, Ganassi's season came to an abrupt end.

At the Michigan 500 on the high-speed, banked oval at Michigan International Speedway, Ganassi lost control and spun when exiting Turn Two, careening across the backstretch and collecting Al Unser Jr. in the process. Both cars skated across the grassy runoff area and slammed into the inside retaining wall. Ganassi's car cartwheeled multiple times, breaking apart and spreading debris over a wide area before coming to a rest right-side up.

When medical personnel arrived, Ganassi was unconscious. Just as they were starting resuscitative efforts, he began breathing on his own. When he regained consciousness, Ganassi suffered from short-term memory loss. Fortunately, over time, he felt he'd made a full recovery.

The next year, Ganassi raced in the Indy 500 for AJ Foyt, where he was classified in twenty-second after retiring with a broken fuel line. In 1985, his lone race was at Michigan, where he exorcized his demons to some extent, finishing in twenty-second while racing for the Machinists Union team.

Ganassi's final race as an Indy car driver was the 1986 Indy 500, once again driving for Machinists Union. An engine failure after 151 laps left him with a twenty-first-place finish.

In 1989, Ganassi partnered with Pat Patrick as a co-owner for Patrick's planned final season in racing. That year, the team won both the Indy 500 and the season championship with driver Emerson Fittipaldi, the grandfather of current racer Pietro Fittipaldi. The next year, Ganassi took over full ownership of the team and renamed it Chip Ganassi Racing.

Ganassi slowly, steadily, and purposefully built his eponymous team, beginning with a one-car effort and growing only as fast as his organization could sustainably operate. Finally, in 1994, the team won its first two races, with Michael Andretti delivering the triumphs on both occasions. Since then, the team has been a contender for race wins and championships.

Over the past three weeks, Ganassi Racing had built out its driver lineup for the 2024 IndyCar season and the 108th running of the Indianapolis 500. The upcoming season had shaped up to be one of the team's most ambitious yet, as CGR would field five full-time entries at all the races.

Joining veteran stalwarts Dixon and Palou would be one second-year driver and two rookies, with all three being rookies at Indianapolis.

On this day, the team confirmed second-year driver Marcus Armstrong would return to the team on a multi-year contract. Armstrong drove for the team this past season, but only on the series' road and street circuits. Still, despite missing the five oval rounds of the series, the twenty-three-year-old New Zealander won the IndyCar Series Rookie of the Year honors on the heels of five top-ten finishes in his twelve race starts.

Armstrong would be joined by IndyCar rookies Kyffin Simpson and Linus Lundqvist, who were confirmed by Ganassi Racing in the previous weeks.

Simpson, an eighteen-year-old from the Cayman Islands, joined Chip Ganassi Racing as a development driver in May 2022. For the past two seasons, Simpson competed in the Indy Lights and INDY NXT developmental series, as well as in sports cars in Asia, Europe, and the United States.

Lundqvist was a twenty-four-year-old Swede who the team signed at the end of August. Simply, Lundqvist was too good of a talent for the team to pass up. After cutting his teeth racing in Europe, Lundqvist started racing full-time in the United States when he campaigned in the Formula Regional Americas Championship in 2020. To say his season was successful would be a dramatic understatement. Lundqvist won fifteen of the seventeen races en route to the championship, easily outpointing his closest competitor, David Malukas.

Graduating to the Indy Lights series in 2021, Lundqvist scored three wins and eight other podium finishes in twenty races and placed third in the season championship. The following year, he earned five wins and another four podium finishes in fourteen races to win the season title.

With little to prove in the feeder series to IndyCar, Lundqvist took a wait-and-see approach to the 2023 season, racing in the Porsche Carrera Cup Scandinavia series and biding his time for an IndyCar ride. His opportunity came when Pagenaud was injured at Mid-Ohio.

Taking over Pagenaud's Meyer Shank entry at Nashville, Lundqvist impressed by qualifying eleventh. He ran up front and set the race's fastest lap, but a crash with just twelve laps remaining left him with just a twenty-fifth-place finish.

After his impressive debut, Lundqvist drove the Meyer Shank car twice more, first on the road course at Indianapolis, where he finished twelfth, the highest finish among rookies, and again on the oval at Gateway, where he finished eighteenth in his first-ever oval race. In that race, Lundqvist again set the race's fastest lap.

With his impressive run as a substitute for Pagenaud, Lundqvist found himself in high demand from teams up and down the paddock. With both he and Ganassi seeing a promising opportunity, they quickly came to terms on a multi-year contract.

Armstrong, Simpson, and Lundqvist will each make their debut on the oval at Indianapolis in May. The track and its incredibly fast speeds would present a steep learning curve for all three. Rookies or not, driving for Ganassi Racing brings with it sky-high expectations, not only from fans but the team itself. However, those rookies would not only be backed by one of the best teams in the business, but they'd also have the experiences of both Palou and Dixon to call upon as needed. And that collective experience would definitely be needed.

Scott Dixon is arguably the best Indy car driver of all time. The forty-two-year-old from New Zealand was a six-time IndyCar Series champion who had won fifty-six races leading into the 2024 IndyCar season, what would be his twenty-fourth year in an Indy car.

Like many racers, Dixon started in the sport by racing karts when he was just seven years old. He showed his natural talent and competitiveness from the start, and he won thirty major karting titles in his age group across both New Zealand and Australia. At thirteen, he started racing cars, and he progressed rapidly, winning four major championships in junior formulas, including the 2000 Indy Lights title.

In 2001, Dixon made his Indy car debut, racing for PacWest in the CART Series. Remarkably, he won in his third start, on the oval at Nazareth Speedway, the hometown track of the famed Andretti family. He completed his rookie campaign with an eighth-place finish in the championship standings.

After PacWest ceased operations just three races into the 2002 season, Dixon signed with Ganassi Racing, and he'd been a stalwart leader of the team ever since.

Over his decades at the highest level of open-wheel racing in North America, Dixon had shown he was good at every aspect of racing, and downright great at some, including an inane ability to conserve fuel while still running very competitive lap times. In 385 career races, he had qualified on the pole thirty-two times and earned 135 podium finishes.

A key to Dixon's past success had been his consistency. In twenty-three seasons, he had won at least one race in twenty-one different years, and when he won on the road course at Indianapolis in August, it marked the nineteenth consecutive year that Dixon had won a race.

Dixon won the 2008 Indy 500, and surprisingly, that victory remains his lone win on the Speedway's oval. In the years since, Dixon had been a major protagonist fighting for the win more often than not.

Dixon qualified on the pole ahead of his 2008 victory and added four subsequent poles, the most recent being ahead of the 2022 race. Additionally, he had recorded six top-five finishes in the 500 since his win, including two second-place finishes. He also finished second in 2007, the year before his victory.

In twenty-one starts in the Indy 500, Dixon had led fifteen different editions of the race for a total of 665 laps, the most laps led in 500 history.

While still stuck on a single 500 victory, Dixon had had a lot of close calls that could have resulted in more wins. He'd also had scary moments, including one of the biggest in recent memory during the 2017 race. For that 500, Dixon qualified on the pole, and he led in the early going. Then, on lap 53, Jay Howard drifted wide in Turn One and brushed the outside wall. After his impact, his car slid across the track and directly into the path of Dixon. Dixon, unable to slow his car, drove into the left rear of Howard's car and launched into a barrel-rolling flip that, improbably, Castroneves drove underneath and escaped to safety.

Dixon's car landed on its right side on top of the inside concrete retaining wall, and the force of the impact tore it into two pieces. Dixon's momentum carried his cartwheeling car down into the inside of Turn Two before coming to a rest right-side up. Almost unbelievably, Dixon escaped without any major injuries.

Having seen the best and worst of Indianapolis, Dixon brought immeasurable experience and counsel to the entire Ganassi team. As a de facto coach and mentor to his three rookie teammates, Dixon would play an important role for them and the team. But his biggest role would be that of a competitor, and the savvy veteran would be one of the favorites to add a second victory in the 500 to his already impressive resume.

FRIDAY, SEPTEMBER 29, 2023

McLaren Racing Sues Palou

Today, McLaren Racing Limited filed a lawsuit against Palou in the High Court of Justice Business and Property Courts of England and Wales Commercial Court. In its filing, McLaren sought at least $23 million to recoup financial losses the team claims it incurred when Palou changed his mind after signing a contract to move over from Chip Ganassi Racing.

With the filing, McLaren sought to recover damages that included losses of $15.5 million of future sponsorship tied to Palou joining McLaren, the costs of using him as a reserve driver for its Formula One team, the expense incurred by McLaren in developing Palou for F1, and a $400,000 advance on his 2024 salary.

In the lawsuit, McLaren stated that after the team had been informed by Palou that he would not honor his contract, the team received a second letter from attorneys representing Palou that incorrectly claimed he had been promised a full-time seat in Formula One, and that because he was only going to be a reserve driver, "a complete severing of the relationship (was) in order."

Additionally, McLaren contended Palou signed two contracts: one with McLaren Racing to serve as its F1 reserve driver and another separate contract with Arrow McLaren to race in the IndyCar Series while simultaneously serving in his F1 reserve role.

Palou has repeatedly declined to comment on the matter since the news broke in early August. On the surface, it appeared that with the McLaren Formula One team having contracts with young drivers Lando Norris and Oscar Piastri, Palou saw no way to earn a race seat unless one of the team's two primary drivers got injured. With racing in F1 being unlikely, Palou felt CGR provided the best opportunity to compete for Indy 500 victories and IndyCar Series championships.

The 2023 IndyCar Series season had been completed, and teams were busily preparing for next year's schedule of seventeen races. Palou would stay at Ganassi Racing, and Arrow McLaren would go forward with O'Ward, Rossi, and Malukas. On the track, the saga of Palou's contractual shenanigans of the past two years would go unnoticed. What was left to be determined, however, was how much of a distraction this legal dispute might cause the two teams off the track, and what impact that might have on racetrack performance.

WEDNESDAY, OCTOBER 11, 2023

Rookie Orientation Program

D riving a race car at the Indianapolis Motor Speedway is a unique endeavor, even for the most experienced racing driver. First, the speeds are higher than anywhere other than a drag racing strip. But racing drivers tend to acquit themselves well with speed. They're almost constantly looking to go faster, at least with respect to their competitors.

The real test at IMS is the nature of the track itself. Called an oval, it's really a rectangle, and the corners, Turns One through Four, represent the biggest challenge. Part of the challenge is the ninety-degree angle of the turns covering a distance of just a quarter mile each. The second part of the challenge is the rather flat 9.2-degree banking of the turns. When drivers new to IMS approach turns at speeds well over 200 mph, the turns look both sharp and flat.

For rookies preparing to race in their first 500, IMS holds a Rookie Orientation Program (ROP), open only to debutantes who have never before raced on IMS's famed oval. To successfully complete the ROP and be cleared for practice during May, drivers must first complete ten laps between 205–210 mph, followed by fifteen laps between 210–215 mph, and finish with fifteen laps faster than 215 mph.

On this cool, crisp autumn day, three aspiring rookies at the Speedway set out to complete their programs. Marcus Armstrong, Tom Blomqvist, and Linus Lundqvist were all three earmarked for full-time rides in the

IndyCar Series in 2024. The buildup to their participation in the ROP, however, had been overshadowed by that of a fourth driver, a driver who, because of scheduling conflicts, would not turn his first laps until the next day.

That driver was Kyle Larson, a former champion and full-time participant of the NASCAR Cup Series and a dirt-track legend who had won in "bullrings" around the country. In May, Larson would attempt to be the fifth driver to compete in the Memorial Day "double," racing in the Indianapolis 500 early in the day, then flying to Charlotte, North Carolina, to participate that evening in the NASCAR Cup Series' Coca-Cola 600.

But first, Larson, a thirty-one-year-old who had won twenty-two NASCAR Cup Series races and was named one of NASCAR's 75 Greatest Drivers in 2023, must complete his first-ever lap in an IndyCar. That would come on October 12, after Armstrong, Blomqvist, and Lundqvist got their first laps in on the oval.

Armstrong and Lundqvist were set to be teammates at Chip Ganassi Racing for the 108th running of the 500. Armstrong just completed his rookie season in the IndyCar Series, where he raced in twelve road- and street-course events and earned Rookie of the Year honors, giving way in his CGR-prepared car to two-time Indy 500 winner Takuma Sato for the Series' five 2023 oval races. Lundqvist raced three events in 2023 as a substitute for Pagenaud at Meyer Shank Racing, including his oval track debut in late August at World Wide Technology Raceway at Gateway Motorsports Park in Madison, Illinois, just east of St. Louis.

Blomqvist also drove his first three races in the IndyCar Series as a Meyer Shank Racing substitute, posting results good enough to earn a full-time ride in 2024. Today's running in the ROP, however, would be his first experience driving an IndyCar on an oval.

The three drivers took to the track like fish to water, undercutting any suspense or drama. Each of the Honda-powered drivers wasted no time in completing their three-phased tests, finishing before noon and the scheduled lunch break.

With their rookie tests completed, after lunch, the drivers set out to build on their experience, and pushed to gradually increase speeds. Together, the three drivers combined to run 285 laps. Blomqvist ended the day fastest overall with a 220.176 mph lap, followed by Lundqvist at 219.504, and Armstrong at 219.252.

The first to complete his test, Lundqvist finished the day with a healthy respect for the track. "It's unbelievable," Lundqvist said. "With the speeds that you're going, it feels so fast. With the history and legacy around this place, it just feels magical. Even though the grandstands are empty, I can only imagine what it will feel like when they're full. Even now it's very, very special."

His CGR teammate Armstrong shared similar feelings and commented, "I've enjoyed it a whole lot more than I expected. I'm not saying I didn't expect to enjoy it, but I think the intensity of it is pretty special, and watching (in-car) onboards and on TV is one thing, but actually feeling how the car moves and how the wind affects you and the tiny details of this place—and Texas—has kind of given me so much enjoyment."

Blomqvist, too, understood the challenge of the Speedway but recognized the day was just the first step in a long, drawn-out process. "There's a bit of a relief, but I still anticipated it being something I would get through," Blomqvist said afterward. "It shouldn't be that much of a challenge, and at the end of the day, I'm coming here to try and compete for victories in the future. But it's all part of the process, and I've also read this is something of a tradition, which has been around for a long, long time.

"But it's definitely rewarding to know that you can do it, to know that it is possible because you're going so fast around here. I'm so fascinated by how your body and how your mind processes everything and slows things down. At some point, you don't feel the speeds that you're doing. I keep saying that it's one thing driving around by yourself, right? Come May, it's a steady thirty-two other cars that you have to navigate your way through and manage with traffic and all the racecraft, so that's another thing. Just baby steps."

It was a day the drivers, like all the drivers before them who drove their initial laps at speed, would never forget. And it also left the drivers wanting so much more, fueling their resolve over the winter to return in May and race for the biggest prize in auto racing.

However, while it was the start of their journey to the Indy 500, it was just the start of ROP, for the highly awaited debut of Larson was still a day away.

THURSDAY, OCTOBER 12, 2023

Rookie Orientation Program & Hybrid Assist Testing

Kyle Larson's ROP program wouldn't be the only session at the Speedway on this day. The day before, he couldn't run with the other three rookies because of a scheduling conflict. Therefore, IndyCar and the Speedway accommodated him on October 12, between 11:00 a.m. and 2:00 p.m., attempting to squeeze his ROP program in on the first day of superspeedway testing for the IndyCar Series' test of its new-for-2024 hybrid engine and energy recovery system.

This would be the first of a two-day test with defending series champion Palou of Chip Ganassi Racing, former 500 winners Will Power of Team Penske and Rossi of Arrow McLaren, and Herta from Andretti Global. The test session followed previous tests with engine suppliers Chevrolet and Honda at road courses at Sebring, Road America, and Barber Motorsports Park, and on the short oval at World Wide Technology Raceway.

The bumpy Sebring short course replicated street circuits, and the road courses at Road America and Barber were great representatives of tracks with big, sweeping corners in both directions, along with sizable straightaways. And, of course, World Wide Technology Raceway outside of St. Louis gave engineers an idea of the challenges facing a hybrid engine on an oval.

However, IMS was an entirely different beast to tame. On a short oval, just as on street and road courses, drivers must lift off the throttle and apply the brakes, both critical components of kinetic recovery systems to capture and store energy, before making the energy available for use later. At Indianapolis, though, if the race car is set up properly, a driver rarely lifts, and when he or she does, it's not for long. Braking, aside from an absolute emergency, is performed only when entering the pits for fuel and tires.

With minimal amounts of braking events on superspeedways like IMS, IndyCar and its engine suppliers have developed a paddle-based hybrid assist system for ovals, where drivers apply pressure to a paddle to trigger energy recovery from a light dragging of the brakes to progressively charge a supercapacitor. Unlike Formula One, whose cars utilize batteries to store energy, IndyCar had selected a supercapacitor for its ability to be charged rapidly, fitting the needs of the series with its wide variety of racetracks, including the biggest of all, the Indianapolis Motor Speedway.

The concept was simple: The drivers would be tasked with manually generating energy using the harvesting paddle on their steering wheels. Then, when they were ready to deploy the stored energy, they would access their stores through the push-to-pass button they were already familiar with on their steering wheels.

It all read well on paper. But how would it work on the track?

Larson, ever the highly esteemed professional racing driver, eliminated any suspense associated with his first driving appearance at the Speedway, which, in hindsight, shouldn't have come as a surprise to anyone. Larson had a well-earned reputation as being a racer capable of competing with any car on any circuit.

Larson had been working with the Arrow McLaren team for months to prepare for the 2024 Indy 500. His program on the day was as uneventful as could be hoped for, and his best lap was a tidy 217.764 mph.

In his press conference, Larson spoke about his expectations and goals for the day. "I guess mostly what I anticipated in a way," he said. "The speed and the grip didn't feel, thankfully, scarier than what I thought it might. But there's, like, how much the car wants to pull left, and you have to kind of fight it back right down the straightaways; all of that was something I didn't expect. The way the wheel was a lot lighter than the simulator but still a little heavier than maybe what I expected.

"Other than that, I thought it went really smooth[ly]. I need more the pit road side of things I'll have to work more on. Just the steering is so slow, you have to turn so far to get in and out—if you're coming in around somebody, if you're leaving, getting out around someone. Just getting used to the steering at a slower speed will be something to get used to. Then just maximizing the apron and braking for pit road; stuff like that I think is stuff I'll have to really focus on and work on. That way we maximize our potential. Overall, I think it was a great day."

While Larson would be keeping busy over the winter with sprint cars and the beginning of the NASCAR season in February, his next appointment with IndyCar and the Speedway would be the open test sessions in April 2024. From then until the checkered flag drops on race day, he would certainly be the subject of both media and fan attention alike.

When the hybrid assist unit was first announced by IndyCar, the vision was to have it paired with a larger, 2.4-liter, twin-turbocharged engine. The desire was to produce over 900 horsepower from the combination of a bigger engine with a hybrid assist energy package.

Earlier in 2023, however, IndyCar and its engine manufacturers, Honda and Chevrolet, announced production of a bigger engine would be paused. As a result, the hybrid assist unit would now get coupled to the existing 2.2-liter engine.

Previous tests of the hybrid assist unit were held in private, away from the prying eyes of the series' regular media members, including its television partner, NBC Sports. On October 12, 2023, the wraps came off on the program, as the media were in attendance.

Testing proved to be . . . well, typical testing. Drivers exited the pits, pounded around for a handful of laps, and then came back into the pits for a data dump.

Ordinarily, testing is centered around the setup of the chassis. One of the most valuable skills of a racing driver isn't racing the car. Rather, when it comes to testing, the most important skill for a driver is the ability to run lap after lap consistently, using the exact same driver inputs to the car. In that way, the entire team can determine whether a change to the setup improved the car's performance or not.

Today, it was all about the power plant, and engineers from the manufacturers and the teams placed a priority on reliability—would the system stand up to the demands of a high-performance racing car, particularly with the heat and vibration it would be exposed to for 500 miles come May?

But for drivers, teams, and fans alike, the big question to be answered was if the hybrid power unit will push cars to lap faster at Indianapolis.

"No, not this year," said two-time IndyCar Series champion and 2018 Indianapolis 500 winner Power of Team Penske. "It's got more capability, but I think reliability comes first. We'll creep up on the amount of power that we use and deploy."

Arrow McLaren's Rossi, the Indy 500 winner in 2016, agreed. "No, it's certainly not faster," he said at the end of the day. "I don't think anything's really optimized yet, so it's hard to say. We're still in a testing process where we are trying different things. The manufacturers want to try different strategies and different ways of doing this. I think that's good."

Lap times were not made public, but the driver testimonies indicated there was still work to be done to wrangle the performance that, on paper, was so abundant. No one with the Speedway or with IndyCar wants the cars to go slower and battle possible reliability issues. A gigantic question remains: Will the power units be ready for primetime with the season opener at St. Petersburg scheduled in just five months?

"We've been working on this for many, many months," Roger Penske told NBC Sports. "We are in the testing stage now, and we have run hundreds of miles through the system. We are getting the different teams to test it and get mileage from it. It's going to be durability and the ability to build enough units by the time we start the season. Right now, we are on schedule. We have to meet certain gates and hurdles to get through."

Like always when it came to building speed and reliability at the Speedway, time would tell.

WEDNESDAY, OCTOBER 25, 2023

Rasmussen Joins Ed Carpenter Racing

Forty-two-year-old racer Ed Carpenter had had a long and distinguished career at the Indianapolis Motor Speedway. It was probably predictable. After all, Carpenter is the stepson of Tony George.

Carpenter was more than the owner of Ed Carpenter Racing. He was also one of the team's drivers, racing all the oval races on the IndyCar Series schedule, including, of course, the Indianapolis 500.

In the past, Carpenter raced the full IndyCar Series, most recently in the 2013 season. Through his career, however, Carpenter excelled on the oval tracks, where his three career victories and nine podium finishes had all taken place. And while he had never won the Indy 500, his hometown race, he and his team had traditionally been key protagonists every May.

Carpenter had qualified for the pole position at Indy on three separate occasions and earned a second, two fifths, a sixth, an eighth, and a tenth-place finish in his twenty appearances at the Speedway. Along the way, he'd led 146 laps in those previous 500s.

Race fans had come to expect strong showings from Carpenter and his team. Their cars are always well prepared, and more years than not, one or more of the ECR cars contended at the front of the field.

A two-car team for the IndyCar Series, ECR annually expanded to a three-car team for the Indy 500. On October 25, the team announced the addition of Danish rookie Christian Rasmussen for the 2024 season, where he'd pilot the No. 20 car on all road and street courses. At Indy, Rasmussen would hand the No. 20 to the boss and take the helm of the team's No. 33 entry.

The twenty-three-year-old Rasmussen started racing in the United States in 2018, and he began his path to racing in the Indy 500 the very next year. He was only the second driver ever to win a championship in each open-wheel junior category that feeds into the IndyCar Series—the USF2000 Championship in 2020, the USF Pro 2000 Championship in 2022, and the INDY NXT Championship in 2023.

In the INDY NXT Championship of the past season, Rasmussen was dominant, winning five of the fourteen races, with three other podium finishes and two more top-five finishes. It was easily enough to catch the eye of Carpenter, always one eager to bring young, new talent into IndyCar.

Rasmussen's championship form earned him a test with the ECR team at the Barber Motorsport Park road course in September, and he excelled. He would now look to create a formidable duo with returning driver Rinus VeeKay.

Rinus van Kalmthout—shortened to VeeKay as his professional name—is a twenty-three-year-old from Belgium who would be entering his fifth season in IndyCar, all with ECR. In his previous sixty-two career races, he had qualified fastest twice and earned four podium finishes, driving to his maiden victory on the road course at Indianapolis in 2021 in just his nineteenth start.

While his formative years as a young racer were groomed on the road courses of Europe, VeeKay had demonstrated a particular knack for quickly getting around the famed Indianapolis oval. In his four attempts at the race, VeeKay had qualified fourth, third, third, and second. As a result, he held Indy 500 records for both recording the best qualifying result by a teenager and for being the youngest ever front-row qualifier.

However, VeeKay had not been able to convert his strong qualifying into equally strong finishes, with his best final classification being an eighth-place finish in 2021.

In the 2023 Indy 500, VeeKay spent the first half of the race dueling with Palou, leading for twenty-four laps. Then, leaving his pit box during a yellow caution period on lap ninety-five, VeeKay spun his rear tires violently, losing control and veering across the front of Palou, both cars coming to a stop along the inside wall.

Both continued, but their best chances for victory had evaporated. Palou, despite having to replace his damaged front wing, recovered brilliantly to finish fourth. VeeKay, who was relegated to the back of the field after serving a drive-through penalty down Pit Lane for causing the incident, drove his car back up to finish tenth.

VeeKay had had potential race-winning cars under him for the previous four years, as had Carpenter for several years before that. At the ECR facility in Indianapolis, a feeling of unfinished business at the Speedway continued to persist. With a driver lineup that included a savvy veteran, a record-setting qualifier, and a promising young rookie, the team looked to take the most difficult step of them all at the Indy 500, that from contender to winner.

THURSDAY, NOVEMBER 2, 2023

Grosjean Joins Canapino at Juncos Hollinger Racing

Argentinian Ricardo Juncos had long been involved in motorsport. The son of a racer, Juncos started racing karts when he was fourteen and moved up the ranks to eventually drive in the Formula Renault series, competing throughout South America.

As his driving career plateaued, Juncos formed his race team in 1997 and based it in Buenos Aires, where it competed successfully in a variety of series until 1993, when Juncos, seeking to compete in higher echelons of motorsport, relocated to the United States.

Now headquartered in Indianapolis, the team made its debut at the Speedway in 2017, fielding cars for Sebastián Saavedra and Spencer Pigot, who finished fifteenth and eighteenth. The next year, in a single-car effort, Kyle Kaiser finished twenty-ninth for the team.

It was in 2019 when Juncos and Kaiser made a lot of noise. Thirty-six cars were entered in the 500 that year, so the last-row qualifying session on Sunday would see three cars eliminated. Battling against the might of McLaren and two-time Formula One champion Fernando Alonso, the lone Juncos car of Kaiser shocked the motorsports community by bumping its way into the field by the scant margin of just 0.0129 seconds over the four-lap, ten-mile qualifying distance.

Following a 2021 investment from Brad Hollinger, a former shareholder and board member of the Williams Formula One team, Juncos Hollinger Racing fielded a one-car team for the full 2022 IndyCar Series schedule, with rookie Callum Ilott piloting the car. Continuing its growth, the team added a second full-time car for rookie Agustin Canapino in the 2023 season.

Today, looking to further spur its growth, the team announced its signing of Romain Grosjean to join Canapino in contesting the entire 2024 IndyCar calendar. Grosjean, who would replace Ilott, is a thirty-seven-year-old French driver who had competed in the IndyCar Series for the previous three seasons. Before that, Grosjean competed in 179 Formula One races over ten years. International motorsports fans remembered him best for his final Formula One race, the 2020 Bahrain Grand Prix.

Driving for Haas, the American Formula One entry, Grosjean survived one of the most spectacular racing crashes in recent memory. On the race's first lap, Grosjean made contact with another car, causing his car to veer off course at high speed. He hit the retaining barrier head-on, the nose of his car splitting through the wall and wedging itself between the upper and lower steel bands of the barrier.

Upon impact, the car was sheared into two, and its fuel cell exploded into a tremendous fireball, instantly engulfing Grosjean in scorching flames. It took an agonizingly long twenty-eight seconds for Grosjean to escape from the cockpit and leap to safety. Amazingly, he suffered only minor burns to his hands and ankles.

Recovered from his injuries, Grosjean made his debut in the IndyCar Series in 2021, driving for the Dale Coyne Racing and Rick Ware Racing team. He found almost immediate success with the small team, earning one pole position and three podium race finishes, including two second-place results.

Grosjean moved over to the Andretti team for 2022 and 2023, and while starting strongly in those years, both seasons brought disappointing thirteenth-place finishes in the championship. With results not meeting expectations and continued run-ins with his teammates on track, Andretti decided in September 2023 to part ways with Grosjean.

Grosjean had raced twice in the Indy 500, finishing thirty-first and thirtieth for Andretti. With three poles and six podium finishes in forty-seven

IndyCar starts, he would look to win both his and Junco Hollinger's first IndyCar race.

For the 2024 season, Grosjean would team with Canapino, a thirty-three-year-old Argentinian who won numerous touring car championships before making his debut in the IndyCar Series in 2023. Although Canapino finished just twenty-first in the season championship, his adaptation to open-wheeled racing was impressive.

Having never raced in an open-wheel, single-seater category before, Canapino raced all seventeen rounds of the Series, recording three twelfth-place finishes and a fourteenth. In his first attempt at the Indy 500, Canapino qualified twenty-sixth and finished in the same position after crashing on lap 192.

Juncos Hollinger was a small team that hadn't tasted success in the IndyCar Series to date. But they had continued to build, and they had a championship pedigree, having won seven previous championships in IndyCar's feeder series, the INDY NXT and Indy PRO 2000 Championships. Their next task was to consistently contend for top-ten finishes. Both Grosjean and Canapino had the experience and racing know-how to help the team make its next steps in development.

MONDAY, NOVEMBER 27, 2023

Palou Admits Breach of Contract

On this day, the Associated Press revealed Palou, a two-time and defending IndyCar champion, conceded in a twenty-page court document filed in the High Court of Justice Business and Property Courts of England and Wales Commercial Court that he breached his contract with McLaren Racing.

In his response to McLaren's original court filing, Palou stated he changed course on his decision to join McLaren for the 2024 season when he "lost trust and confidence that [McLaren] genuinely intended to support his ambition to race in the Formula One Series and decided to continue racing with CGR in the IndyCar Series instead."

The document further stated that Palou "therefore admits that he renounced his contractual obligations" with McLaren Racing and "the real issue between the parties is as to the quantum of any damages which the Defendants are liable to pay."

The week before, Palou's IndyCar Series rival, Pato O'Ward, was named as Palou's replacement as McLaren's F1 reserve driver, and he participated in a practice session during the season-ending race weekend in Abu Dhabi. O'Ward, of course, races full-time in the IndyCar Series, driving the No. 5 Arrow McLaren Chevrolet.

This ongoing silly season saga appeared to be nearing its end. Palou would not race for McLaren, either in IndyCar or Formula One, and

McLaren was set in its driver lineups for both series. All that was left to be determined were the financial penalties, and that total, what with McLaren's eye-popping ask of at least $23 million, would undoubtedly continue to be hotly contested.

Palou's counter-filing stated, "This claim is embarrassing for want of particularity and speculative in the extreme. The performance of any team in a future IndyCar Series cannot be predicted with any degree of certainty. Driver performance is variable."

Moreover, Palou disputed McLaren's claim of lost revenues that Palou "would otherwise have earned in relation to the Formula One Series," arguing the claim would be valid only if Palou raced as a McLaren F1 driver. Lastly, Palou's response declared if Palou were an F1 driver, all McLaren's claims to IndyCar financial losses would be moot.

On the racetrack, "Palougate" was over, and thank goodness for that, as race fans could focus on the racing. In the courtroom, however, the legal race appeared to be in its early days.

THURSDAY, DECEMBER 7, 2023

Hybrid Power Unit Delayed—Yet Again

The IndyCar Series once again delayed the rollout of its new hybrid engine program, the third time it had been forced to do so. When the series originally announced the new regulation in the summer of 2019, the target date was to have it operational for the 2022 season. Now, according to today's announcement, the hybrid engine program will be introduced "after the 108th Indianapolis 500," and sometime "during the second half of the (2024 season)." No specific date or race was clarified for the power unit's debut.

IndyCar didn't specify a cause for the delay, but the announcement came as no surprise to those in the paddock. Despite unprecedented collaboration between Chevrolet and Honda on the new technology, rumors persisted that the manufacturers simply didn't have an adequate production lead time to service all ten teams and their twenty-seven full-time cars with the new power unit well in advance of the season's first race weekend just three months hence.

The delay was foreshadowed the week before when IndyCar scrapped planned testing for the six teams who had yet to test the new technology. That cancellation was a big hint that the manufacturers were experiencing difficulties in producing enough units for every team to have an ample supply of testing, racing, and spare parts components.

The delay continued the saga of the hybrid engine. The COVID-19 pandemic and its impact on the worldwide supply chain forced the first delay from 2022 to 2023. Then, continued supply chain issues forced another bump out to 2024.

One year ago, IndyCar, in partnership with Honda and Chevrolet, announced they would abandon plans to pair the still-in-development hybrid unit with a brand-new, 2.4-liter V-6 engine and instead integrate the hybrid technology into the 2.2-liter engine that had been in use since 2012.

Initially, Mahle, a German automotive parts manufacturer based in Stuttgart, had been contracted to develop the hybrid system. However, shortcomings at Mahle forced both Honda and Chevrolet to take on increased roles—along with increased investment—to complete the hybrid project. That meant there was less time and, of course, less money, to develop a new V-6 engine.

Development and innovation continued to be sticky problems for the IndyCar Series, one that got a bit more problematic with each passing year. In addition to entering its thirteenth season with the same engine, the series was also using the same chassis for its thirteenth season, the Dallara DW-12, named after two-time Indy 500 winner Dan Wheldon, who was instrumental in the initial design testing.

It wasn't long ago the IndyCar field had multiple chassis and engine manufacturers in which to mix and match to race a competitive entry. It was part of the charm of the build-up to each year's Indianapolis 500.

Every year, chassis designers would develop and implement innovations, but that didn't stop some teams from using cars from previous seasons in an attempt to bootstrap themselves into the 500. Many car owners designed their chassis, including Indianapolis 500 winning entries for both Team Penske and Galles Racing.

Then, of course, there were engines, including bespoke, one-of-a-kind creations like Roger Rager's stock block Chevrolet, which he built in his garage ahead of the 1980 Indy 500. The block for Rager's engine came from a wrecked school bus found in a junkyard. Rager's working theory was that a block taken from a truck or bus would have numerous heat cycles under heavy loads that would make it practically immune to failure.

It worked brilliantly. Rager qualified for his first 500 tenth fastest, ahead of such notables as AJ Foyt, Tom Sneva, and Gordon Johncock. When the race started, Rager charged toward the front.

Alas, the Cinderella story ended for Rager on lap fifty-six when, swerving low in Turn One to avoid the spinning car of lapped runner Jim McElreath, his tires found the grass of the infield, causing him to lose control and crash out of the race. Rager was credited with a twenty-third-place finish. Sneva and Johncock finished second and fourth, respectfully.

Speedway lore was filled with stories like Rager's, but those days of garage innovations had gone the way of the dodo, at least currently. Gone too, at least for this generation of racers, was the ongoing development of multiple chassis and engine manufacturers.

Today, development by race teams was severely limited and focused primarily on components that produced mechanical grip, like springs and dampers, or shock absorbers. It was not a lot to develop, but development in dampers was a must. It created a potential competitive advantage, and in a "spec series" like IndyCar, where everyone competed with the same equipment specifications, a better damper could be the difference between a trip to Victory Lane and a trip back to the garage to think of what might had been.

FRIDAY, DECEMBER 15, 2023

The Borg-Warner Trophy Adds a New Face

To the victor go the spoils. Today, in an evening ceremony at the Stutz Museum in downtown Indianapolis, reigning 500-winner Newgarden's facial likeness was revealed on the Borg-Warner Trophy, where it joined 109 other faces on one of the most recognizable trophies in sports.

After the IndyCar season was over, Newgarden traveled to the Tryon, North Carolina studio of sculptor William Behrends so the artist could put finer details on a life-sized, clay bust of Newgarden's face—a critical step in the process that eventually produced a sterling silver cast image permanently attached to the Borg-Warner Trophy. However, from there, Newgarden, along with almost everyone else, was kept in the dark.

That is until the evening's unveiling when Indianapolis Motor Speedway President Doug Boles and BorgWarner Global Director of Marketing and Communications Michelle Collins lifted the wraps on the updated Borg-Warner Trophy.

With the giant trophy shining under the lights, Newgarden, with more than a little dreamy twinkle in his eyes, commented, "It looks amazing. The work that goes into this is intimate; it's very precise. Just like this race, I don't know another trophy like this in sport anywhere. It's another special part of what the Indianapolis 500 and the Borg-Warner Trophy represents.

"To everybody at BorgWarner, we are all custodians of this event with the duty to carry it forward and make it bigger and better every year. To know that it is there, and it is going to stay forever, it's the highest honor."

After the 2023 race, 795 drivers had started the Indianapolis 500 race, and Newgarden was the seventy-fifth winner. As for the trophy, Newgarden was the 110th face to be immortalized in sterling silver, a number that accounts for shared drives that resulted in victory. Of the 110 faces, Newgarden was the 109th face cast in sterling silver. Tony Hulman, who rescued the Speedway when he purchased it from Rickenbacker in 1945, was the only non-race winner to be represented on the trophy. His likeness, unlike the others in sterling silver, was cast in gold.

The Borg-Warner Trophy first appeared in Victory Lane after the 1936 Indy 500, won by Louis Meyer, the last of his three victories in the race. Since that time, it has become a regular fixture at the Speedway every May, not only in post-race ceremonies but throughout the month as a promotional symbol for the 500.

In the lead-up to the 1936 race, Borg-Warner Automotive commissioned designer Robert J. Hill and Gorham, Inc., of Providence, Rhode Island, to create the trophy at the cost of $10,000. The current trophy stands at just over five feet tall and tips the scales at over 100 pounds.

The original hollow body had space for seventy winners of the 500 and reached its capacity after it was affixed with the likeness of 1986 winner Bobby Rahal. In addition to Rahal's likeness, a base was added in 1986 to accommodate additional winners, very similar to how the National Hockey League expanded the capacity of its Stanley Cup.

The Borg-Warner Trophy features the faces of all seventy-five drivers who have won the 500, displayed in a checkerboard pattern and inscribed with the winners' names, years of victory, and average speeds. Of course, four-time winners Foyt, Unser, Mears, and Castroneves appear most on the storied trophy.

The removable dome-shaped top features a nude man, in the tradition of ancient Greek athletes, waving a checkered flag. Most likely because of the figure's nudity, the trophy is most often seen in images with the flag waving in front of him, obscuring his nakedness.

In its early years, the Borg-Warner Trophy was seldom out on display, so it was maintained with a simple polish. As a result, early photos of it show it with a relatively matte-like finish. Today, the trophy is maintained with a showstopping, mirror-like finish.

The trophy went through restorations in 1991 and 2004, and the second featured a larger base to accommodate additional winners. With its current design, the Borg-Warner Trophy has space to feature winners through the 2033 race.

Naturally, given the perpetual nature of the Borg-Warner Trophy, the winner doesn't get to take it home. Throughout the year, it is displayed at the Indianapolis Motor Speedway Museum, nestled on the infield grounds of the Speedway between Turns One and Two.

Instead of the big trophy, winning drivers now receive what has become known as the "Baby Borg," an eighteen-inch tall, free-standing replica of the trophy. Officially known as the Indianapolis 500 Champion Driver's Trophy, the Baby Borg is usually presented to the winning driver in January.

As for the winning car owners, since 1997, they have been bestowed with the Indianapolis 500 Champion Owner's Trophy, which is nearly identical to the Baby Borg.

As for that $10,000 commissioned trophy back in 1936, the Borg-Warner Trophy is today insured in excess of $1.3 million. To racers and race fans around the world, it's priceless.

TUESDAY, JANUARY 9, 2024

Foyt Finalizes Lineup by Confirming Ferrucci

AJ Foyt Racing finalized its IndyCar lineup for 2024 by confirming twenty-five-year-old Santino Ferrucci's return to Foyt's famous No. 14 car, based out of its Waller, Texas, race shop near Houston. This season would mark Ferrucci's second consecutive year with the team.

Ferrucci qualified fourth for last year's Indy 500, where he finished third, his fifth top-ten finish in as many 500 starts in his career. In the race, he led eleven laps in his patriotic red, white, and blue-liveried race car, including ten in the race's hotly contested final fifty laps. His result marked Foyt's best 500 result since Eliseo Salazar both qualified and finished third in 2000.

Despite the great run in the Indianapolis 500, Ferrucci's 2023 campaign was rather dismal. However, thanks to his high finish in the 500, his car finished the season twentieth in the championship standings, securing one of the final three positions of the IndyCar Series' Leaders Circle program and earning a payout of nearly one million dollars to the team.

Today's news followed the December announcement that Foyt had retained the services of twenty-two-year-old Sting Ray Robb. Robb, who would be entering his second season in IndyCar, had also endured a dismal 2023 campaign as a rookie driving for the joint Dale Coyne Racing with Rick Ware Racing team.

Robb started his rookie season horribly, recording five DNFs (did not finish) in his first six races, including a crash in the Indy 500 that left him with a thirty-first-place finish. Robb's best result came at the season finale at Laguna Seca, where he finished twelfth, and for the season, he finished next to last in the championship standings.

Last place in the season championship in 2023 was Ferrucci's teammate at Foyt, Benjamin Pedersen, who won Indy's Rookie of the Year Award. With the confirmation of Ferrucci in the second Foyt entry, it meant Pedersen was now without a ride.

Racing, like every sport, is very much a "what have you done for me lately" affair. A racer is only as good as his last race, or his last season. In Pedersen's case, it wasn't good enough for him to secure a race seat, at least not yet.

Less than a year and a half ago, Foyt signed what was believed to be a multi-year contract with Pedersen, who brought substantial sponsorship funding with him. He may well have simply been outbid by Robb for a seat, as Robb was rumored to bring with him a high-seven-figure full-season budget.

Seemingly perpetually underfunded, the Foyt team needed to take a pay driver who could help finance the 2024 campaign. However, with an eye toward more competitive results, it also needed to keep a talent like Ferrucci with the team.

Ferrucci was once an up-and-coming American driver racing in Europe with an eye toward competing in Formula One. As a fifteen-year-old, he signed a deal to race in Europe, but he had to wait until he turned sixteen before he could race, making his debut at the fabled Spa-Francorchamps course in Belgium in 2014.

He moved quickly through the junior formulas and found himself racing in Formula Two in 2017. Despite joining the series in the middle of the season, Ferrucci recorded a best finish of ninth on the way to the twenty-second position in the final season standings.

In 2018, however, things fell apart for Ferrucci. Racing in Formula Two at Silverstone, on the undercard of the Formula One race weekend,

Ferrucci was involved in two separate incidents. He was disqualified from the Saturday Sprint race, which set the field for the feature race on Sunday, when he made what was judged as deliberate contact with his Trident F2 teammate, Arjun Maini. Additionally, he was found to have driven his race car between the F2 and F1 paddocks without one glove and while holding his phone, infractions that resulted in a €6,000 fine.

For his deliberate contact with Maini, Ferrucci was suspended for four races. Soon after, Trident terminated its contract with Ferrucci, citing his behavioral issues as well as the non-payment of money required by his contract. Subsequently, an Italian court ruled Ferrucci to pay Trident €502,000, plus interest and legal fees.

Ferrucci found his refuge, and a much-needed lifeline for his racing career, in the form of Dale Coyne Racing, for which he raced in three IndyCar events in 2018. Returning to DCR in 2019, Ferrucci made his debut at the Speedway that May. After having qualified twenty-third for the Indy 500, he drove his way up the field during the race to finish seventh, earning Rookie of the Year accolades.

It was in that 2019 Indianapolis 500 that Ferrucci became somewhat of a darling of race fans around the country. In the later stages of the race, having already improved his position with crafty racing, Ferrucci found himself trailing a pack of cars heading into Turn Three. Ahead of him, Sébastien Bourdais and Graham Rahal made contact entering the turn, triggering a five-car crash.

Amid the carnage in front of him, Ferrucci slowed only a bit, keeping his foot on the throttle, weaving through the debris, and eventually driving through the grass and onto the warm-up lane. During the yellow flag period used to clean up the mess, television commentator Dale Earnhardt Jr. raved about Ferrucci's poise and racecraft. When the popular Earnhardt heaped praise, his fans, of which there are legions, took immediate notice.

Ferrucci had shown a special knack at the Speedway. He had suffered costly accidents in practice. But, on race day, he had excelled, posting far better results than at other courses. As to whether he would be the driver to bring Foyt back to glory in May remained to be seen.

Sting Ray Robb's real name is . . . Sting Ray. It's on his birth certificate, and it is not a reference to the marine animal.

Rather, Sting Ray's parents, Kimmie Serrano and Larry Robb, are long-time Chevrolet enthusiasts, who founded two Corvette clubs in their hometown of Payette, Idaho. When it came to naming their son, they found inspiration in the Corvette Stingray.

Oddly, Robb debuted in IndyCar driving a Honda-powered entry for DCR. This coming season, with Foyt, he would find himself behind the wheel of a Chevrolet-powered racer. Before the timid start of his IndyCar career, Robb finished second in the Indy Lights feeder season in 2022. Despite bringing a large amount of funding with him, Robb would be under pressure in the coming season to significantly improve upon his past IndyCar results.

MONDAY, JANUARY 22, 2024

Preseason Testing at Homestead

Ten IndyCar teams converged on the Homestead-Miami Speedway to get their first opportunity to run laps with the technical configuration the series will compete with this season through the Indianapolis 500. All the teams arrived eager to garner first impressions and begin to come to terms with new, lighter chassis components—specifically the aeroscreen, bellhousing, and gearbox.

However, teams were limited in their approach to this three-day test. As the new, lighter-weight components were continuing to be manufactured, there weren't enough parts to go around to the full field of almost thirty cars. Thus, teams were limited to bringing one car to the test on the track's "roval" configuration and rotating their drivers over the three days.

For Bobby Rahal, winner of the Indianapolis 500 in 1986 and a three-time Series champion, this test was less about the car and more about the drivers. After the test, he said, "The biggest part of this week was just to get the drivers in the car. It was a chance to knock off the rust since the last time they raced."

The Rahal Letterman Lanigan (RLL) team approached the test differently than they would approach tests at both Sebring and Indianapolis later in the spring. "First, we don't race at Homestead, and while we don't race at Sebring either, the nature of that track, with its bumpy surface, is very similar to a lot of tracks we race on, like the season-opener at St.

Petersburg," said Rahal, the team founder and co-owner. "Secondly, the tires brought to the test were designed to have high degradation, and that prevented long, race-simulation types of runs.

"We tried to put a lot of laps in, but we weren't really chasing a time. When we got quick laps, yes, that was good, but really, how was the rest of the run?

"There's always questions with testing. Typically, you're not there for a time, specifically. But you are looking for where you might be losing time. Maybe it was because we didn't put tires on at the right time, or maybe one damper wasn't as good as a different one. But testing helps point you in directions. And, hopefully, it's relevant for later, at races, where it really counts."

Testing can be a fickle process. A car setup on one day can be perfect, but that very same setup on another day at the same circuit can result in a handful of a car that is difficult to drive.

"In my career, I've returned to a track two weeks after a great test only to have a horrible test," said Rahal. "It was the same car at the same track, but weather, track temperatures, and all the other variables came together to produce a completely different result."

Interestingly, Rahal wasn't concerned about the new, lighter-weight components but welcomed them. "We've had a weight creep over the years with this chassis," continued Rahal. "Every year or other year, for safety considerations, we've ended up with more weight on the car. Its weight has swelled by over one hundred pounds, and, of course, the heaviest addition was the 'halo' (aeroscreen), which put a lot of weight very high on the car, resulting in a big learning curve for all the teams."

For the RLL team, weight distribution posed a unique challenge for one of its cars, the No. 15, driven by Bobby's son, Graham, who simply is taller and heavier than every other driver in the paddock. And it's not really that close of a contest either.

"Our competitors don't ballast up to meet Graham's weight," said Rahal, with a chuckle. "What we're learning about with the new components will show up for us on road courses, where fore and aft weight distribution is so important. Graham is an easy ten to fifteen pounds heavier than other drivers, and that's three gallons of fuel. Lighter chassis components will allow us to better tune the car setup with weight.

"But, after Indianapolis, when we start to run the hybrid components of the engine, more weight will be added. I hate to say it, but by the second half of the season, with respect to total weight, it will probably be a wash."

Thirty-five-year-old Graham Rahal was the second-youngest driver to ever compete in an Indy car race when he made his debut in 2007 at just eighteen. Competing in the CART Series, he finished second in his third race, becoming the youngest-ever podium finisher.

Ahead of Rahal's second season, the IndyCar Series was created as the singular premiere open-wheel racing series in the United States. And Rahal's debut in that series was even more spectacular than the year before.

Rahal missed the first race of the season after a crash in testing left his car unable to be repaired in time. Thus, he made his IndyCar debut at the second race of the season, contested on the street circuit in St. Petersburg. Remarkably, Rahal overcame a spin early in the race and drove to a convincing victory over two-time defending race winner Castroneves. In doing so, Rahal became the youngest driver to win a major American open-wheel race—just nineteen years, ninety-three days old—and the fourth-ever driver to win in his debut in the IndyCar Series.

In May, Rahal would attempt to qualify for his seventeenth Indianapolis 500 race, a race he had never won. But Rahal had come oh-so-close to victory at the Brickyard. He finished third in the 500 twice, in both 2011 and 2020. However, it was the 2021 race where Rahal had his best chance to be immortalized on the Borg-Warner Trophy along with his father.

Rahal qualified just eighteenth for the race, but once the green flag flew, he smartly raced himself into contention, all the while saving fuel. Thanks to his fuel-saving drive, Rahal pretty much had his competition covered—he looked to complete the race with one less pit stop than his rivals. Rahal had them right where he and his team wanted them. When the other racers made their final pit stops, he would cycle into the lead of the Indy 500.

On lap 118, Rahal entered the pits for a routine stop. However, while there to take on fuel and tires, his left rear wheel was fastened incorrectly—Rahal was told to leave the pit box before the left rear wheel nut had been secured. Exiting the pits, Rahal built up speed on the warm-up lane inside of Turns One and Two, and that's where his race would end.

The left rear wheel came off as Rahal was steering through the Turn Two warm-up lane to get back on the racing surface on the backstretch. At that speed, in the middle of the corner, Rahal had no control of his car after the wheel came off. He spun and crashed heavily into the Turn Two wall, right in front of the lead pack he was set to rejoin.

As Rahal got out of his car, he collapsed to his knees in anguish, for he knew exactly the opportunity that had just slipped away.

Last May, Rahal was involved in a completely different sort of drama in qualifying for the 2023 Indy 500. All through practice, he and his RLL teammates struggled for speed. The result was that they would be competing against themselves to fill the final slot on the starting grid.

Rahal was bumped at the last moment by his then-teammate, Jack Harvey, and it appeared as though he would miss the race. However, the day after Rahal's disappointment at failing to qualify, Stefan Wilson crashed in practice, suffering a vertebral fracture that would require surgery and cause him to miss the race. Wilson's team, Dreyer & Reinbold, tapped Rahal as its replacement driver.

Starting thirty-third, Rahal raced to a twenty-second-place finish in the 500, his first career race in a Chevy-powered car. For 2024, he would look to avoiding any qualifying drama and secure a career-defining victory in the world's biggest race.

TUESDAY, JANUARY 23, 2024

An Entry to End the Andretti Curse?

On this day, as was generally expected throughout the racing community, Andretti Global announced that thirty-six-year-old Marco Andretti would return to race at the Indianapolis 500. He would pilot the No. 98 Honda-powered entry, sporting livery of new sponsor Mapei, a chemical company based in Milan, Italy. The race would be Andretti's nineteenth Indianapolis 500.

Andretti, the son of team owner and former racer Michael and the grandson of racing icon Mario, burst upon the scene in IndyCar his rookie year in 2006. Qualifying ninth and starting on the outside of the third row, Andretti nearly won the 500 on his debut.

He probably couldn't have come closer to winning the race without actually winning it. Andretti only led two laps the entire afternoon, but he nearly led the one that mattered most, the final lap.

He made his last pit stop on lap 190, and while Andretti was in the pits getting fuel and tires, the yellow flag came out for Felipe Giaffone's crash in Turn Two. Andretti got out of the pits without losing a lap, and as several of the leading cars entered the pits for service under the yellow, he cycled up the running order to second place, trailing only his father, fan favorite Michael, a storied racer who, despite all his racing success, had never made it to Indianapolis's famed Victory Lane.

Michael Andretti came out of retirement just for that race, so he could race alongside his nineteen-year-old son. And there they were, running first and second with just a handful of laps to go.

Racing resumed when the green flag waved with four laps remaining, with Michael leading Marco into Turn One, followed closely by Dixon and Scott Hornish.

Hornish, driving for Team Penske and having qualified fastest for the race, lunged past Dixon for third as the field exited Turn Two and tore down the backstretch, chasing the two Andretti cars out front.

On the front stretch, coming down to begin lap 198, Marco pulled out of his father's slipstream and overtook him entering Turn One. It looked as though Marco would end the famed "Andretti Curse" that had kept the family out of the Speedway's Victory Lane since Mario's win in 1969.

Hornish, however, had a different idea.

Hornish got by Michael on the backstretch and closed in on Marco. Coming around to start lap 199, Marco led by about a half second.

Down the backstretch, with just under one and a half laps to go, Hornish made a late move into Turn Three, where Marco, racing for the win, swiftly shut the door. Hornish, with no place to go but off the racing surface, backed off. Losing all his momentum, Hornish fell back considerably and, as Marco zoomed past the start/finish line to begin the last lap, Andretti's lead was up to one second.

Hornish kept after it, and as they entered Turn Three for the last time, his faster, better-handling car clawed back the gap to Andretti. Through the short chute and Turn Four, the two cars were nose to tail coming down the straightaway. With the crowd standing and screaming, Hornish pulled out of Andretti's slipstream with a seemingly impossible short length of racetrack remaining to complete the overtake.

Hornish made it work, though, beating Marco to the yard of bricks by just 0.0635 seconds, or the equivalent of fifteen feet after 500 miles of racing. To this day, it remains the third-closest finish in Indy 500 history. It was also the first time in the race's history that a driver made an overtake for the lead on the final lap.

In that 2006 race, Marco had to settle for second place and Rookie of the Year honors, joining his father, Michael, who shared Rookie of the

Year honors with Roberto Guerrero after finishing fifth in his first Indy 500 in 1984.

The confirmation of an entry for Andretti brought the total number of drivers locked into the field to twenty-nine of the possible thirty-three starting spots. There were, however, more teams looking to add entries to the list, and if more than thirty-three car and driver entries were reached, qualifying would feature bumping for the second year in a row.

In his eighteen Indy 500 starts, Marco had four top-three and eight top-ten finishes. He also qualified on the pole for the 2020 race. Would 2024 be the year he cracked the fifty-four-year Andretti drought at the Speedway?

Despite just one Indy 500 victory to the family's name, make no mistake about it: the Andrettis are IndyCar royalty.

The twisting, interlocking tales of both the Andrettis and the Indianapolis Motor Speedway began with family patriarch Mario, who first raced in the Indy 500 in 1965, finishing third and earning Rookie of the Year honors. Riding that momentum, Andretti won the season's Indy car championship, then known as the USAC National Championship. At twenty-five, he was the youngest-ever series champion.

In 1969, Mario won the Indy 500 and eight other champ car races, including the famed Pikes Peak International Hill Climb, on his way to his second season title. On top of his racing exploits being splashed across newspapers everywhere, Mario was named ABC's *Wide World of Sports* Athlete of the Year. Having won twenty-nine of eighty-five USAC championship races between 1966 and 1969, it looked like Andretti would be an unstoppable force at any racetrack where he competed.

In many ways, Mario Andretti turned out to be that unstoppable force. He is the only driver ever to win the Indianapolis 500, the Daytona 500 (1967), and the Formula One World Championship (1978). He won fifty-two IndyCar races in four different decades and was named United States Driver of the Year in three decades (1967, 1978, and 1984).

But unbelievably, Mario Andretti won only one Indianapolis 500.

It wasn't for a lack of trying, and Andretti's bad luck at the Speedway became somewhat of a tradition. Always a crowd favorite, you could hear the crowd's collective groan over the racing engines as the public address announcer often repeated, "Andretti is slowing down."

Mario raced in twenty-nine Indy 500s, and he almost always seemed to have a very competitive car. Yet, Andretti finished the full 500-mile race distance just five times. There were so many near-misses at another race win were it not for the now infamous Andretti Curse.

In 1981, Andretti finished second in the 500 behind Bobby Unser. The following day, however, Unser was penalized a lap for passing cars under the yellow caution flag, and as a result, Andretti was awarded the victory. It was a victory that lasted just four months, though. Considering a protest from Unser and his car owner, Roger Penske, USAC, the governing body of the race, rescinded the penalty and declared Unser the rightful victor yet again.

In the 1985 race, Andretti was leading on lap 120 when Danny Sullivan, mistakenly thinking the race was closer to its end, pulled alongside down the front stretch and then desperately went low, very low, into Turn One to complete the overtake. Just on the exit of the turn, though, Sullivan's car wiggled at the rear. He reined it in momentarily, but then lost it completely, spinning right in front of Andretti's car.

Andretti jumped on the brakes, locking up his front tires as Sullivan spun toward the wall. Off the brakes, Andretti swerved low to avoid Sullivan's spinning car. Miraculously, Sullivan avoided contact with the wall and found his car straightened out and headed toward Turn Two. Twenty laps later, Sullivan repeated the same overtaking attempt for the lead, this time without incident. He went on to win the race, with Andretti finishing second.

In the 1987 edition of the Indy 500, Andretti dominated from the wave of the green flag, rather easily leading 170 of the first 177 laps. Surely the day would see to reward Mario with his second race win. It was not to be, however, as a broken valve spring in his engine ended his race with twenty laps remaining.

In 1992, Mario started the race as one of four Andrettis to take the green flag, joined by sons Michael and Jeff, and nephew John. Unfortunately, Mario and Jeff were eliminated in crashes, both suffering injuries, with Jeff suffering multiple leg fractures.

The 1992 race was eerily similar to the 1987 race with Andretti domination. In this case, it was Michael's race for most of the day, leading 160 laps and enjoying a thirty-second lead before a fuel pump failure ended his race with just eleven laps to go.

In total, five Andrettis have raced in the Indianapolis 500, for a total of seventy-eight starts—and with Marco's entry for 2024, still counting. Mario started the Indy 500 twenty-nine times, Marco eighteen, Michael sixteen, John twelve, and Jeff three. All of them, save John, were named Rookie of the Year on debut.

How competitive have the Andrettis been at Indianapolis? Incredibly competitive. How much back luck have they experienced? An incredibly large amount. Consider that on the all-time lap leaders' chart, Mario ranks fourth with 556 laps led, while Michael ranks eleventh, with 441 laps led, two more laps than four-time Indy 500 winner, Rick Mears.

Of the top twenty-one lap leaders all-time at Indianapolis, Michael is the only driver to have never won the race. As an owner, however, Michael has guided his eponymous team to five Indy 500 victories.

Would 2024 see the end of the dreaded Andretti Curse? As always, the greatest spectacle in racing would have its say come the last Sunday of May.

THURSDAY, FEBRUARY 1, 2024

Dreyer & Reinbold Confirm Hunter-Reay & Daly

Dennis Reinbold is a successful Indianapolis car dealer with a long familial history with auto racing and the Indianapolis 500. His grandfather, Floyd "Pop" Dreyer, was a mechanic and car builder of Indy cars in the 1920s and 1930s, and deeply involved with championship-winning sprint and midget cars.

With racing running so deep in his blood, Reinbold formed Dreyer & Reinbold Racing in 1999 and created a small, underdog racing team that annually holds its own against IndyCar juggernauts like Chip Ganassi Racing and Team Penske. Dreyer & Reinbold Racing runs only one IndyCar race a year—the Indy 500—and it has successfully qualified forty-eight entries in its history at the Speedway, often at the expense of bigger, more well-funded teams, like Rahal Letterman Lanigan in 2023.

If race fans want cheer on a dark horse candidate to pull off an Indy 500 upset, they need to search no further than Dreyer & Reinbold's two cars.

Today, the team announced its drivers for the 2024 race: Ryan Hunter-Reay, the 2014 winner who finished eleventh in the 500 for the team in 2023, and local hometown hero, Conor Daly, the driver Hunter-Reay replaced at Ed Carpenter Racing for the last half of 2023's IndyCar Series schedule.

In addition to its drivers, Dreyer & Reinbold also announced its continued partnership with Cusick Motorsports for the race, allowing the two organizations to leverage their expertise and resources, along with a large collective dose of auto racing passion, to bring the battle to the competition.

In a statement released by the team, Hunter-Reay said, "It has been an absolute pleasure to work with Dreyer & Reinbold Racing since joining them in 2023. I'm thrilled to be back and ready to build on where we left off last year. We had a very strong showing at the 500 last year, and if it were not for a failed front wing adjuster early in the race, I truly feel we would have been fighting in the top-five to the finish."

He and Daly would have an opportunity to bring the fight in a pair of Dallara-Chevrolets, Hunter-Reay in the team's No. 23 and Daly in the matching No. 24.

The forty-three-year-old Hunter-Reay had run 293 Indy car races over a nineteen career in the highest form of open-wheel racing in the United States, winning eighteen races and the 2012 IndyCar Series Championship. Known as "Captain America," for years Hunter-Reay drove the No. 28 car to represent the estimated 28 million people living worldwide with a cancer diagnosis. After his mother, Lydia, died from complications of colon cancer in 2009, Hunter-Reay founded Racing For Cancer, a nonprofit organization dedicated to bringing the motorsport community together to beat cancer.

Hunter-Reay had raced fifteen times in the Indy 500, for five different teams. In addition to his 2014 victory, Hunter-Reay finished in the top ten in the 500 on five other occasions, just missing out with Dreyer & Reinbold last year in eleventh.

Daly is a thirty-one-year-old native of Noblesville, Indiana, part of the northern suburbs of Indianapolis. To say that racing and the Indy 500 course through the fabric of Daly's being would be an understatement—his father is former Formula One and Indy car driver, Derek Daly, who raced in six 500s, and his stepfather is Doug Boles, President of the Indianapolis Motor Speedway.

Daly raced both full-time and part-time in the IndyCar Series for ten years but secured only one podium finish, a second place on the Detroit street circuit for Dale Coyne Racing in 2016. In his previous ten Indy 500s, Daly produced finishes of sixth, eighth, and tenth to his credit, and he'd been a frontrunner who led laps two of the last three years.

Despite his relative lack of success over his 107-race IndyCar career, Daly is a fan favorite. Together with Alexander Rossi, he competed in the thirtieth season of CBS's *The Amazing Race*, where the duo finished in fourth place. But television only showed part of Daly's character and charm. A case in point was an Instagram post of his on December 23, 2015, where he showed a picture of himself kneeling between two local children. In his caption, he explained how they asked him in a tweet if he would like to see the latest *Star Wars* movie with them, to which he answered, emphatically, "Yes!"

A local team with a local driver paired with a former race winner would make the Dreyer & Reinbold Racing with Cusick Motorsports a team to watch for come May.

THURSDAY, FEBRUARY 15, 2024

Sato to Return with Rahal Letterman Lanigan

Today, Rahal Letterman Lanigan Racing announced two-time Indianapolis 500 winter Takuma Sato would once again drive for the team at the 2024 race. Sato, winner of the Indy 500 in 2017 for Andretti Global and again in 2020 for RLL, would return to the team for the Indy 500 only, piloting the team's fourth Honda-powered entry alongside teammates Graham Rahal, Christian Lundgaard, and Pietro Fittipaldi.

In a statement, Sato said, "I'm absolutely thrilled to make my return to the 108th Indy 500 with Rahal Letterman Lanigan Racing. A heartfelt thank you to Bobby (Rahal), Mike (Lanigan), and David (Letterman) and the entire organization for this incredible opportunity. My journey with RLL spans over a decade, marked by shared successes and rejoining the team fills me with immense excitement. Here's to reconnecting with familiar faces and forging new alliances. I just can't wait to get to work."

Sato delivered RLL its second Indy 500 win in 2020, joining Buddy Rice (2004) as the team's only winners of the race. Co-owner Bobby Rahal also won the Indy 500 in 1986, driving for Jim Trueman's Truesports team.

The forty-seven-year-old Sato had long been a fan favorite at the Speedway, in no small part to his driving style, fueled by his motto, "No attack, no chance." Experienced fans knew watching Sato race is a thrill, and he would never disappoint come race day .

Sato began his racing career relatively late, karting first at the age of nineteen. After winning Japan's national karting title, he received financial backing from Honda and moved to Europe, where he steadily climbed the ranks of junior formulas.

In 2002, Sato graduated to Formula One with the Honda-powered Jordan team, and he raced in the world's premier single-seater category for seven seasons, scoring forty-four total points and securing a podium finish at the 2004 United States Grand Prix held on the Indianapolis Motor Speedway's road course.

Sato visited the Indianapolis Motor Speedway in 2009 as a spectator, networking for an opportunity to join the IndyCar Series, which he did when he joined KV Racing Technology ahead of the 2010 season. He raced his first 500 that year, finishing twentieth.

However, Sato indelibly left his mark on the Speedway and race fans in 2012. Having qualified nineteenth, Sato sliced through the field from the start and raced with the leaders by the halfway mark. Sato became the nineteenth driver to lead that year's race when he did so on lap 120, and he continued to feature as one of the race's main protagonists as the laps counted down.

In the final circuits of the Speedway, Ganassi teammates Dixon and Dario Franchitti battled, with Sato tucked behind them in third. Starting lap 199, Franchitti got past his teammate, with Sato aggressively following behind, slipping by Dixon on the inside of Turn One and setting up a final lap shootout for the race win.

On the final lap, racing down the frontstretch and into Turn One at nearly 220 miles per hour, Franchitti went low, entering Turn One at an unusually low angle. Sato, already on the inside line, was fully committed. He would make the pass, or he wouldn't, but one thing was certain: Sato was going to go for it.

Side by side that low on the track, however, was never destined to work. Forced down the track to the point where his left side tires went over the white line, Sato lost control of the rear of his car early in Turn One, spinning toward the outside retaining wall.

By the slimmest of margins, Sato's car missed the rear of Franchitti's car, but he heavily impacted the outside retaining wall, bringing out the caution flag and allowing Franchitti to secure his third Indy 500 triumph.

Sato may have finished seventeenth in that 500, but he cemented himself as a Brickyard legend. For Sato, like almost every racer, second place represented nothing more than "first loser." It was either win or not win. But Sato had to try, and fans respected him for the effort. His name has drawn rousing cheers from the grandstands ever since.

TUESDAY, FEBRUARY 26, 2024

New Suspension Uprights Mandated

Today, IndyCar and Dallara, the official chassis partner of the series, informed race teams of new rear suspension uprights that would be mandatory for all cars on oval tracks. The mandate would take effect at the Indy 500 Open Test in April and would be in place in competition for the first time at May's Indianapolis 500.

The new component comes in response to a spectacular crash in 2023's Indy 500 when Felix Rosenqvist lost control of his Arrow McLaren and collected Kyle Kirkwood's Andretti Global car. Protecting his sixth-place position with just seventeen laps remaining, Rosenqvist tried mightily to keep Newgarden from passing him down the frontstretch, moving to his left and taking away the inside. Right after they crossed the yard of bricks, however, Newgarden drifted to his right and rode the momentum he had created by following in Rosenqvist's slipstream to overtake entering Turn One.

Because of Rosenqvist's defensive driving in trying to keep Newgarden behind, his line entering Turn One was compromised. To make matters worse, the wake from Newgarden's car took air off of Rosenqvist's front wing, eliminating a significant amount of downforce and causing his Arrow McLaren to understeer toward the wall.

Rosenqvist tried to keep his car off the wall at the exit of Turn One, but he brushed it just enough to damage his right rear suspension before tapping the wall yet a second time. With a damaged car, Rosenqvist lifted off the throttle and tried to get off the racing line. It was then when he lost the car completely, spinning into the entry of Turn Two.

Kirkwood, running a strong tenth in his second Indy 500, had nowhere to go. Racing a car length behind Ferrucci, the two tried to get around Rosenqvist's spinning car. Ferrucci made it by the slimmest of margins. Kirkwood, however, wasn't as fortunate.

As Rosenqvist's car moved up the track toward the Turn Two wall, Kirkwood made contact with his left rear tire, shearing it free from his car. Minus his rear wheel, Kirkwood's car made a half spin before contacting its left side heavily with the Turn Two wall, then immediately flipped onto its top and slid along the wall before coming to a stop, upside down, on the backstretch.

As spectacular as the accident was, even more alarming was what happened to Kirkwood's left rear tire and wheel assembly, which soared through the air and narrowly missed the fans packed into the Southeast Vista stand on the outside of Turn Two. Simply, if the wheel assembly, traveling well over a hundred miles an hour, had landed in a group of spectators, the results would have been catastrophic.

In the 1987 Indy 500, a wheel from Tony Bettenhausen's car was struck by the nose cone of Roberto Guerrero's car, sending it flying over the catch fence. The wheel almost cleared what was then Grandstand K in Turn Four. Tragically, however, it struck and killed Lyle Kurtenbach, a spectator who was watching the race from the top row. Kurtenbach, a forty-one-year-old race fan from Rothschild, Wisconsin, was killed instantly, becoming the first spectator to die at the Speedway since 1960.

In 2023, tragedy was narrowly avoided, with Kirkwood's wheel missing the grandstand and landing in a parking lot. Luckily, no people were injured, although race fan Robin Matthews's Chevy Cruze was damaged enough to be a complete write-off. For its part, IMS gifted Matthews a 2023 Chevrolet Equinox as a replacement.

In the aftermath of the accident, an investigation found Kirkwood's suspension failed at the retaining nut that held the hub within the wheel bearing and upright. A new retaining nut with a larger flange was designed and mandated by IndyCar as an immediate preventative measure.

But the quest for safety, both drivers' and spectators', didn't stop there.

Further evaluation led to Dallara's newly redesigned, stronger rear uprights that would attach to the suspension A-arms and carry the wheel bearings, axles, brakes, and the hubs that spin in the bearing and connect the transmission's axles to the wheels. With the new configuration, wheel tethers would now be mounted to the upright rather than the caliper studs. Lastly, new and larger retaining nuts were manufactured for the front uprights.

While the new components were necessary to increase safety all around, they provide yet another variable for race teams to consider as they approached the 2024 Indianapolis 500, just ninety days away.

MARCH 5, 2024

Coyne Rounds Out the Season's Field

Dale Coyne Racing (DCR) had traditionally been notorious for announcing last-minute driver lineups. As a smaller team that had competed at the top level of open wheel racing in the US for forty years, Coyne funded his eponymous team but was always looking for drivers who might bring sponsorship funding with them. Thus, late calls were routinely made on lineups.

With last season's full-time drivers David Malukas and Sting Ray Robb moving onto other teams—Malukas to Arrow McLaren and Robb to AJ Foyt Racing—DCR had been on the lookout for a new driver lineup for the entire offseason. Today the team announced some of its drivers for the upcoming season, although questions remained about its roster for the Indy 500.

With practice set to start in just three days for the opening race weekend of the year, the team announced that its No. 18 car would be shared by veteran Jack Harvey and INDY NXT Rookie of the Year, Nolan Siegel, with Harvey in the cockpit for the season-opener in St. Petersburg. For its No. 51 Rick Ware Racing-supported car, thirty-five-year-old sportscar veteran Colin Braun would make his IndyCar debut, racing the season opener and the second race, a non-points-paying exhibition race at Thermal Auto Club on March 24.

Throughout the season, the nineteen-year-old Siegel would race primarily in the INDY NXT feeder series. However, on the weekends when the INDY NXT Series would not support the IndyCar Series as a preliminary race, he would race the No. 18 DCR car. Importantly, that meant the seat for the Indianapolis 500 would be his, not Harvey's.

Thirty-year-old Harvey made his IndyCar debut at the 2017 Indianapolis 500, where he drove for Meyer Shank Racing, in an entry supported by Andretti Autosport. As Meyer Shank Racing, long a successful sportscar racing team, slowly, steadily built its IndyCar program, Harvey was its driver, racing in sixteen races over the 2018 and 2019 seasons.

In the 2020 and 2021 seasons, Harvey firmly established himself and Meyer Shank Racing on the IndyCar grid, particularly in qualifying, where he earned three front-row starting positions for the relatively new team.

However, in 2022, Harvey moved to RLL, and his career, once very much a promising one, unraveled. The team struggled with an understaffed race engineering department, and his results trailed his two teammates. With three races remaining in the 2023 season, RLL parted ways with Harvey, who was now looking to rebuild his career.

But would that rebuilding effort be bolstered by a ride at this year's Indy 500?

Siegel would get the No. 18. Kathryn Legge, who teamed with Harvey at RLL at 2023's Indy 500, was still putting together a sponsorship package that, if fulfilled, might see her join the DCR team for Indianapolis.

Then, there was Braun, who was confirmed for the seat in the No. 51 for the first two races of the year but nothing further. Coyne likely would field three cars for the Indianapolis 500 but only one driver, Siegel, was set. That left three drivers in talks for the other two seats, with Harvey and Braun getting the opportunity to let their driving do the talking to some extent at the season-opening race weekend.

MARCH 10, 2024

Newgarden, Team Penske Dominate at St. Pete

At the season-opening Firestone Grand Prix of St. Petersburg, Newgarden dominated from the pole position, racing his PPG Team Penske Chevrolet to a nearly eight-second victory over the Arrow McLaren Chevrolet piloted by Pato O'Ward. In front of a capacity crowd on a sun-soaked Florida afternoon, Newgarden led ninety-two of the one hundred laps and easily earned his thirtieth career victory. In doing so, he moved ahead of four-time Indianapolis 500 winner Mears for thirteenth on the all-time win list.

Newgarden led a dominant Team Penske presence, as Scott McLaughlin finished third in his DEX Imaging Chevrolet and two-time IndyCar Series champion Will Power finished fourth in his Verizon Business Team Penske Chevrolet. Colton Herta and Alex Palou rounded out the top six, representing the highest-placed Honda-powered entries.

The race was run on a bumpy, fourteen-turn, 1.8-mile temporary street circuit, which was about as polar opposite of the Indianapolis Motor Speedway's billiard-table smooth, superspeedway oval. As such, there was absolutely zero setup data to be gleaned from the entire race weekend to better prepare for the 500 in May. Still, drivers and teams did not race for racing's sake; they raced to win.

While chassis setup data won't be applicable to getting ready for the Indy 500, a great many other variables were refined over the race weekend, like pit stop execution. Then there were the entire preparation processes that took place before practices, qualifying sessions, and the race. The first race of the year allowed teams to "check for leaks," in a manner of speaking. Team Penske passed the first test with flying colors and would bring momentum and high morale into the early season.

Scott McLaughlin is a thirty-year-old racer from Christchurch, New Zealand, who broke into the IndyCar Series in 2020, leaping straight into the deep end of the pool with Team Penske and its ever-high expectations to compete for race wins and championships.

Like so many racers of his generation, McLaughlin started in karting, and his early success, including a championship in 2002, led his family to relocate to the Gold Coast of Australia so he could compete both there and in New Zealand. In five seasons of karting, he finished second in three different championships, catching the attention of team owners in bigger, faster categories.

The biggest category of racing in Australia and New Zealand had long been the Supercars Championship, an international series governed by the FIA. Supercars are absolute beasts—custom-made racers loosely based on production road cars and powered by enormous normally aspirated V-8 engines.

It was in Supercars that McLaughlin excelled. Over 253 races, he qualified for seventy-six poles, won fifty-six races, and finished on the podium 106 times. In his last three years in the series, he won the season title, all in cars owned by DJR Team Penske, a partnership between Dick Johnson Racing and Team Penske.

Originally, Team Penske earmarked McLaughlin to race for the team's sports car programs, both in the United States and Europe. McLaughlin had a different idea. He wanted to move up to Team Penske's IndyCar operation for three reasons: 1) to meet the challenge of moving from a full-bodied racer to an open-wheel race car, 2) to compete wheel-to-wheel against his childhood racing hero and fellow Kiwi Scott Dixon, and 3) to realize his life-long dream of racing in the Indianapolis 500.

McLaughlin, though, had to first prove he was capable on the racetrack. In January 2020, he tested for Team Penske on the bumpy road course at Sebring and dutifully impressed long-time Penske driver Power. Then, the next month, he tested on the oval at Texas Motor Speedway, where he similarly impressed Newgarden. Later that year, he made his IndyCar debut at the season-ending race at St. Petersburg, where he finished a nondescript twenty-second.

In his rookie season of 2021, McLaughlin acquainted himself well with open-wheel racing in the United States, posting five top-ten finishes in the season's sixteen races, including a second-place finish in just his third race, the banked oval in Texas. In his first Indianapolis 500, he qualified best of his teammates at seventeenth and finished the race at twentieth to capture Rookie of the Year honors.

In 2022, McLaughlin won the first race of the season in St. Petersburg for his maiden IndyCar victory. He would win two additional races on his way to a fourth-place finish in the season championship. He followed that up in 2023 with one victory and three second-place finishes on the way to another third place in the championship standings. That year's fourteenth-place finish in the Indianapolis 500 was also his best finish in his three attempts at the biggest race of them all.

Completing the strong trio of drivers at Team Penske is Power, a native of Toowoomba, Australia, who recently turned forty-three. Power had won the IndyCar Series title twice, both in 2014 and 2022, and also won the Indy 500 in 2018.

Growing up a road course expert in Australia, Power made his Indy car debut in the CART Series race in Surfers Paradise in 2005. Running two races that season earned Power a full-time ride in the Series with Team Australia for 2006, where he scored one podium finish on the way to a sixth-place finish in the championship standings. He also earned his first career pole position that rookie season, qualifying first at his home race in Australia.

That pole position was the first of what was now a record seventy pole positions in CART and IndyCar. Power deservedly held the reputation for consistently being the fastest driver over a single qualifying lap. Ever.

Power had raced for Penske since 2009 and had delivered thirty-eight victories for The Captain, including at least one victory every year for a remarkable fourteen consecutive seasons. That streak was broken in 2023, but Power's competitive spark was far from extinguished.

Always one to wear his emotions on his sleeve, a solid start for Power in 2024 was a good omen for his Verizon Chevy crew. A potential big lift ahead of the Indy 500 would be the race on Indy's road course on May 11. It's a course that Power had won on four times previously, and another victory this year would provide him and the rest of Team Penske a strong start to the month of May.

TUESDAY, APRIL 9, 2024

Coyne Adds Katherine Legge to Push Entries to Thirty-Four

In 2023, British driver Katherine Legge returned to the Indianapolis 500 for her third attempt at the race, ten years after she had made her last appearance. She wouldn't wait nearly that long to return to the Brickyard, as Dale Coyne Racing announced she would drive its No. 51 Honda-powered entry in the 2024 race, teaming with rookie Nolan Siegel in the No. 18 car.

DCR's pink and black No. 51 car would carry primary sponsorship from e.l.f. Cosmetics, an online American cosmetics brand keen on expanding its partnership with Legge. With its sponsorship, e.l.f. Cosmetics would become the first-ever beauty brand to serve as the primary sponsor of an Indy 500 entry.

In a press release, Legge said, "I'm honored to be back at the 500 to represent such a groundbreaking and historic effort put forward by e.l.f. When I was nine years old, I decided I wanted to be a racecar driver, and I never would have dreamed a beauty brand would one day be my primary sponsor in the Indy 500. Together with DCR, Honda and e.l.f., we will truly empower women who are breaking barriers, pushing boundaries and testing the limits by giving them the confidence and a path towards realizing their dreams, whatever they may be."

Legge was an experienced racer and had spent time in a variety of race cars, including making twenty-eight CART starts and twelve Indy-Car starts. While she raced full-time in the IMSA SportsCar Championship, she had served as a test driver in Formula One, raced touring cars in the incredibly competitive Deutsche Tourenwagen Masters (DTM) series, and had essentially raced most anything with an engine and four wheels.

The previous year, driving only the Indy 500 for Rahal Letterman Lanigan, Legge struggled alongside her three full-time teammates: Graham Rahal, Christian Lundgaard, and Jack Harvey. Ahead of qualifying, all four desperately—and, ultimately, fruitlessly—searched for speed.

Remarkably, Legge out-qualified them all, just barely placing her car into the field on the first day of qualifying. On the second day, in the Last Chance Qualifying session, Lundgaard and Harvey squeezed into the field, leaving Rahal as the lone entry to not qualify for the race.

Even though Legge qualified for the race, her 2023 Indy 500 campaign didn't get any easier for her. During a practice session on the Monday after the qualifying weekend, Legge was in a long train of cars entering Turn One. As drivers ahead of her unexpectedly backed out of the throttle and slowed, the pack compressed in a concertina-like effect. Unable to react to the slowing cars quickly enough, Legge ran into the rear of the car driven by Stefan Wilson, sending them both into the outside wall in a heavy crash.

Legge was uninjured, but Wilson suffered vertebral fractures, which would cause him to miss the 500 just six days later. In an odd turn of events, the driver who replaced Wilson in the cockpit of his Dreyer & Reinbold racer was Legge's teammate at RLL, Rahal.

The month to forget ended for Legge much as it had begun, with an Indy 500 to forget. Making her first pit stop on lap thirty-two, she spun leaving her pit box and impacted the inside Pit Lane wall. Her RLL team tried to repair her car, but after three additional pit stops, Legge was forced to retire from the race. With just forty-one laps run, Legge was classified in thirty-third place—last.

Legge was the only woman entered thus far in the Indy 500 this year, but she was not the only woman to have raced at the famed oval. Nine women had competed in the 500, with Janet Guthrie first blazing the trail in 1977.

It hadn't been easy for women to break into the male-dominated field of auto racing. There had been a stubborn stigma attached to nearly every woman in nearly every category of racing around the world. The driver wasn't a driver. Rather, she was a "woman driver," and it had been difficult for women to earn seats in the most competitive cars in the biggest of teams.

It was not a situation unique to the IndyCar Series. Women drivers experienced difficulty breaking into all series, and it started at the entry-level, junior formula categories, which tended not to draw the interest of young girls as competitors. Legge and her effort with e.l.f. Cosmetics set out to change that. Just imagine the booming interest in motorsports for young women if Legge should pull off a victory in the 500.

Sarah Fisher held the mark for the most Indy 500 starts for women with nine between 2000 and 2010. However, the most famous woman racer and the most successful at Indianapolis was Danica Patrick, who started eight races between 2005 and 2018, posting six top-ten finishes, with a best finish of third in 2009.

Patrick remained the only woman to have won an Indy car race, driving to victory in the Indy Racing League's Japan 300 at Twin Ring Motegi in 2008. She had a long racing career, first in open-wheel Indy cars and then in stock cars in the NASCAR Series. However, she never broke through to become a consistent contender for race victories and podium finishes.

The knock on Patrick was her ability to qualify well, and she struggled in that aspect on different courses throughout her career. However, Indianapolis wasn't one of them. Simply, Patrick knew how to get around the Indianapolis Motor Speedway quickly. In her rookie year of 2005, Patrick electrified the crowd all month long, qualifying fourth, leading nineteen laps in the race, finishing in fourth place, and earning the Rookie of the Year Award.

Her star didn't stop shining at the checkered flag either. The morning after the race, she was interviewed on ABC's *Good Morning America* news program, and later in the week, she was featured on the cover of *Sports Illustrated*.

While it might have ruffled the feathers of some of her competitors that Patrick received so much attention for not winning the Indy 500, in time, some embraced it with a sense of humor. Winner Dan Wheldon sported a T-shirt exclaiming, "I actually 'won' the Indy 500," while Patrick's Rahal Letterman (Mike Lanigan had yet to partner with the team) teammates Buddy Rice, the 2004 Indy 500 champion, and Vitor Meira, 2005's runner-up, wore shirts exclaiming, "Danica's teammate" and "Danica's other teammate."

The time for more women in racing had been long overdue. There had been moments when the door looked ready to be kicked in once and for all, like in 2010, when Patrick was joined in the field by Fisher, Ana Beatriz, and Simona de Silvestro. Patrick ended that race in sixth place, and de Silvestro was named Rookie of the Year.

Four women also qualified in 2013. But, by 2020, there wasn't a single woman in the field, the first time since 1999. In fact, in 2020, there wasn't even an entry for a woman driver, marking the first time that had happened since 1991.

Legge would likely be the only woman driver attached to an entry at this year's 500. Hopefully, she would produce a good result that inspired other women to get involved in motorsports.

The addition of Legge to the 2024 Indy 500 entry list brought the total number of confirmed car-and-driver pairings to thirty-four, and that had racing fans thrilled. Fans were excited because only thirty-three cars qualify for the running of the Indianapolis 500. At present, one team would miss out on the biggest race in the world, and that would bring a considerable element of drama to qualifications, scheduled for Saturday and Sunday, May 18 and 19. Qualifying always brought plenty of drama as drivers fought for the fastest qualifying run and the pole position. However, there was arguably even more drama at the other end of the spectrum, where teams and drivers did all they could to avoid being the odd car or cars that didn't qualify for the race.

Rumors abounded that another entry was imminent, that being an announcement on who would drive Abel Motorsports's No. 50 car.

In 2023, RC Enerson qualified twenty-eighth for Abel but suffered a mechanical failure that forced his retirement after seventy-five laps. In the final classification, he was credited with thirty-second, one position better than Legge.

The Enerson family owned the Dallara chassis that Abel Motorsports prepared and ran at Indianapolis in 2023. To keep its options open to other potential drivers, Abel Motorsports ordered a new Dallara chassis during the off-season.

With the month of May quickly approaching, ongoing speculation had the Enerson family continuing to search for a primary sponsor to help fund their Indy 500 effort, and should that land, they could formalize another arrangement with Abel Motorsports.

However, Enerson isn't the only driver who would love an opportunity to participate in this year's Indy 500. That very same silly season speculation around the IndyCar paddock had drivers like Wilson, Charlie Kimball, Benjamin Pedersen, Devlin DeFrancesco, and others attempting to put together financial packages to get the Abel Motorsports ride.

If fans were excited about the prospects of thirty-four cars fighting for thirty-three starting positions, they would be ecstatic about a thirty-fifth car entering the fray.

WEDNESDAY, APRIL 10, 2024

Open Testing at IMS

Two days ago, on April 8, nearly 50,000 people entered the grounds of the Indianapolis Motor Speedway, and it had nothing to do with any on-track activity. Or, rather, nearly nothing.

Those in attendance were there for a special watch party for a total solar eclipse. It turned out that Indianapolis was the biggest city outside of Texas to be on the path of totality for the Western Hemisphere's 2024 eclipse. With its abundance of both space and seating, the Speedway made for a perfect watch party location.

With it being the Speedway and all, IndyCar couldn't resist the temptation to run a few laps early in the day to not only give spectators something to see ahead of the eclipse but maybe also make some new fans for the race itself, just a month and a half away. Doing the honors on the demonstration laps was local driver/owner and three-time fastest qualifier Ed Carpenter in his No. 20 Ed Carpenter Racing Chevrolet.

On April 10, however, the track was open for an entirely different kind of activity, the activity it was created for more than a century ago. Indy cars took to the track for an open test ahead of next month's race.

The weather was anticipated to be cool, with temperatures expected to top out just below sixty degrees—much lower than the Indianapolis area temperatures most often experienced in late May. Still, no IndyCar team would consider missing the open test, as it allowed teams their only opportunity to prepare for May, and it gave drivers, both young and experienced alike, a chance to get acquainted, or reacquainted as the case might be, with the Brickyard.

As the teams prepared for the day, the track was still damp from overnight showers, delaying the start. Nervous energy abounded, particularly among the drivers. Drivers weren't ordinarily nervous in their cars, the one place at the racetrack they felt the most comfortable. It was the waiting where nerves could sometimes fray, eyes glancing back and forth between the track and the sky, looking for one to dry and the other to stop threatening more rain.

Race cars could run in the rain, and the IndyCar Series runs on wet tracks at both street and road circuits. At an oval, however, and especially at a superspeedway like IMS, cars don't go out on a wet surface.

Indy cars are too powerful and have too much torque from the rear wheels to run "in the wet" on an oval track. Sure, teams *could* mount grooved, wet-weather tires—on dry surfaces they run non-grooved slick tires constructed especially for racing—but speeds would be diminished greatly, far below the cars' capacities. Plus, racing drivers being racing drivers, most would push and push ever faster until they lost control and wrecked into the retaining wall. All in all, it would be a different kind of spectacle, and one that no one would be interested in watching.

Therefore, when it rained at the Speedway, everyone waited.

Sunshine, of course, helps the track dry, as does a breeze. Additionally, the Speedway will run service cars and trucks on the track, their tires lifting the standing water to be blown away by the wind. Lastly, the Speedway deploys several jet dryers—jet engines mounted on trailers, with the jet wash exhaust blowing moisture from the outside of the track down and off into the apron and warm-up lane, and onto the grass of the infield along the backstretch.

As the track continued to dry, teams rolled their cars out to Pit Lane, where they made final preparations. There was a lot to get prepared, and safety was paramount. Important, though, was to avoid making any silly mistakes in preparation that would cause the car to miss time turning laps. Crews learned from their cars moving, at speed, on the track, not sitting still getting repaired either on Pit Lane or in the garages in Gasoline Alley.

Finally, the safety lights around the track turned green, signifying cars could go on track. Initially, it was a simple "installation lap" for all participants. Drivers ran a slow lap around the track, testing their radio communications with their crews, ensuring they could hear, and in turn be heard, at all points of the large oval. Then the drivers drove down Pit Lane and stopped in front of their respective crews, where they turned off their engines. They did so for the crew to check for leaks. Was everything on the car installed properly?

With the installation laps completed, the day's scheduled activities then took off in earnest. The morning session was earmarked for veterans and full-time drivers in the IndyCar Series.

Lapping at speed on the IMS oval is a learned practice. Leaving Pit Lane, drivers stay on the warm-up lane on the inside of the circuit through Turns One and Two, before entering onto the racing surface on the backstretch. Depending on traffic and other considerations, drivers will either build up speed and drift to the right to enter Turn Three or stay low on the track and go through the warm-up lane inside of Turns Three and Four.

The racing line at Indianapolis, the quickest way around the track, is called "the groove," and it develops and becomes visible over time, as cars repeatedly lap the Speedway. When cars go through each of the four turns, the incredible friction placed on the tires results in a tiny bit of rubber left on the racing surface. Lap after lap, that rubber build-up gets deeper and darker in color.

As the groove develops, it affords more traction, allowing drivers to feel more comfortable and drive faster. But if a driver should venture above the groove into "the gray" in any of the four turns, there's a dramatic decrease in the levels of grip. That's precisely when drivers find themselves out of control, and possibly into the wall.

At speed, drivers roar down the five-eighths-mile frontstretch a car width or more away from the outside retaining wall, as any closer, the turbulent wake of the air pushing off the side of the car creates a buffeting effect that can disrupt the car's handling.

As drivers approach Turn One, they quickly move to their right, close to the wall, to gain the preferred entry into the turn, diving low to clip the apex and then piloting the car dangerously close to the wall at the corner exit. Drivers aim to be smooth, minimizing their driver inputs on the steering wheel through the quarter-mile turns to scrub off as little speed as possible.

In the turns, almost every driver will dip the left front tire just below the white line that marks the edge of the racetrack. There's just a little bit more asphalt below the white line for the tires to safely grip. Drivers can't go too low, however, for each turn has a concrete curb that rests between the asphalt of the track and the grass of the infield. Touching that concrete curb will unsettle the car, shifting weight and momentum in a way that threatens to spin the car out of control. Thus, drivers have to be incredibly accurate in hitting their mark at the apex of each turn.

That driving line, going just below the white line with the left front tire, was popularized by Carlos Muñoz, a Colombian driver who finished second in both the 2013 and 2016 Indy 500s. At first, other drivers thought Muñoz was crazy for taking that line. Then they saw his results and copied him.

All except for Castroneves, that is. The "Castroneves line" sweeps around each turn at a higher radius, the left-side tires rarely, if ever threatening to roll over the white line. Castroneves feels comfortable there, and his results—four Indy 500 victories, three second-place finishes, one third-place finish, and seven other top-ten finishes—have proven his preferred line certainly works for him.

Still, year after year, Castroneves is pretty much the only driver who ventures high in the turns. Interestingly, it makes him one of the easier cars to follow in the turns, as there is more "clean," undisturbed air to flow over the left front wing of the following car, allowing it to experience more aerodynamic grip and, in turn, go just a touch faster.

The one-eighth-mile-long short chute between Turns One and Two goes by quickly, with driver and car close to the wall, entering Turn Two and aiming for the apex on the far left, or inside, of the track. The car's momentum, well over 220 miles an hour, again carries the car to the outside of the track at the corner exit, right up against—but not quite touching—the concrete wall on the outside of the track.

Drivers then get an opportunity to catch their breath as they rocket down the backstretch, drifting slightly toward the left to keep a little distance between the right side of the car and the outside wall. Then they approach Turn Three much like they approached Turn One twenty seconds earlier.

In theory, the four turns of the Indianapolis Motor Speedway are identical. They're each a quarter-mile-long, and they're banked at nine degrees, twelve minutes. In practice, however, as any Indy car driver can tell you, the turns are far from being the same. To make matters even more difficult, they can be different from day to day and, sometimes, even within a day.

The modern-day Indy car is very much a finely-tuned, aerodynamically dependent vehicle, and as such, it's greatly affected by wind. Therefore, cars will handle differently at opposite ends of the track if the wind is blowing. Additionally, speeds at the end of the long straightaways entering Turns One and Three are higher than the speeds entering Turns Two and Four. During a qualifying attempt, it's not uncommon for a car to have scrubbed four or five miles an hour going through Turn One before entering Turn Two. That same differential of speed is repeated at the north end of the track in Turns Three and Four.

Speed is also dependent on the tires, which, in many respects, might be the most important component of the car. A driver can have the most powerful engine in the world, but without tires, he or she isn't going anywhere.

Tires offer their maximum grip when they're within their prime range of operating temperatures. They get warmer as they slide through the turns, the friction heating the surface of the tire and, eventually, the tire's inner core.

The IndyCar Series does not utilize tire-warming blankets like Formula One, so it's incumbent upon the drivers to warm up their tires appropriately. Ordinarily, that takes a lap or two of scrubbing the tires along in the turns to get them in the optimum temperature window.

Tire temperatures are critical. Tires that are too cold offer less grip in the turns, greatly impacting the speed that can be carried through the turns. With turns making up a total of one mile of the Speedway's two-and-a-half-mile length, drivers cannot afford to be off the pace while cornering. At the other end of the spectrum, tires that are too hot also lose grip, causing the car to slide more in the turns which, of course, creates even more friction and therefore more heat. It's a cycle that just gets worse and worse. The only remedy is to slow down, and no driver wants to do that. As a result, managing tires is an important skill developed over time by Indy car drivers.

Ambient air temperature and clouds are yet more performance-impacting variables. The track's temperature is closely monitored by teams, and it changes over time. Passing clouds can drop the temperature of the track, and on a hot qualifying day, a lucky break with cloud cover can help a driver tremendously. Unlike the tires, engines thrive in cooler weather. The cooler the air entering, the more powerful an engine's output.

Today's cool weather would be perfect for the engines. But it would also require drivers to carefully work their tires into the optimal tire temperature window before really sending it on a fast lap.

The morning session for veterans went off without incident. Defending race winner Newgarden turned the fastest lap, posting a 228.811-mph speed. That result didn't come as much of a surprise. The second-fastest driver, however, raised more than a few eyebrows up and down Pit Lane.

NASCAR star Larson, running with the veterans after completing his Rookie Orientation Program in October, went second fastest with a lap of 226.384 mph in his Arrow McLaren Chevrolet, just a whisker in front of six-time IndyCar Series champion and 2008 Indy 500 winner Dixon at 226.346 mph.

After stepping from the cockpit, Larson told NBC Sports's Dillon Welch that he benefited from following Newgarden and learning how to run in the turbulent wake of other cars. "I'm trying to learn all that and process all that and learn what I can do in the car to compete. Timing the runs behind me and trying to figure out any bit of racecraft today, which is tough. But I get an idea of things and notes in my head. So far, so good."

So far, so good, indeed.

For the day, thirty-four drivers completed a total of 1,327 laps. Included in those were refresher tests for three drivers: Marco Andretti,

Pietro Fittipaldi, and Katherine Legge. After the morning practice session for the veterans, three rookies took to the track to tackle the Rookie Orientation Program. Christian Rasmussen, Kyffin Simpson, and Nolan Siegel each completed the three-phased program without incident. With the ROP behind them, they were cleared to practice during any green-flag session.

The rookies would still have a lot of work to do come May. Inclement weather shortened today's test by washing out most of the afternoon session, and the weather forecast was not promising for tomorrow, the second and final scheduled day of testing at IMS before practice for the 500 starts on Tuesday, May 14.

Thus, the anxiety-ridden countdown to the start of the 108th running of the Indianapolis 500 began in earnest . . . now!

SUNDAY, APRIL 21, 2024

Dixie Triumphs on the Streets of Long Beach

───

Scott Dixon arrived at this weekend's race in Long Beach with fifty-six victories, second only to AJ Foyt on the all-time win list. Today, on the street circuit at the Acura Grand Prix, "Dixie" picked up his fifty-seventh victory displaying what has become, in many ways, his trademark style.

Dixon had demonstrated repeatedly an uncommon knack for saving fuel while, at the same time, turning in racy laps. It's a skill he had mastered like no one else, and he used it to full effect by stretching his last load of fuel for the final thirty-four laps of the eighty-five-lap event. In the end, he held off the hard-charging Colton Herta by just under a second.

"That was tough; that was really tough," Dixon said immediately after the race. "Honestly, I didn't think we were going to make it, and they kept giving me a (fuel) number, and it just wasn't getting . . . I was close but not enough. Luckily, we were on the safe side there."

Herta was on a different fuel strategy, one that allowed him to run full throttle to the end before eventually falling just short. Reigning Series champion Palou finished third, while Team Penske's Newgarden placed a disappointing fourth after having led much of the race and later bumped out of second position by Herta.

The Long Beach course is a bumpy, eleven-turn, 1.968-mile circuit that uses public streets. As such, there are no chassis setup learnings for teams and drivers to take forward and better prepare for the Indy 500. Fuel conservation, though, is an area of constant development, and it's a skill Dixon had put to good use throughout his storied career.

One way to conserve fuel is mechanically, within the car. On the steering wheel, there is a dial where the driver can change the fuel mapping of the engine. Running the fuel full rich provides maximum power to the engine but uses the most fuel. Running full lean minimizes fuel consumption but reduces power. Then there are various settings between full rich and full lean.

The other way to affect fuel mileage is through driver inputs into the car. On a street course like Long Beach, drivers like Dixon will lift off the throttle as they approach the braking zone for a corner—the longer the lift, the greater the fuel savings. Then, upon accelerating out of the corner, the driver will gently roll onto the throttle instead of instantly mashing it to the floor. Lastly, while shifting gears through an acceleration phase, the driver will short shift, shifting into a lower gear earlier than usual, causing the engine to spin fewer revolutions per minute (RPM), and saving a bit of fuel.

When a driver like Dixon starts saving fuel at the beginning of a stint and works hard at it at every brake zone, corner, and acceleration phase, the fuel savings can be substantial. And, if a driver can make one less pit stop than his competitors, then he just might find himself celebrating a victory.

Of course, there's a tradeoff. Saving fuel means going slower. Except, maybe, if you're Scott Dixon.

At the Indy 500, saving fuel is an important strategy in the race. Fuel mapping is important, as is following closely in the slipstream of the car in front, saving fuel. Then, if more fuel needs to be saved, drivers will ease off the throttle gently before entering all four turns.

Saving fuel in the Indy 500 often helps a car move up in the field early in the race, gaining better track position for those who may have started toward the end of the grid. Then, late in the race, fuel savings can mean the difference between victory and defeat. Fuel runs have won the Indy 500 many times before, maybe most famously when Alexander Rossi won the 100th running of the race in 2016.

Rossi etched his name in the history books that afternoon by crawling along on his last lap, desperately hoping he wouldn't run out of fuel. His last lap was recorded at just 179.784 mph. By comparison, his teammate Carlos Muñoz, who finished second, just 4.4975 seconds behind, recorded a final lap speed of 218.789 mph.

Victory in the Indy 500, as in any race, goes to the driver who completes the race distance the quickest and not necessarily the driver who completes the last lap the quickest. Conserving fuel won't make a car go faster. But conserving fuel to eliminate the need to make as many pit stops as others can make a driver complete the race distance the fastest. And no one has done that better in the past than Dixon. He further proved that point again in today's victory.

FRIDAY, APRIL 26, 2024

Scandal Blazes Through the IndyCar Paddock

On Wednesday, April 24, IndyCar handed down stiff penalties to Team Penske for rules infractions incurred at the season-opening race in St. Petersburg on March 10. The penalties included disqualifications for drivers Newgarden and McLaughlin, and a ten-point penalty for their teammate, Power. Additionally, all three entries were fined $25,000 and forced to forfeit prize money associated with the Streets of St. Petersburg race.

As a result of the penalties, Pato O'Ward was named the official winner of the race. Power, who was penalized points but not disqualified, was promoted to second place. Third place was officially awarded to Colton Herta.

This story is an incendiary cheating scandal at its core. After all, it's a severe penalty leveled at a team owned and operated by the owner of the entire IndyCar Series. The story will likely continue to, and through, the Indy 500 next month.

At issue is the use of the push-to-pass system on race starts and restarts. The push-to-pass button is on the driver's steering wheel, on the lower right side. When operated by the driver, it engages a system that delivers increased power—approximately sixty additional horsepower—to the engine through added turbocharger boost for a predetermined period during a race. Depending on the circuit, drivers are allocated between 150 and 200 seconds of push-to-pass to use at their discretion.

However, IndyCar prohibits the use of the push-to-pass system on race starts and restarts. Moreover, the button on the steering wheel is supposed to be deactivated, unable to be used in those circumstances.

The previous week at Long Beach, the issue was discovered when a software glitch in the system knocked out the push-to-pass system on all cars during the Sunday morning warm-up session before the race. The glitch affected every car . . . except the three Penske entries.

After the issue was identified by IndyCar officials, they took immediate action to rectify it before the race. Then they moved to investigate exactly how long the system had been compromised. Their in-depth investigation included onboard camera footage that showed Newgarden deploy his push-to-pass system on at least one restart at St. Petersburg.

Team Penske claimed it modified the push-to-pass system on all three cars to use specifically for a test session for the upcoming hybrid assist system. Afterward, they were mistakenly not replaced before the start of the season.

Late Wednesday, McLaughlin took to X and posted a statement where he wrote, in part, "I was not aware of the situation with the software. In this instance, I used a single, very brief (1.9 seconds) deployment of push to pass in a section of the track exit of turn 9 where it is typically utilized throughout the race. I hit the button out of habit, but I did not pass any cars nor did I gain any time advantage. The data, which IndyCar has, confirms all of this information. While I accept the penalty, I want to be clear that I did not gain an advantage over my competitors."

Thursday, Power offered his thoughts on his own post on X, where he wrote, "I was disappointed to learn about the penalty that we received this week from IndyCar. There was an oversight by our team and I was unaware of the situation until it was brought to our attention following Long Beach.

"As per the rules, I did not utilize the P2P capabilities during any start or restart during the St. Petersburg race. While I accept the penalty, I want it to be known that I did nothing wrong and followed the rules. Now we move forward and my focus is on Barber."

Newgarden, however, was silent. Until, that is, he spoke at a press conference today, ahead of the on-track activities for the Children's of Alabama Grand Prix at Barber Motorsports Park in Birmingham, Alabama.

Newgarden was emotional at his thirty-minute news conference, and his voice wavered throughout. "The facts are extremely clear," he said. "There's no doubt we were in breach of the rules at St. Pete. I used push to pass at an unauthorized time on two different restarts.

"Those are the rules, and we did not adhere to them. What's really important about that, too, is there's only one person sitting in the car. It's just me. It's my responsibility to know the rules and regulations at all points and make sure I get that right; with that regard, I failed my team miserably. I failed completely to get that right. You can't make a mistake like that at this level in that situation. There's no room for it. I don't want to hide from that. It's an embarrassing situation to have to go through. It's demoralizing in a lot of ways. There's nothing I can say that changes the fact of what happened. It's pretty clear. I think the facts are most important; that's what really matters. I also think the truth is really important. There can be space for both those things."

Newgarden claimed to have not remembered the push-to-pass rules in the heat of competition, where every racer is doing everything in his or her control to improve their position. His position remained that he broke the rules but without intent. "You guys can call me every name in the book, you can call me incompetent, call me an idiot, . . . call me stupid, whatever you want to call me. But I'm not a liar."

When asked how this emerging scandal might affect him leading up to next month's Indy 500 as the defending winner, Newgarden paused to collect himself. "Well, I'm still happy," he replied. "Look, I got the best job in the world. I'm excited. I'm still excited. I'm excited for this weekend. It should be good."

The IndyCar paddock wasn't completely buying what Newgarden was selling. Herta expressed perhaps the strongest opinion.

When asked if he believed Newgarden's explanation that the push-to-pass rules had been changed to allow its use on the starts and restarts of a race, he replied, "No. That's (expletive). That's wrong. No. He knows. But if he thought that, why didn't he push it at the start? He didn't push it at the start. He pushed it on the restarts. You would think when everybody stacked up the most, you would push it. So that's a lie.

"I think some of what Josef said wasn't true, I don't believe it. Their hybrid testing car was probably a different chassis and they probably just took whatever the coding is, I don't know exactly how it works, but they probably implemented it. I believe that and that that's possible. But what's not possible is to go to Long Beach again with it, with the intent to use it again.

"At the end of the day, it's a Penske problem. Even though they took advantage of it and that's wrong. It shouldn't have been in the car to begin with."

Six-time IndyCar champion and respected series elder statesman Dixon also shared strong opinions. When asked if he believed the explanation that the software had been left in Newgarden's car since the most recent hybrid assist test, Dixon said, "No. Every team did a hybrid testing. It's not a part of code that you needed to change for hybrid testing. So, I don't . . . I don't know where they're going with that one.

"It's not a good look. The issue you have is separation of church and state. You've got a team that owns the series—owns one of the engines that's raced in it."

Seeking a welcomed respite from the firestorm, Newgarden quickly found solace in the cockpit of his race car. In the first practice session of the weekend, Newgarden put his name at the top of the chart with the session's fastest time.

SUNDAY, APRIL 28, 2024

McLaughlin Rebounds with a Decisive Victory

In the world of sports, there's no greater salve for what ails than a victory. Today, McLaughlin put an emphatic end to a tumultuous week for all of Team Penske with a resounding victory in the Children's of Alabama Indy Grand Prix.

With the victory, McLaughlin successfully defended his win in last year's race at Barber. It was the Kiwi's fifth career win in the IndyCar Series. Joining McLaughlin on the podium were his Team Penske teammate Will Power and Chip Ganassi Racing's Linus Lundqvist.

Heading into May at Indianapolis, first for the Sonsio Grand Prix on the road course on May 11 and then the 500 on May 26, Andretti Global's Colton Herta topped the championships standings, one point ahead of Power and three points clear of Palou, in third.

McLaughlin qualified just ahead of Power on Saturday, and the two drivers were clearly the class of the field on race day too. Caution flags during the race created three very different strategies on which teams could embark. In the end, though, the top three finishers made a three-pit-stop strategy work, allowing them to race hard through the final stint and overtake drivers who were conserving fuel on a two-stop strategy, like Palou, who ultimately finished fifth.

After leading fifty-eight of the race's ninety laps, McLaughlin did his best to shrug off the controversy of the last four days, saying, "We know our job; we know what we need to do. I'm just super proud of the execution. A couple of yellows didn't fall our way, but we just showed our pace. We just keep rolling, man.

"Definitely one of my best drives in terms of execution and just knocking out the laps. Very happy we could advance to the checkered flag there and bring home a *W* for Team Penske and for Roger."

Earning the second step of the podium, Power joined in on the celebrations after a trying week for Team Penske. "It was a hard-fought one-two for Penske," he said. "We were certainly fast, but obviously, a lot of strategy played into that. We were able to use our speed to come out in front again."

Like other sports, momentum plays an important role, if nothing else, to have drivers and crews confident in their abilities. After having their feet to the fire since the push-to-pass scandal erupted, Team Penske needed an elixir. While Newgarden struggled to a sixteenth-place finish, he showed his pace by qualifying eighth on Saturday.

Team Penske got a lot of its mojo back today, and that would prove instrumental as the IndyCar Series took up residence at the Indianapolis Motor Speedway. However, no one was expecting the push-to-pass scandal to go away quietly.

MONDAY, APRIL 29, 2024

Arrow McLaren Moves on from Malukas

Racing an Indy car is physically demanding, and as such, today's racers train intensely—to not only stand up to the rigors of driving but to possibly gain an edge over their competitors. Drivers don't want to be the weak link in the performance chain, and as such, they work on their strength and conditioning throughout the year.

In February, David Malukas broke his left wrist in a mountain bike accident while training for the IndyCar season. On February 13, he underwent extensive surgery to repair the damage. Pins and screws were implanted during the surgery, and as of the most recent race, Malukas was still wearing a cast and unable to compete.

With Malukas out with his injury, Arrow McLaren had been forced to turn to substitute drivers for the four races contested thus far this season. That fourth race, in which rookie and reigning Formula Two champion Theo Pourchaire drove the No. 6 Arrow McLaren to a twenty-second-place finish at yesterday's race on the road course at Barber Motorsports Park, triggered a clause in Malukas's driving contract, allowing Arrow McLaren the option to terminate his services.

On this day, rather surprisingly, Arrow McLaren did just that.

Racing can be a heartless, cut-throat business, and this served as yet another a prime example. But, at the same time, the teams are in the business of winning, not just for themselves but for their financial sponsors.

Drivers are only as good as their last race, and memories in the paddock can be short.

Malukas was injured outside of the car. But the sport can be cruel even for those injured in the car. Simon Pagenaud, 2016 IndyCar champion and 2019 Indy 500 winner, was still without a ride after suffering a concussion last season practicing for the race at Mid-Ohio. His Meyer Shank Racing-prepared car suffered a mechanical failure, to no fault of Pagenaud. Still, Pagenaud was the one whose career was on hold.

So, what would be next for Malukas? It was unlikely he could race on the road course at Indianapolis on May 11, as the twisting and turning course, with both right and left turns and multiple gear shifts each lap, would have overly taxed his wrist. However, for the Indy 500 on May 26, he would possibly be ready.

Drivers have driven the 500 with orthopedic injuries before. Buddy Lazier famously won the 1996 Indy 500 with sixteen fractures in his vertebrae and twenty-five large chips out of his sacrum, the triangular bone just below the lumbar vertebrae. In 1989, Danny Sullivan raced the 500 with a cast on his broken right forearm.

Malukas might be a candidate for another car for the 500. As for the Arrow McLaren No. 6 entry, there had been no word yet on who might grab that seat. In its statement today, the team said, "Arrow McLaren is finalizing its driver assignments for the remainder of the 2024 season and will announce confirmations for upcoming races in due course."

Callum Illot, a veteran of thirty-seven IndyCar races, substituted for Malukas at St. Pete and drove the No. 6 car home to a thirteenth-place finish. He had appeared in the last two Indy 500s with Juncos Hollinger Racing, finishing a best of twelfth in 2023.

Pourchaire would also be an option. However, he had never raced on an oval and would need to complete his Rookie Orientation Program.

Then there was fan favorite Tony Kanaan, the 2013 Indy 500 champion. Kanaan currently worked for Arrow McLaren as a special advisor to its drivers, coaching and mentoring the team's stable of drivers. For the past three months, he had been working with Malukas to help his physical recovery.

The forty-nine-year-old Kanaan is revered by race fans, and the Indianapolis community has essentially adopted the Brazilian as one of their own. He had also been at the forefront of driver fitness for decades, so there is little doubt he could still handle the physical strain of racing even though he hadn't raced since the 2023 Indy 500.

An announcement would be forthcoming. In the meantime, Malukas would look for a new team in which to restart his career. He was a young driver with a lot of potential, and he brought financial backing that would make him an attractive driver to every team in the mid-field. Thus, in a way, silly season 2024 had just begun—early.

MONDAY, MAY 6, 2024

Pourchaire Completes IndyCar Oval Test

Twenty-year-old Frenchman Théo Pourchaire took to the 1.33-mile oval circuit at World Wide Technology Raceway outside of St. Louis today with a single mission in mind: pass his IndyCar Series oval test. He did so with ease.

Pourchaire was the current defending Formula Two champion and was the youngest-ever race winner in Formula 2 history. Clearly, he knew how to race cars. But, having grown up racing in Europe, Pourchaire had never experienced the unique nature of an oval track.

Until today. However, to make matters just a touch more difficult, Pourchaire had to contend with the distinctive layout of the WWTR track, which resembles more of an egg than a true oval, with Turns One and Two being considerably tighter than Turns Three and Four at the opposite end.

By passing his oval test, Pourchaire, driving for Arrow McLaren in relief of Malukas, was cleared by IndyCar to compete at all the oval tracks the series would visit this season, including Iowa Speedway in July, a return to WWTR in August, The Milwaukee Mile on Labor Day weekend, and Nashville Superspeedway in September. And, of course, the Indianapolis Motor Speedway later in May.

It's Indy where Pourchaire and Arrow McLaren directed their focus. The team had not thus far announced a new driver for its No. 6 car to replace Malukas, but all signs indicated it would likely be either Pourchaire or Illot, the two drivers who had competed in the car this season. However, if Arrow McLaren chose Pourchaire for the 500, he would still have to complete the Rookie Orientation Program at the Speedway once the track opened for practice on Tuesday, May 14.

Of his on-track experience, Pourchaire said, "The first time for me on an oval was really exciting. I couldn't wait to feel the driving on an oval. I can say it now, it's really quick, really impressive. You have to be really smooth on the steering wheel, the steering inputs going back on power and be really smooth in the car.

"It feels amazing. I'm really happy. I'm really tired mentally as well because it's super quick and you don't want to do a mistake on a track like this. If you do a small mistake you can end up in the wall, and we all know that ending up in the wall on an oval is really dangerous."

Time quickly ticked away for Arrow McLaren to confirm a driver for the No. 6 for the 500. But whether Pourchaire received the nod or not, he would most likely be in the seat of the No. 6 for the remainder of this, his rookie IndyCar season.

TUESDAY, MAY 7, 2024

Penske Suspends Four

The push-to-past scandal that rocked IndyCar racing the past two weeks reared up again today, and it was poised to affect the sport's most successful team as it made final preparations for the Indy 500. Team owner Roger Penske suspended Tim Cindric, the president of Team Penske, along with three others for two races for their roles in the scandal.

In an interview with The Associated Press, Penske said a review conducted by his general counsel found the team had no "malicious intent by anyone," and concluded the incident was a breakdown in both internal processes and intra-team communication. The suspensions covered this week's race on the IMS road course and the showcase Indianapolis 500 at the end of the month.

The Associated Press quoted Penske as saying, "We're the same company we have been for fifty years and I'm going to hold my head high. This is an unfortunate situation and when you're the leader, you have to take action. We've done that and we're going to move on. I am not trying to run a popularity contest."

In addition to Cindric, who has been at Team Penske since 1999, Penske suspended team managing director Ron Ruzewski and engineers Luke Mason and Robbie Atkinson. The suspensions affected the entirety of Team Penske, especially the cars of both Newgarden and Power.

Cindric oversees all of Team Penske's operations, and the impact of his absence will be felt throughout the organization. In addition, he serves as the strategist for Newgarden, calling the shots and making the decisions during races—he is widely considered to be one of the best strategists in the sport. Meanwhile, Mason serves as the engineer for Newgarden and is ultimately responsible for the car's performance.

Ruzewski serves as the strategist to Power, and Atkinson fulfills the role of car engineer. Atkinson, it seemed, was the Team Penske team member who uploaded the modified push-to-pass software late last summer.

There were no suspensions on the crew that oversees Team Penske's third entry, that of McLaughlin.

The suspensions were handed out in part to appease the outrage that continues to emerge from the IndyCar paddock. Since the scandal emerged, there had been consistent skepticism expressed by team owners and drivers on how an entire team's pit crew could not be aware its driver used push-to-pass against the rules during a race. After all, routine data from the power unit would show its usage, and Team Penske is renowned for leaving absolutely no stone unturned to be "Penske Perfect."

The push-to-pass scandal would be a story that underscores the narrative leading up to the running of the 500. Rival teams would likely bring it up if nothing more than to serve up a distraction to Team Penske. Then, there was the curious case of Newgarden.

Newgarden was, of course, the defending 500 champion. He was also a two-time IndyCar Series champion with twenty-nine victories and fifty-two podiums over a 201-race career. Importantly, he would be a free agent at the end of the season when he would be out of a driving contract with Team Penske.

Newgarden had driven for Penske since 2017, and Penske relayed to The Associated Press that he remained committed to his driver. Together, they'd had tremendous success. However, would Newgarden feel betrayed by the suspensions impacting his chances to repeat as 500 champion? Even if so, would other race-winning teams like Ganassi and Andretti be interested in a driver they considered, at least publicly, to have purposely violated rules to create a competitive advantage?

The push-to-pass story would grow more deeply and broadly before it began to slowly fade away.

SATURDAY, MAY 11, 2024

Palou Roars into May

After qualifying fastest yesterday, Ganassi's Alex Palou drove to victory today in the Sonsio Grand Prix, contested on the road course at Indianapolis Motor Speedway, building momentum for both him and his team as attention now turned to the Indianapolis 500. Pulling away after a late-race caution period bunched up the field, Palou drove his No. 10 DHL Honda to a 6.6106-second victory over the No. 12 Verizon Business Chevrolet of Team Penske's Will Power.

The win was Palou's second consecutive win in this event on the Speedway's fourteen-turn, 2.439-mile road course.

After struggling in Friday's practice sessions, Palou found pace in qualifying to narrowly edge out RLL's Lundgaard for the pole position. However, going into Turn One on the first lap, Lundgaard turned the tables on him, cutting underneath Palou and setting himself up on the inside of the circuit going into Turn Two. From there, Lundgaard led comfortably for the first stint of the race.

Holding his competitors at bay, it looked as if Lundgaard was in line for his second-ever IndyCar Series victory. But, as they often do, pit strategy and pit stop execution played a hand in determining final results among him, Palou, and Power.

The decisive moment of the race occurred at the end of the second stint. Power pitted first, diving into the pits in an attempt to undercut

Lundgaard, the leader. The idea was to take advantage of a blistering lap out of the pits on fresh tires, turning in a quicker time for that lap than Lundgaard, who would be struggling on worn-out tires on his in-lap for his subsequent pit stop. If all worked out, once Lundgaard left the pits, Power would be in the lead.

That didn't happen, though, as Power was held up just slightly by the car of Marcus Ericsson, allowing Lundgaard to keep his position on Power. However, one lap later, Palou and his Ganassi team did it better than anyone else, and Palou exited the pits ahead of both Lundgaard and Power. From there, he ran a steady race, slowly stretching his lead lap after lap.

On the third sequence of pit stops, Power got out ahead of Lundgaard, and that settled the battle for the podium positions.

Palou and his team now turned their sights toward preparing for the 500. From Victory Lane, Palou said, "A win helps a lot, especially if it's a pole and a win and the way we won it. We're going to celebrate, for sure, but we're going to switch this afternoon our focus to the big one."

The entire Chip Ganassi Racing organization would ride a wave of momentum as the team took three of the Grand Prix's top five spots, with Dixon and Armstrong finishing fourth and fifth.

There would not be a lot of carryovers from the Grand Prix to the Indy 500, as the racing circuits are completely different. The road course features left and right turns, with several hard braking and acceleration points. The oval, of course, requires only left turns, albeit at speeds of well over 220 miles per hour. Chassis setups would be completely different.

However, some aspects would carry over, like pit stop execution, and Ganassi showed the field they were prepared for the tests ahead. Additionally, driving had always been a game of confidence, and no greater confidence came to a driver than that associated with a victory over their rivals.

After echoing with the roar of IndyCar engines for two days, the Speedway fell silent for now, save for the teams' preparations of their cars for the 500. That silence would break when the green flag fell to open practice for the Indy 500 on Tuesday morning.

MONDAY, MAY 13, 2024

Silence before the Storm

Cars sat silently today at the Speedway, but there was a beehive of activity across the facility's 559 acres. Not only were the teams busily preparing their cars for the opening day of practice the following day, but the Speedway crew was preparing both the circuit and the grounds.

Immediately after the Grand Prix on Saturday, the IMS crew shifted its focus to transitioning the Speedway from its road course layout to its oval configuration. It was no easy task.

Safety remained paramount at the Speedway, and the safety precautions put in place for the Grand Prix needed to be removed and placed appropriately for the oval. As a result, a number of concrete retaining walls, tire barriers, and catch fencing needed to be relocated. On the track surface itself, painted lines for the road course were removed with a pressure washer, while simultaneously at other locations, new lines were reapplied for the oval.

The previous week, walls were opened to allow the race cars to sweep into the track's infield and use Hulman Boulevard, the road that bisects the Speedway's infield, as the road course's backstretch. For the remainder of the month, Hulman Boulevard would become the biggest sidewalk in the city as it served as the best way for fans to walk from one end of the infield to the other.

And, of course, nothing happened in the expensive world of auto racing without corporate sponsorship. The finishing touches for the grounds crew required the removal of the previous weekend's banners, signs, and wraps and the installation of new signage, especially that of the 500's title sponsor, Gainbridge, a digital insurance agency.

In Gasoline Alley, the garages at the Speedway, there was a different beehive buzz of activity altogether.

A casual race fan might not notice the difference between an IndyCar setup for a road course and that of one set up for a superspeedway like Indianapolis. However, if you placed two cars side-by-side, several differences would become immediately visible.

In racing, aerodynamic downforce is a critical attribute. Downforce presses the car onto its tires and provides grip through the corners. The more grip a driver feels, the faster they can go, and racing is about going faster than your competitors.

In theory, an IndyCar at speed creates enough downforce that a driver could operate the car upside down—if only one could find an inverted track and a driver crazy enough to attempt it. A considerable amount of that aerodynamic downforce is generated by the car's front and rear wings.

In road and street course configurations, those wings are enormous. On Saturday, all the IndyCars featured multi-element front and rear wings, with multiple layers of aerodynamic aids to create much-needed downforce. That downforce was required for the road course's twisting and turning layout.

For the Speedway's oval, the cars will be outfitted with single-element front and rear wings, with just one horizontal mainplane element on each. The reason for the smaller wings is a tradeoff between the grip needed in the four corners and the flat-out straightaway speed needed for the oval's long straightaways.

Aerodynamic wings generate downforce, but at the same time, they also generate drag. The trick for every team is to balance those two effects to achieve the fastest possible lap time. More grip means more speed in the turns, but more drag and slower straightaway speeds. Less drag means faster straightaway speeds, but at the sacrifice of grip, and therefore corresponding speed, in the turns.

In placing a road course-prepared IndyCar next to an oval course-prepared car, the difference in the sizes of wings is readily apparent. In comparison to the road course car, an oval car's rear wing is minimal and sits low behind the rear wheels.

Another visible change is that of brake ducting. Drivers repeatedly use the brakes on road and street courses, and ducting prevents the braking system from overheating. On the oval course, however, drivers will use the brakes only to enter Pit Lane for service. Out on the track, brakes are used only in the event of an absolute emergency. As brake ducts are bulky and produce speed-sapping drag, they're removed from the car.

More subtle changes occur in the cockpit, where additional padding is added to the right of the driver's helmet. At 225 miles per hour in one of the oval's four turns, a driver experiences a gravitational force (g-force) load of four lateral *g*s. With the 500-mile race entailing 800 turns, even the strongest of necks appreciate the added padding to help hold the head upright.

Lastly, there's the camber of the tires to reconfigure. For oval tracks, tire camber adjustments are made to have both front tires lean ever-so-slightly to the driver's right. This setup allows the car to sit more balanced on its tires at speed on the banking of the turns, and it's solely used for courses, like Indy, that require only left turns.

Most of the large, well-funded teams arrived at the Speedway last week with two different cars, one set up for the road course, and another preliminarily set up for the oval. Smaller teams and those with budget constraints unloaded a single primary car and thus had been busier since the checkered flag flew after the Grand Prix.

Even the big teams who had a car specially built out for the road course were busy converting it into an oval-ready backup car. No team could afford downtime that kept a car off track, and if a team suffered a mechanical failure or crash damage, they would need to roll out a backup car as quickly as possible. Never would that be more critical than on Saturday, when everyone attempted to qualify.

As IndyCars haven't changed for over a decade, experienced teams unloaded at the Speedway for the April Open Test with a baseline setup based primarily on what worked best the previous year. Adjustments were made by engineering teams before arriving to factor in both new, lighter-weight components and where the weight distribution now resided in the car, both fore and aft as well as vertically. Their limited runs in the weather-shortened test confirmed some settings and raised questions about others. Those who participated in the Open Test developed an initial car setup based on what was learned that day.

In addition to setting up the chassis, teams busily prepared their bodywork to make the most slippery car possible to cut through the air. Last year, Abel Motorsports received a lot of attention for hiring experienced mechanics to properly fit their car's bodywork, ensuring it would slip through the air with as little drag as possible. The small team's reward was qualifying for the world's biggest race, beating out one of the cars from the much bigger Rahal Letterman Lanigan team.

It was a lesson relearned for the RLL team. According to Bobby Rahal, body fitting was an exercise performed in the off-season to particularly prepare for Indianapolis, but one that was also an ongoing exercise throughout the year.

"We want to make sure the car is as slippery as it can be," Rahal said. "Back when I was racing in CART, it wasn't that big of a deal because we had a 900-horsepower engine pushing us through the air. Now, with less power and closer racing, fit and finish is important to take mechanical drag out of the car. It's part of our offseason process, and we tweak it often during the season."

Across Gasoline Alley sat the garages of local team Dreyer & Reinbold Racing/Cusick Motorsports, who fielded Indy cars only at the Indianapolis 500. Today, they were putting the final touches on the cars of 2014 winner Ryan Hunter-Reay and local fan favorite Conor Daly. Being a one-race team only, they would start practice on their back feet, compared to their competitors. Every practice session would be critically important for them, and they couldn't afford to miss time because of lax preparation. In the garages, mechanics pored over their cars with a proverbial fine-toothed comb as they looked to find speed quickly once the track opened for practice and build upon it leading up to qualifications.

In a widely-anticipated move, Arrow McLaren today confirmed Callum Ilott would drive its No. 6 car. While Theo Pourchaire passed his IndyCar oval test the week before and was named the car's permanent driver for the remainder of the season, save the Indy 500, Ilott was considered the leading candidate for the 500 because of his experience in the race. As a veteran of two Indy 500s, Ilott was not required to pass the Rookie Orientation Program and thus could get to work on building qualifying speed immediately. Plus, he finished an impressive twelfth in the previous year's 500 for Juncos Hollinger.

Relatively new to the Arrow McLaren team, Ilott had some experience with the crew. He raced in the season opener as a replacement for Malukas, and he drove the car in April's Open Test session.

Ilott would step into the car brimming with confidence from the previous weekend's World Endurance Championship race at the legendary Spa-Francorchamps course that winds through the Ardennes Forest in Belgium. He drove the final stint of the six-hour race to clinch the overall victory for his Hertz Team Jota crew, the team's first overall WEC race win.

In a press release from Arrow McLaren, Ilott said, "I'm grateful to step into this race with a familiar car and a familiar team now in Arrow McLaren. While our April Open Test at the Indianapolis Motor Speedway was shortened by weather, the runs we did have were productive. I feel comfortable with the team and know that we can come together throughout the month of May to put our best foot forward come race day."

Ilott completed a formidable lineup for Arrow McLaren, joining full-time Series regulars Pato O'Ward and Alexander Rossi—the latter, the winner of the 2016 Indy 500. And, of course, the team also featured a one-off entry for the 500 for NASCAR superstar Kyle Larson.

Arrow McLaren would be one of the teams to watch once the track opened for practice on Tuesday morning. That is *if* the track opened for practice on Tuesday morning.

Every eye that was not on a race car, preparing it for practice, was looking at the weather forecast for Tuesday. The news wasn't great—a ninety percent chance of rain, including scattered thunderstorms throughout the day. The good news was the weather in Indianapolis often flipped at a moment's notice.

In his song, "Little Green Apples," Roger Miller sang somewhat sarcastically that it doesn't rain in Indianapolis in the summertime. It's an earworm refrain that has gone through the minds of Speedway watchers since the song was released in 1968, and it continued today and, likely, tomorrow too.

In years past, weather forecasting at the Speedway was an art mastered by experience. With a look to the skies and a wealthy reservoir of past knowledge, racers would anticipate the very best conditions for their runs, particularly on qualifying days.

Today, everyone had their favorite online weather application, and weather forecasting was much more science than the art of yesteryear. Still, its importance remained high. The modern-day IndyCar is very susceptible to even the slightest weather changes, particularly ambient temperatures and wind.

Moreover, track closures due to rain would throw a gigantic curveball into every team's preparation. Practice time was crucial, particularly if a team should roll out of its garage with a poor initial setup and found itself chasing speed. Thirty-four racers were going to attempt to qualify for just thirty-three positions on the grid. Time to get up to speed was short, and every team and driver would want as much time on the track as possible to ensure they were not the odd car out.

Cloudy skies and the threat of rain only ratcheted up the pressure cooker that was life inside Gasoline Alley. Which team's preparations would see them languishing at the bottom of the timing charts once practice commenced?

TUESDAY, MAY 14, 2024

Déjà vu All Over Again

The ever-quotable former New York Yankee and baseball Hall of Famer Yogi Berra once said, "It's like déjà vu all over again." For those in the IndyCar paddock this morning at the Indianapolis Motor Speedway, the day was eerily reminiscent of the Open Test day at the track on April 10.

The preliminary schedule for the opening day of practice for the Indy 500 had a two-hour session at 9:00 a.m., followed by a two-hour break. Practice was then scheduled to resume at 1:00 p.m. and run until 6:00 p.m. No one, however, expected that schedule to be kept, as heavy rain was forecasted for most of the day.

Weather forecasts indicated the best opportunity to run laps would be early in the day before the rain came, but it remained to be seen exactly when the rain would arrive.

Needing to be ready to go at literally a moment's notice, crew members and drivers wasted no time letting the last vestiges of the morning's breakfast and coffee settle. Crews rolled out their pit stands, tools, tires, and race cars onto Pit Lane and set themselves working through their pre-session checklists. All the while, they kept a watchful eye on the sky.

As 9:00 approached, a fine mist hung in the air and foreshadowed a delay. But drivers pulled on their helmets and gloves, sat in their cockpits, and tugged their safety belts tight, all in anticipation.

Finally, at 9:03, the track opened. Immediately starters turned engines down the length of Pit Lane, and, as the rumbling sound of race engines echoed between the Speedway's grandstands, drivers sped out to get on the track.

Single file, over twenty cars exited Pit Lane and drove onto the warm-up lane on the inside of Turns One and Two, before popping out on the backstretch. While most everyone completed that first installation lap by taking the warm-up lane inside Turns Three and Four, Power led a couple of cars through the racing circuit itself, opting for another installation lap.

Soon, all the cars were back on Pit Lane, with crews removing engine covers and checking to determine if everything was in working order, from electronic connections to hoses and everything in between.

Not every car sailed through its installation laps. Newgarden's crew went to work on what they believed was a faulty electronic sensor. It was too early to take chances with equipment, so they set out to troubleshoot whether it was a faulty sensor, or a deeper, more serious problem identified by the sensor.

With installation lap checks complete, cars filed back out onto the circuit. Dreyer & Reinbold Racing/Cusick Motorsports running mates Hunter-Reay and Daly ramped up the speed, hitting laps of 221.700 and 220.883. Then two-time winner Sato upped the ante to 225.551 in his RLL Racing Honda No. 75. Marco Andretti looked racy early, zipping through traffic and utilizing an aerodynamic tow to top 228 miles per hour. Then at the seventeen-minute mark, Dixon shot to the top with a 229.107 lap, benefiting from a tow down both straightaways.

And that was as good as it got. The yellow flag flew soon after for moisture on the track surface, and then the rain came in earnest. Experienced observers knew the day was likely done when wily veteran Dixon emerged from his car, took off his helmet, and summarily zipped it away in his bag. He knew then it was unlikely to come out for the rest of the day.

In a Team Penske stall on Pit Lane, Power laid down on the top of the wall, collecting his thoughts. He had managed to turn just those two installation laps. His quest for a second 500 victory hadn't really begun before the rain called it to a halt.

In all, twenty-nine of the thirty-four entered drivers turned in laps, although Power, Newgarden, and Larson did only install shake-down laps. Rosenqvist, McLaughlin, and Kirkwood each turned in thirteen laps to lead the field.

Noticeably absent from the track was Saturday's Grand Prix winner Palou and his CGR teammates, rookies Kyffin Simpson, Marcus Armstrong, and Linus Lundqvist, along with Dale Coyne Racing with Rick Ware Racing's Legge.

It's a long-held opinion that cars ready to run on the opening day of practice would be the ones best positioned to qualify and race well. For the powerhouse CGR team, it was probably not critical to miss out on practice with four of their five 500 entries. After all, their fifth car, that of Dixon, topped the charts. However, the three rookie drivers would benefit from every bit of practice they could get, particularly with other cars on the track.

Legge's absence, however, raised an early alarm. She had not run a single event with the team this season, and they would start, when they all eventually started, from square one. While they were not behind by much so far, they were behind, and one driver was destined to miss out this coming weekend in qualifying for the biggest race in the world.

No team wants to miss a practice session, be it at Indianapolis or another circuit. Practice is a finite commodity, and teams are constantly learning how to set up their cars for maximum performance. When it comes to practice time, the old adage, "Waste not, want not" rings particularly true.

At no racetrack, however, is practice time as plentiful as it is at Indianapolis ahead of the 500. At every other race during the season, there are a couple of short, intense practice sessions on Friday and Saturday ahead of qualifications, and then there is the race. Indy, by its tradition, is unique.

If the rain hadn't washed out practice after just over twenty minutes today, teams would have had the opportunity to run for seven hours, or over three times the amount of time they typically get to practice for a race weekend. And, of course, there's the rest of the week to consider as well.

There used to be even more practice time. Not too long ago, the Speedway would open for practice at the beginning of the month, and there would be two weeks of practice before the first of two qualifying weekends. In between those qualifying weekends was another week of practice.

The abundant track time at Indy had proven valuable to younger, less-experienced racers. It allowed them to learn the intricacies of racing on this unique racetrack and to slowly, but steadily, build their confidence in preparation for race day.

Stories abounded of rookies taking advantage of practice, like sportscar ace Al Holbert running repeated race simulation stints in practice before his rookie race in 1984, and those practice laps returning immediate dividends with a fourth-place finish and Rookie of the Year honors.

It's more difficult for rookies now. While there are a lot of hours to practice at the Speedway, there's still not quite enough to close the gap to competitors much less leapfrog past them—not all of them, at least. This year's rookie class—Simpson, Lundqvist, Armstrong, Larson, Blomqvist, Rasmussen, and Siegel—had their work cut out for them. After today's abbreviated start, they would look to figuratively and literally get "back on track" Wednesday.

Last year, Rahal Letterman Lanigan Racing had a disastrous week of practice ahead of qualifications, and that was without wrecking any cars. Simply, they couldn't find speed in any of their four entries. After their struggles all week in practice, it came as no surprise they were slow come qualifying.

Legge was a one-off entry for the team, running only the 500, but as a part-timer. Somehow, she managed to squeak into the field on the first day of qualifications by posting the thirtieth-fastest time. She was locked into the starting grid. But her teammates weren't.

Almost unbelievably, RLL's other three cars, those of Graham Rahal, Lundgaard, and Harvey were, along with the DCR entry of Sting Ray Robb, among the four slowest qualifiers. They would battle it out on Sunday to determine which three would qualify for the race—and which singular one would miss out.

Rahal, of course, proved to be the odd driver out, bumped off the grid on the last run by his then-teammate, Harvey. Sure, he started the race a week later in relief of an injured Stefan Wilson, but the damage to the team's collective psyche had already been done.

The team rallied after Indy, winning one race with Lundgaard and earning a pole position later in the year with Rahal. Over the winter, they worked concertedly to be better at Indy.

It was too early to tell if they'd found the speed they needed. Sato's third-fastest time today, coupled with Lundgaard's fifth-fastest time, were good omens. But those speeds were still well off what would be required to avoid missing out on the race.

For his part, Rahal tested two different front wing configurations during his six laps on track today. There was still a lot of work to be done, but the team had begun to progress through its months-in-the-making plan to make their cars capable of running toward the front of the field.

WEDNESDAY, MAY 15, 2024

Rain, Rain, Go Away

To make up for lost track time the day before, officials bumped up the start of Wednesday's practice session two hours to 10:00 a.m., particularly good news for the field's seven rookies. However, Mother Nature wasn't consulted ahead of time.

A continuation of Tuesday's rain left the track wet, delaying the start of the session. As the green flag was scheduled to wave, the rain had pretty much ended. But that didn't mean cars would run soon.

Once it stops raining, it takes roughly two hours for the Speedway's track to dry. It can be shorter depending on both sunlight and wind. On an overcast day like today though, drying took much longer.

The Speedway sped up the drying process with its jet dryers and service vehicles as much as it could, but it could only do so much. The rest laid in Mother Nature's hands, and she'd made it clear that practice would probably commence at its regularly scheduled time, if not later.

Waiting out the delay, all teams had their cars back in their garages in Gasoline Alley. Their pit stands, however, were loaded with telemetry equipment, video monitors, and other tools of their trade, sitting zipped up on Pit Lane, ready to be opened once the day's practice session looked ready to get started.

In general, there are two primary handling characteristics of a racing car, whether it's an IndyCar, a Formula One car, a NASCAR stock car, or a sports car. Actually, there are three, the third being a perfectly balanced car. That's the ideal condition every team and driver work so hard to achieve. It's often an elusive target, and once reached, it's fleeting, not usually held for very long as so many variables continue to change, like temperatures, tire wear, fuel loads, and the amount of tire rubber on the track. Finding the proper balance is a never-ending quest.

Most often, a car suffers, to some degree, from either oversteer or understeer. Oversteer, also referred to as "loose" and "free," is a feeling where the car wants to over-rotate in the corner, with the rear end sliding out, threatening to break away completely and result in a spin. A minimal amount of oversteer at Indy is preferred by some drivers, and it's typically a sign of a fast car. One reason a car might have a bit of oversteer is because there's less aerodynamic drag at the rear of the car, and less drag means faster straightaway speeds.

Understeer, also known as a "push" or being "tight," occurs when the car underrotates in the corner, its front tires sliding out toward the wall. An understeering car loses grip on its front tires and doesn't turn in a corner like the driver ideally wants. One cause of an understeering car is a lack of downforce at the front of the car, especially that generated by the front wing angle.

Race teams have a variety of ways they can address oversteer and understeer, both mechanically and aerodynamically. A quick potential remedy is adding or subtracting wing downforce at either the front, the back, or a combination of the two.

During a race, those sorts of quick fixes are really all that's available to the crew, and it's most often seen performed on the front wing. A driver suffering from understeer might ask for additional downforce at the front of the car, and at the next stop, a crew member will add increased front wing angle, and therefore additional downforce, by twisting a T-shaped adjuster. Sometimes those adjustments are as small as a quarter turn; other times they might be as large as two full turns or more.

Teams can also make adjustments at one end of the car to offset a problem at the other end. For example, if a car is loose, or suffering from oversteer, the crew can reduce the amount of front wing on the car, freeing up the front to better match the rear.

Drivers can also affect changes to their car handling with, of all things, their right foot. If a car is suffering from understeer and not wanting to turn in the corner, a slight lift of the throttle will cause the car's center of gravity, its fore/aft weight distribution, to shift forward. The result is more pressure on the front tires, producing more traction at the front and less pressure on the rear tires, producing less traction and freeing up the rear. Ideally, it balances out and the turn is made.

Inside the car, drivers can also change the handling characteristics of their car by using one or both of their in-car tools, the weight jacker and anti-roll bars (ARBs), also known as sway bars and anti-sway bars.

The weight jacker is an electronically activated mechanical device only used on oval courses. Activated by buttons on the steering wheel, the weight jacker changes the height of the right rear suspension, allowing the driver to adjust the car's handling to better suit conditions, be it traffic in the race, wind conditions at different ends or sides of the track, tire wear, fuel loads, or most any other variable.

Situated between the top of the damper housing and the coil over spring, the weight jacker can be extended to push the spring away from the damper housing, lifting the right rear suspension and placing added diagonal force across the car, onto the left front tire. When the weight jacker is extended, it helps reduce understeer.

Retracting the weight jacker has the opposite effect, lowering the right rear suspension, taking the weight off the left front tire, and placing more on the right rear tire, reducing oversteer or, if the driver prefers, inducing a bit of understeer.

Manipulating the weight jacker also has an impact on straight-line speed down the long straightaways at Indianapolis. By retracting the weight jacker on the exits of Turns Two and Four, the car will tilt ever so slightly, nose-up, as the right rear suspension is lowered, reducing the downforce created by the floor of the car. The benefit of doing so is an estimated 0.5- to one-mile-an-hour increase in top speed. However, it makes for a busy driver in the cockpit, for they need to return the weight jacker to its normal position just before entering the turn.

There are two ARBs on an IndyCar, one for the front suspension and another for the rear. They, too, are mechanical devices, not electronic, and are couplings between the suspension on opposite sides of the car. As a car corners at high speed, the ARBs resist the rolling motion of the car, keeping it flat as the car absorbs lateral g-forces in the turns.

Effectively, ARBs act as a weight transfer device, much like the weight jacker. If a driver stiffens the front ARB, it will reduce front tire grip and add stability by adding a degree of understeer to make the car more neutral handling. Stiffening the rear ARB reduces the rear grip, inducing more oversteer to find a better cornering balance.

Once the action gets started on the track, every driver will be searching for that chassis setup that is both fast and comfortable to drive. The thing is, what's comfortable for one driver can be decidedly uncomfortable for another.

Take the Rahal Letterman Lanigan's stable of drivers, for instance. According to Bobby Rahal, Lundgaard and Sato both prefer a loose, understeering car. On the other hand, Fittipaldi and Graham Rahal both prefer a car that is more planted at the rear. Thus, the RLL team will roll out their four cars for practice with two different baseline setups. From there, each driver and team will work on making adjustments, some big and some minute, in an attempt to get a perfectly balanced, comfortable to drive, and, most importantly, fast race car.

Because of the persistent morning rains, the start of practice was delayed by more than five hours. Then, once it got started, the session was interrupted three additional times by sprinkles. Finally, a heavy rain came and washed out the entire last hour.

Between raindrops, however, all thirty-four cars got out on the track and tried their best to make up for lost time. Together, they ran a total of nearly 2,100 laps, usually in large packs of cars. While not ideal for understanding how a car would handle during qualification attempts, where cars run by themselves on an otherwise empty track, the pack running gave drivers and teams an idea of how their cars might handle in the race.

McLaughlin turned in the day's fastest lap, and the fastest lap of the two abbreviated practice days thus far, at 229.493 mph. Power and Newgarden, his Team Penske teammates, slotted in at second and fourth on the speed chart, separated by the Andretti Global No. 26 Gainbridge car of Herta. Arrow McLaren's Rossi rounded out the top five.

Larson was the fastest of the seven rookies, posting the fifteenth-fastest overall lap at 225.245 mph. However, the lack of practice time because of the rain was a concern for a driver new to driving an Indy car. Speaking to the media, Larson said, "It's a little bit frustrating. But it is what it is. There's plenty of track time. I'm trying to remember that. I'm glad to have gotten out there and got running. I'm still trying to figure a lot out and work through the car balance, timing of runs, and all that. Just trying to play around with things and make runs and pass people."

An Indy car is equipped with a six-speed gearbox, or transmission. On a street or road course, drivers work their way up and down through the gearbox on every lap. Not so on the oval at Indianapolis.

On the oval, drivers engage first gear only to get out of the pits. They'll then work their way through to fourth gear on the warm-up lane before popping out onto the backstretch. Fifth and six gears are where most of the running takes place. The gear ratio for the fifth gear makes it the fastest, the gear that pulls the highest revolutions per minute (RPMs) from the engine. Sixth gear is built to run in traffic and reduce fuel consumption.

In a race setup, drivers will typically run in sixth gear. In qualifying mode, they'll run in fifth gear if there's not much wind. If there is wind, however, drivers will frequently choose to shift between fifth and sixth, one working best at one end or side of the track, the other gear the best for the opposite side. The key to a fast lap is to pull every last RPM from the engine, and gear ratios are a determining factor.

Lessons are learned running in practice. Each engine is fitted with a rev limiter, limiting the engine to 12,000 RPMs. If a car hits 12,000 RPMs, the limiter activates and decreases the power produced, significantly slowing the car. Ideally, cars hit 11,999 RPMs just at the point of entering both Turns One and Three at the end of the Speedway's long straightaways.

A tailwind is fully capable of pushing a car past 12,000 RPMs, as well as a long string of cars creating a slipstream for following cars. Teams need to adjust their gear ratios to avoid hitting the limiter at the end of the straights.

Today, O'Ward was among the drivers hitting the limiter heading into Turn One. His Arrow McLaren crew would be analyzing data that night to determine if a change was needed for the rest of the week. It's a relatively easy change, but it does require the car to be back in the garage in Gasoline Alley.

Tires play an important role every time a race car goes onto a track. Typically, Firestone, the supplier of tires to the IndyCar Series, allocates thirty-two full sets of tires to every car. This year, however, while unintentional, the tire allocation for each team had increased significantly.

Since April's Open Test was considerably abbreviated because of rain, Firestone found itself with more tires available. As a result, they allocated an additional five sets for teams to use for the entire month of May.

Ordinarily, race teams needed to carefully plan out their tire usage. They started with determining the number of sets they would likely need for the race, then worked themselves backward, planning out their daily programs. Importantly, they sought to have brand new tires—called "sticker tires," for the Firestone sticker still attached to its surface before rolling out of the pits—for every qualifying simulation and qualifying attempt.

An extra five sets of tires now provided teams a luxury. Plus, since running on both Tuesday and Wednesday was greatly limited, tires not used on those days were still available. For the remainder of the month, tires would not be a limiting factor for teams; they had more than enough tires available than both time and preferred engine mileage would allow for use.

This year's tires presented a learning opportunity for drivers and teams. Firestone constructed a harder, more durable tire in anticipation of heavier cars weighted down with IndyCar's hybrid assist engine program. However, with the deployment of the hybrid assist technology delayed until after the Indy 500, the race cars remained lighter than what was anticipated when the tires were designed and constructed.

Tires, while plentiful, represented a bit of an unknown as teams prepared for qualifications. Teams had yet to use this new tire formulation in hotter temperatures, as were expected over the weekend. Every lap of practice would provide the data to drivers and crews to more finely tune their cars.

THURSDAY, MAY 16, 2024

The Weather Cooperates... Mostly

A glorious Indiana dawn greeted the race teams this morning, with brilliant sunshine falling over the grounds of the Speedway for the first time this week. Teams spent the early morning busily preparing their cars and the programs they wanted to progress through in what promised to be a full eight-hour day of practice.

Today loomed important, too, as it could very well be the final day of practice available to the teams before qualifications on Saturday. The weather forecast suggested Friday's session was under threat of heavy rain, especially in the afternoon.

With Friday being uncertain, race teams prepared two different programs for the day: race stint simulations and qualifying simulations. The difference between the teams came on when during the day the different simulations would take place.

The track opened as scheduled at 10:00 a.m., and that, in and of itself, presented a bit of an uncertain variable. Qualifying on Saturday and Sunday would start at 11:00 a.m. and 12:00 noon, respectively, and the race would start at 12:35 p.m. With weather dramatically affecting car setup and performance, teams tended to learn the most in practice by running in similar weather conditions they would experience later. However, beggars—in this case, in the form of teams needing as much track time as possible—couldn't afford to be choosers.

Qualifying at Indianapolis is single-car, one car on the track at a time. As a result, teams looked to run their qualification simulations in clean air, without the benefit of a tow. That, of course, got to be difficult as teams could not control when other teams took to the track.

Some teams jumped out early with qualifying simulations right from the start, when traffic was light. Arrow McLaren sent out Rossi, O'Ward, and Ilott, with Larson's car still back in the garage getting an engine replaced on the advice of Chevrolet. Andretti Global followed quickly with Herta, and he immediately raised eyebrows with no-tow laps of 223.143 and 223.537 mph. Herta clearly had a comfortable, fast race car.

An hour and a half into the session, the Speedway's concrete walls claimed its first victim of the month. CGR's Lundqvist was working his No. 8 American Legion Honda in traffic when he lost the rear end after dipping too low and touching the curbing on the apex of Turn Two.

Lundqvist slapped the outside wall heavily with the right rear of the car, then careened at high speed across the track and into the grass on the inside of the backstretch. Working frantically to slow his damaged racer while on the slippery grass, he gently glanced off the inside retaining wall with his left rear before spinning to a stop several hundred feet down the backstretch.

Unhurt, Lundqvist immediately radioed his crew to tell them he was okay and apologize. His day was done, but his crew's day had just grown longer, as once they received the car back in the garage, they would need to determine whether they should rebuild it or prepare a backup car—both time-intensive tasks.

Either way, rookie Lundqvist missed out on valuable practice time. However, he learned a big lesson. There's an adage at the Speedway that says there are two kinds of Indy drivers: those who have hit the wall and those who will hit the wall.

Lundqvist's lesson was a costly one, for both team and driver. He learned that at racing speeds, driving too low in the corner and hitting the concrete curb upsets the car's balance. Sometimes a driver can "catch" the car and recover; other times, the driver can't, and a spin, and likely contact with the wall, is the result. It was a difficult lesson to learn, but Lundqvist would be a better racing driver for it.

Larson continued to receive the lion's share of attention at the Speedway, both on the track and off. His story, as a young, American racing superstar who competes at all levels, from little dirt tracks in front of a few hundred spectators to events as big as the Daytona 500, was as compelling as it got. The media scrum around Larson was bigger than around defending 500 champion Newgarden.

The result was the other rookies in the field had flown a bit under the radar, at least to the casual observer. To the teams up and down Pit Lane, however, many of them made quite an impression.

They'd all accounted well for themselves, even Lundqvist, despite his crash earlier in the day. But, one rookie, other than Larson and his high speeds, to have made an impression was Ed Carpenter Racing's Christian Rasmussen, in his No. 33 car. He hadn't been at the top of the speed charts. Today, for example, he posted just the thirty-second quickest one-lap time with a 221.862 mph speed, the fastest of his forty-two laps completed. Where he'd received more notice was for his moxie, particularly his willingness to simulate racing around the 2.5-mile oval.

Rasmussen showed no hesitation in going into corners side-by-side with his fellow drivers, much to the surprise, and sometimes condemnation, of his rivals. Herta shared his feelings, both with gestures in his car and with comments to the media on Pit Lane.

At Indy, the timing of passes is important, and it's a learned skill mastered by experience. Drivers learn to time their runs just right, ideally allowing for an overtake on a straightaway that allows both cars to line up properly to enter a turn nose to tail. Late passes involve a car lunging down into the turn once both cars have entered it, and that often comes as quite a surprise to the car in front, whose driver unexpectedly finds themself on the outside of a one-groove racetrack.

Nobody wants to crash at Indy, ever. But, especially, no one wants to crash in practice by getting into any unnecessary scraps with other drivers. There's nothing to be won in practice. The prizes all come on race day.

Rasmussen had a few instances of late overtakes, including the one that drew the ire of Herta. But he'd also overtaken on the outside entering turns and running high in the corner. It's a practice that added much-needed experience for what Rasmussen would likely need on race day.

Come race day, particularly in the later stages of the 200 laps, drivers would be desperate to improve their positions however they could. As a result, side-by-side racing through the turns would become common—not as frequent as overtakes ahead of the turns but far from rare.

Rasmussen was learning exactly how his car was handling, both in traffic and in less-than-ideal conditions with other cars and on different parts of the track. Like a great learner, he was filing those lessons away and sure to draw upon them when opportunities presented themselves.

There's often one big difference on race day, though. Throughout the race, the track surface just outside the groove gets dusted with little pieces of rubber called "marbles" that get rubbed off the tires from all the laps turned by racing cars. Driving onto those marbles can be treacherous—drivers describe it as like driving on ice. A car's warm tire surfaces will pick up those marbles and lose grip immediately. Those marbles won't get worn off from friction for another couple of turns.

Rasmussen was learning his way around the Speedway in practice sessions when fewer marbles were seen on the track. Race day, as usual, both for rookies and veterans alike, would no doubt produce a different set of challenges.

As the clock approached 4:00 p.m., the Speedway's retaining wall reached out and grabbed another car for its daily collection.

Running fourth in a line of cars, Ericsson, in his No. 28 Delaware Life Honda, clipped the concrete curbing on the inside of Turn Four and immediately experienced a bobble from the rear of the car. He tried to catch it by steering into the spin, but once the car was out of the groove and into the gray and the marbles, it was too late. After a half spin, he smashed the left side of the car into the SAFER barrier and the outside retaining wall. With broken front and rear suspensions, Ericsson was a passenger from that point onward.

The car turned a lazy half-spin as it crossed the track, then struck the inside retaining wall nose first. Still scrubbing off speed, the car bounced off the inside wall and continued to spin until it hit the Pit Lane attenuator with the left side. Ericsson's car then came to a stop just beyond the Pit Lane entrance, blocking the pits.

Of his crash, Ericsson told Jenna Fryer of the AP, "Obviously it was quite a decent hit, but the safety in these cars is pretty impressive, so (I'm) feeling okay. I'm very disappointed and very sorry for my team. They've done a very good job, and they have a lot of work ahead of them now, and that's probably the worst. I think we were in good shape, but obviously, you have a big crash like this, it sets everything back to zero. It is what it is—we just have to bounce back."

As Ericsson's car came to rest at the entry to Pit Lane, it was a relatively short trip on the wrecker to the Andretti Global garages in Gasoline Alley. There the team quickly confirmed the significant damage they had seen from the video replays and decided to move to a backup car for the rest of the month.

Well-funded teams like Andretti Global typically have a backup chassis for each of their primary cars, for situations just like what Ericsson and his crew faced. Attempts are made to make the backup car identical in every aspect to the primary car, but they are never, ever the same.

Manufacturing tolerances mean components that look identical don't exactly perform identically. For example, one front wing might have a little more flex than another when it's being pushed through the air at over 200 miles an hour. That results in a different handling characteristic for the driver when turning into a corner.

Ericsson's crew now had a lot of work to prepare the backup car for Friday's practice session. They started the work, knowing it was just the beginning, for when they finally got back on track, the real work would commence to get the car up to speed. And, like Lundqvist's Ganassi team, they worried about the possible impact of rain on Friday, for both teams would need all the practice time they could get.

In the ongoing effort to increase safety, the Indianapolis Motor Speedway, with financial sponsorship from both the IRL and NASCAR, began a collaborative effort in 1998 with engineers at the University of Nebraska-Lincoln to develop safer walls. The walls of the Speedway were originally built to protect spectators. For nearly one hundred years, drivers alone had to deal with the consequences of the concrete's unforgiving nature.

Finally, ahead of the 2002 Indy 500, the SAFER (Steel and Foam Energy Reduction) barrier was installed along the outside walls of the Speedway's four turns. Known also as a "soft wall," the SAFER barrier is a system designed to absorb kinetic energy during a crash to reduce the injury-causing forces experienced by the driver.

The SAFER barrier is built from structural steel tubes welded together in a flush mounting and strapped into place along the existing concrete retaining wall. Behind the steel tubes are bundles of closed-cell polystyrene foam, placed between the barrier and wall.

When a car impacts the barrier, it moves outward toward the concrete wall as it compresses. The effect is the kinetic energy of the car is dissipated along a longer portion of the wall, reducing the impact on both car and driver.

The SAFER barrier returned immediate benefits once installed at tracks around the world. Racing is still a dangerous sport, but extreme injuries and fatalities have been greatly reduced. There's not a driver in the world who has hit both a concrete wall and one with the SAFER barrier who isn't grateful for the safety innovation. Both Lundqvist and Ericsson walked away from their accidents in large part to the SAFER barrier.

The day's scheduled eight-hour practice session was delayed not only for the two on-track incidents but also for over an hour in the late afternoon for a rain shower. Eventually, more rain caused the session to be called thirteen minutes short of schedule.

Despite the interruptions, all thirty-four entries got on the track, and together they turned 1,896 total laps. The busiest driver of them all was veteran driver Conor Daly, driving for Dreyer & Reinbold, who turned in eighty-six laps in his No. 24 Polkadot Chevrolet. With the Indy 500 a one-off effort for both Daly and his team, the extended running allowed for both to close ground on the full-time entrants in the IndyCar Series. In addition to running a lot of laps, Daly was quick, too, posting a fast lap of 225.613 mph, eleventh fastest on the day.

Fastest of all today was Arrow McLaren's O'Ward in his No. 5 car, benefiting from an aerodynamic tow to record a 228.861-mph lap. In terms of single-lap pace, Herta was fourth-fastest in his No. 26 car, posting a 226.828-mph lap. However, running without the benefit of a tow, which the Speedway's timing and scoring system filters to include only laps run at least ten seconds behind any car or cars in front, Herta turned a lap of 224.182 mph, the fastest of any no-tow lap in the session. That speed boded well for a strong qualifying attempt if he could replicate it for the four laps needed in a qualifying run.

Rounding out the top five on the speed chart were McLaughlin and Palou, in second and fourth, and Newgarden in fifth. At the opposite end of the spectrum, Siegel and Robb were slowest at 220.904 and 219.990 mph, respectively. Robb's day was hampered by technical problems that limited him to just fourteen laps in total.

Two-time winner Sato, driving the No. 75 Mata Honda in an Indy-only run for RLL, had an interesting day, and quite different from most of the field. Sato and his crew weren't interested in developing their race car setup. Rather, just like the day before, they focused on getting a qualifying setup ready for almost the entire practice session. While he ran fifty-four laps with the quickest being 223.435 mph, he spent the day working through chassis adjustments to prepare for the weekend and qualifications.

Sato's work was meticulous. So much so, he didn't complete a single four-lap qualifying simulation. He aborted each early, coming into the pits to confer with his team about the performance adjustments needed for speed. A veteran of fourteen Indy 500s, Sato knew that to race, you must first qualify. If they first qualified on the upcoming weekend, Sato and his crew would then focus on developing the correct race-day setup.

With the struggles to find speed the RLL team had encountered both last year and this—his teammates Rahal, Lundgaard, and Fittipaldi were twenty-seventh, thirtieth, and thirty-first today—Sato's approach might pay dividends. He and his team would find out this weekend, as the stopwatch never lies.

FRIDAY, MAY 17, 2024

Fast Friday

"Fast Friday" has long been the name given to the final full day of practice ahead of qualifying for the Indianapolis 500. This is the day when every team sets aside race preparation and focuses intently on one of the most difficult feats in auto racing: qualifying for the Indy 500.

There would be a lot less nervous energy vibrating through Gasoline Alley if there were just thirty-three entries for the thirty-three starting spots in the race a week from Sunday. But there were thirty-four entries, and that meant the dreams of one entire team would be vanquished come Sunday afternoon.

No one wanted to experience what Graham Rahal and his RLL crew experienced last year.

For the marketing purposes of the Speedway, IndyCar, and their television broadcasting partners, Fast Friday wasn't coined as a formal designation until the 1990s. But drivers and teams long ago used the term. If you're not fast on Friday, you're probably not going to be fast on Saturday and Sunday, and that presents a very real problem.

Marketing, though, plays an enormous part in Fast Friday, and it greatly affects the crews and drivers as they tackle the track. Simply, speed sells.

While the Indianapolis Motor Speedway was built as a testing ground for the automotive industry, Fisher and his partners knew the true commercial appeal would lie in revenue generated by spectators. And, back in the early 1900s, incredible, record-setting speeds captivated the public's attention, making activities at the Speedway, for some, must-see events.

Nothing much has changed over the ensuing one hundred-plus years. Speed captures attention, first of the media, then of the fans. Especially casual fans who might not have already been bitten by the Indy 500 bug.

To goose speeds upward and spur noteworthy headlines, when the latest engine formula was adopted, the Speedway allowed an elevated turbocharger boost level for qualifying only. The added turbocharger boost for qualifications adds approximately one hundred horsepower to the performance of both the Chevrolet and Honda engines.

With the additional boost now available on their cars, drivers had a big adjustment to make. With the increase in power, their lap times around the Speedway would be a second or more quicker. Where the faster speed would be really felt was at the end of the front and back straightaways, where drivers would enter Turns One and Three over ten miles an hour faster than they had been all week—some would be over 240 miles per hour. For rookies, in particular, the added power and speed presented another ramp-up on the learning curve.

Some drivers were nonplussed about the increase. Ed Carpenter, for instance, believed the increase in speed was balanced out by an increase in aerodynamic downforce created by that increase in speed. The added grip, in his mind, offset the increase in speed.

Of course, Carpenter was a master of oval-track racing who had twenty previous Indy 500s under his belt, including being the fastest qualifier and sitting on the pole position on three different occasions. There was not much that could ruffle the feathers of one of IndyCar's most experienced drivers.

Going into the practice session, every team up and down Pit Lane had the same to-do list. Each wanted to run multiple simulated qualifying attempts.

Qualifying at Indianapolis for the 500 is unlike qualifying for any other race in any racing series, including IndyCar itself. Most qualifying sessions at races involve a single-lap time. For the 500, qualifying requires a four-lap average. Four laps means sixteen heart-pumping corners at the absolute limit.

Drivers push their cars to their fullest capabilities, running right on the thin razor's-edge line between being in control and out of control. It's a line that, when crossed, can produce disastrous results. Rarely can a team suffer a serious crash and recover in time to qualify for the world's biggest race.

The first lap of the four-lap run will almost always be the driver's fastest because the tires have their maximum grip. However, the tires soon start to "go off" and degrade. Every corner has the car at the limit of its traction, and the lateral load at speed slides the car sideways as it corners. Each slide on each corner wears the tire and raises its temperature, and higher tire temperatures produce less grip for the next corner, where the traction spiral continues downward.

In addition to tire degradation, cars also suffer a degree of engine degradation on a qualifying attempt, as internal temperatures rise and sap horsepower. Ahead of their runs, teams look to gain an aerodynamic edge by blocking cooling airflow through the bodywork and into the engine. But they can't go too far, as replacing a blown engine from inadequate cooling can be almost as difficult to recover from as a serious crash.

In practice today, drivers would seek not only flat-out pace but also consistency over four laps. The difference in positions up and down the grid of qualified cars is typically very thin. Those drivers who can desperately hold onto their cars for four full laps as their tires lose grip, especially on that critical fourth lap, can improve their positions considerably.

Qualifying over the weekend would occur with just a single car on the track. Therefore, teams ideally wanted a clear racetrack today so they could get an accurate representation of their car's performance. Aerodynamic tows from cars in front were not wanted or welcomed, for they would give a false promise of speed.

Since every team was in the same situation, an informal agreement covered the entirety of Pit Lane today. Teams would look to only have three or four cars on the track at any given time, spaced out appropriately to minimize the effects of a slipstream. It wouldn't always work, of course, and as the time remaining grew shorter, desperate teams searching for speed would spark an increase in track activity. It wouldn't be surprising that some drivers aborted their simulated four-lap qualifying runs early because of a tow from a car, or cars, in front of them. Not only would the team not benefit from knowing their real pace relative to others, but it also wouldn't benefit from knowing exactly how the tires would respond on the critical third and fourth qualifying laps.

The green flag flew promptly at noon, and Penske's Newgarden quickly shot out of the pits on sticker tires for a qualifying simulation. With the track to himself, he gave his team—and every other team up and down Pit Lane—an idea of what pace might be needed, not only to contend for the pole position but, eventually, what it would take to make the race.

Running in clean air, Newgarden left a few jaws agape with a first lap of 233.8 mph, hitting 241 mph at the end of both straightaways. Tire wear slowed his second lap to 232.6. For his third and fourth laps, he benefitted ever-so-slightly from a draft from O'Ward about a quarter mile ahead of him on the track. Still, his 233.259 four-lap average speed set a new benchmark for the field.

Team Penske had struggled the past few years in qualifying, with Power being the quickest of the team last year but only twelfth overall. Newgarden's first qualifying simulation showed the team had made vast improvements in its outright qualifying pace.

One team needing considerable improvement in qualifying pace was that of the entire Rahal Letterman Lanigan organization. Graham Rahal went out for his first qualifying simulation, and in clean air, reeled off laps of 231.236, 231.011, 230.594, and 230.631 mph.

On his radio, Rahal reported his car sliding through the turns, signifying a need for more grip, either aerodynamic, with wing adjustments, or mechanical, with changes to tire pressures, damper adjustments, and more. He was faster than he was the previous year, but weather conditions were nearly perfect when he went out today. Warmer days forecasted for the weekend would likely sap some degree of performance from his car, so making changes now became a top priority.

Rookie Nolan Siegel went out in his No. 18 Dale Coyne car and ran a first lap of just over 228 mph, discovering his car was unsettled at the rear, suffering from oversteer. On advice from his team over the radio, he aborted his simulated run on the second lap. Discretion being the better of valor, it was smart advice from an experienced crew to an inexperienced driver. There would be nothing to gain in risking it all in a simulation, and the consequences of pushing it too far could be significant.

At 12:30 p.m., Herta began his qualifying simulation, and as he had posted fast no-tow laps the previous three days, observers were keen to see his speed in qualifying trim. It didn't take long to see that he was a bit off the early pace.

Herta's first lap was a 231.025, with speed trap speeds at the end of the straightaways clocked at 238 mph. He remained fairly consistent over the last three laps, posting speeds of 231.018, 230.805, and 230.718 for a four-lap average of 230.891 mph, placing him just above Rahal.

Both Herta's and Rahal's average speeds, as compared to that of Team Penske, presented what perhaps might be a trend and an emerging storyline. Herta and Rahal drove Honda-powered cars. Penske, Ed Carpenter Racing, and AJ Foyt racing cars, all Chevrolet-powered cars, had proven to be faster so far on the day.

Would the Chevy runners have an advantage over the weekend? It was still too early for Honda and its teams to be too worried. That time would come at the end of today's practice session—if it came at all. Plus, the front-running Honda-powered cars of Chip Ganassi Racing, including that of last year's polesitter Palou, had yet to show their capability.

When Palou started his run a little after 1:00, he didn't immediately ease concerns of the Honda contingent. His second lap was his fastest, a 231.799, and his four-lap average was just 231.337 mph. While still very early in the simulated qualifying attempts, the best Honda-powered cars seemed to be consistent in lap speed over four laps but a touch off the pace at the very front.

Dixon, Palou's CGR teammate, went next in his No. 9 PNC Bank Honda. Dixon, true to his career where he had proven to be one of the most successful Indy car drivers ever, had also proven in the past to be a master at qualifying for Indianapolis. Dixon had won the pole five times, including two of the last three years, and four of the last nine. In his previous twenty-one appearances in the Indy 500, Dixon qualified on the front row seven times.

Dixon alleviated Honda worries slightly by posting speeds of more than 232 mph over his first two laps. He dropped off, however, over his final two laps, leaving him with a 231.549 mph four-lap average, good for ninth fastest, and the second fastest Honda behind that of Marco Andretti on the speed chart.

Two drivers and teams with early struggles were Katherine Legge in her Dale Coyne Racing with RWR entry and Juncos Hollinger Racing's Romain Grosjean. Legge completed her initial run with a four-lap average of 229.984 mph and aborted her subsequent runs after not finding speed on her first lap. Grosjean was not comfortable, or fast, at the start of his runs and didn't complete a four-lap run.

Frustrated with a relative lack of on-track practice early in the week, Larson looked to make up for lost time with repeated qualifying simulations. He improved on each of his first three runs, eventually posting a 232.549 mph four-lap average, good for sixth on the speed charts and just off the 232.565 average of his more experienced teammate, O'Ward. With his quick learning and performance, Larson had thrown his name into consideration as a top-twelve qualifier on Saturday and a very real contender to win the pole on Sunday.

At 1:45, Siegel's day went from bad to worse. On another qualifying simulation, Siegel's car broke loose late in Turn Two, after the apex. After an early wiggle entering the turn, the rear end snapped around, and after a 180-degree spin, Siegel hit the outside retaining wall twice, first with a big slap to the left front of the car, then with a softer, yet still significant hit to the left rear.

Rolling backward down the back straight, the front of the car drifted to the right, toward the infield, and as the air hit the leading edge of the side of his still quickly moving race car, it launched Siegel upside down. Siegel slammed back down to the asphalt, where his car slid on its top several hundred feet before coming to a stop.

Almost as soon as his car came to a rest, Siegel was on his radio, first apologizing to his crew, then letting them know he was okay. That the apology came first was fitting as to where Siegel's head was.

Unlike the teams who fell victim to the Speedway's unforgiving walls yesterday—Ganassi and Andretti—Siegel's DCR team was not nearly as well-funded. Siegel's car was relatively devoid of stickers and didn't have a primary sponsor to foot much of the bills.

Siegel's accident put the team significantly behind on their planned program. They weren't safely fast to begin with. Now the team needed to prepare its spare, a car driven by Jack Harvey in last Saturday's road course race, for qualifying over the weekend. There was no doubt about it: rookie Siegel and his DCR team were now decidedly on their back feet in attempting to qualify for this year's race. Of course, for those other drivers and teams currently at the bottom of the speed charts, including Legge, Siegel's teammate at DCR, their monumental struggle allowed for a bit of relief.

After an extended stoppage to clear Siegel's car and its debris from the racing surface and repair a divot in the circuit from where the car landed after its flip, the track opened again for practice. One of the first cars out was that of Ericsson, trying to again shake down his new race car, which was prepared for him by his Andretti crew last night, after yesterday's big crash.

Ericsson's first run was quite slow in comparison to the rest of the day's runs, but that wasn't a particular surprise. Those laps were primarily to get Ericsson comfortable in the car again, ensuring all the car's systems were in prime working order and determining if the car's preliminary setup was close to that of the primary car Ericsson was so comfortable with before his crash.

His second run was also off the pace as the team looked to continue to make setup changes. Finally, Ericsson took to the track to make a concerted qualifying simulation attempt. The results were not what either the team or Ericsson wanted, although they weren't entirely unexpected.

Ericsson's best lap was his first, a 229.458. His speed dropped each subsequent lap, leaving him with an average four-lap speed of just 229.040 mph. Like the rest of the Andretti team—and most of the Honda-powered cars, for that matter—they would be searching to find incremental speed improvements.

After Ericsson, Lundqvist went out again to wrestle out the demons of yesterday and get his program back on track. Under a bright sun, he grappled to find speed, but it turned out to be elusive, at least so far. His average speed of 228.951 mph was well below what was expected from a Ganassi car at the Speedway.

As the sun broke out and the track temperature rose to 112 degrees, traffic activity slowed down in the middle of the session. Team Penske ran its three cars early when conditions were ideal for both the engines and tires. It showed, with Newgarden and McLaughlin positioned one-two, and Power close at sixth-fastest. After that, knowing track conditions would change throughout the day, the team covered everything up and took a break.

The weather, particularly ambient air temperature and cloud cover, or the lack of cloud cover, as the case may be, always presented a strategic challenge for teams. Weather conditions often delivered considerable good fortune—or bad fortune—come qualifying attempts. A well-timed "qualifying cloud" could help a car's speed considerably.

Initial qualifying attempts were to be determined by a random draw, to take place after the Fast Friday practice session. With qualifications scheduled to start at 11:00 a.m. on Saturday, eyes along Pit Lane continued to look at weather forecasts. Thus far, those forecasts called for a partly sunny day with a bump in ambient air temperatures, to a high of 83 degrees. Therefore, teams desired an early draw number. First would be best, the top ten would be good, and anything after that . . . less than ideal.

To get a representative feeling of what to expect in the heat of the day for tomorrow, Power went out and immediately impressed. Despite a small bobble in Turn Two that scrubbed off some speed on his third lap, he shot to second on the chart with an average speed of 233.174 mph.

Defending champion Newgarden followed up and threw down the gauntlet to both his Team Penske teammates and the rest of the field. Newgarden's first lap was the first lap of the month over 234 mph, a 234.260, and he didn't slow much from there. His fourth lap, a 234.087, was faster than his second and third laps. His average speed of 234.063 mph set a new high mark.

Later, Palou, on the first lap of yet another run, suffered a power unit failure, with blue smoke billowing from the right-side exhaust as he barreled down the back straight. Typically not a sign of an easy fix, Palou exited his Honda-powered car in the pits and immediately put away his helmet and gloves, his program for the day interrupted.

Palou, Dixon, and the rest of CGR Racing unexpectedly struggled to find pace today. Ordinarily a threat for the front row and the pole, all five Ganassi entries had work to do overnight to find competitive qualifying speed.

At 4:00, Larson started yet another qualification simulation and showed his reputation for being fast in any car with four wheels. With McLaughlin providing him only a slight slipstream, Larson banked laps of 234.271 and 234.037 mph, before backing out of the throttle under instruction from his team because of high engine temperatures. In their quest for speed, the Arrow McLaren had buttoned up the bodywork perhaps a bit too much. Still, Larson's first lap was the fastest lap turned this month and confirmed him as a solid contender for the pole position.

"Happy Hour" is the term given to the last hour of practice every day, from 5:00 to 6:00 p.m. Air temperatures drop from the heat of the day, and shadows from the massive grandstands along the front stretch and Turn One cool the track temperature even more. It's the prime opportunity to clock fast times, and almost every team wants to get out to gain valuable insights into what changes are needed to get to a muscle-flexing stage.

While speeds during Happy Hour can grab headlines, they don't often translate to either qualifying or race day. Unless rain or other circumstances dictate a delay on race day, even the post-race celebrations would have wound down by the time 5:00 p.m. rolls around.

Being the last hour of practice, however, meant every driver needing additional time on track needed to take advantage of the opportunity. Earlier in the day, there was an informal agreement among teams to send their cars out with adequate spacing to get a reflective no-tow time. Come Happy Hour, those agreements flew right out the window.

Therefore, speeds during Happy Hour weren't usually the best indicator of a car's qualifying pace. Cooler air and track temperatures, as well as more tows from traffic, lifted speeds slightly above the pace they'd show tomorrow, and tended to make teams feel their cars were better than they actually were. Still, those speeds would make for great headlines.

Today was a Chevrolet day, with only the Honda-powered Andretti entry of Kirkwood, ninth fastest, and Andretti-affiliated Meyer Shank Racing entry Rosenqvist, sixth fastest, breaking the Chevrolet stranglehold on the top ten in four-lap qualifying simulations.

In single-lap speeds, the results weren't much better. Rosenqvist posted the second-fastest lap of the day, 233.485 mph, behind only Newgarden, and Kirkwood and Sato ended up in the top-ten at fifth and eighth.

Manufacturers participate in racing for several reasons, including using racing as a research and development testing ground. However, the primary reason is to market their passenger cars. "Win on Sunday, sell on Monday" is a mantra often repeated, and every manufacturer—and every car sponsor, for that matter—wants to be associated with a winner.

Honda and Chevrolet were the only current engine providers to the IndyCar Series and, somewhat counterintuitively, both continued to be keen to see a third manufacturer enter the series. The reason was simple: a third engine supplier would decrease their costs.

Currently, Honda supported just over half the field, and despite each engine costing teams about $125,000, the company's involvement in IndyCar was, standing entirely on its own, a money-losing proposition. Honda hoped that while its HPD engine division might lose money, it was an investment that delivered returns through the sale of more Honda passenger cars and trucks.

No new engine manufacturer would break into the IndyCar Series until after the hybrid-assist program took full effect. And, even then, it would take more than a year to get up to speed, both literally and figuratively.

Until then, it would be Chevrolet and Honda, or at least IndyCar officials hoped. Honda had been public about its uncertain participation in the series beyond 2026.

That would be the future, and for executives to decide. At the close of practice, Honda engineers were in close consultation with their teams, looking for any potential ways to coax just a bit more power from their engines, all without negatively affecting reliability. The big test for all-out speed loomed tomorrow. Eight days later, the dual test of both speed and reliability would come with the running of the 2024 Indy 500.

When interviewed on Pit Lane earlier in the afternoon, Graham Rahal was asked about the draw to determine the qualifying order. He replied, "An early draw will be God's gift to whoever gets it; hopefully it's us."

Alas, true to his form at the Speedway the past two years, he proved not to be that fortunate. Rahal would go thirty-second out of the thirty-four entries.

An early draw would allow cars to perform in temperatures more ideal for both engines and tires. The later the draw, the greater the likelihood of higher temperatures. Stuck with a late draw, one could only hope for the fortunate qualifying cloud to drift over the track and cool the track temperature just as their car entered the track for a qualifying attempt.

As it was, Andretti's Kyle Kirkwood would be the first car on track, followed by Penske's McLaughlin. The rest of the first ten were to be Simpson, VeeKay, Grosjean, Larson, Canapino, Ilott, Power, and Newgarden.

The early draw would probably benefit Grosjean, who had struggled to find qualifying speed. Siegel's twelfth-place draw would also benefit him in his quest to recover from today's crash. The Penske trio, already at the top of the speed charts, were also positioned very well.

One driver looking for speed who wouldn't be helped with his qualifying order was Carpenter's Christian Rasmussen, who would go off thirty-first, one spot ahead of Rahal. Palou, Dixon, and Herta also received no favors with the draw and would go off twenty-fifth, twenty-seventh, and twenty-ninth. The final two drivers to make their initial qualifying runs were scheduled to be Castroneves and Rossi.

SATURDAY, MAY 18, 2024

Go Fast Day

Yesterday evening's draw established the order of every car and driver's initial qualifying attempt. Every entry would have a guaranteed initial qualifying attempt, if the entrant chose to take it. However, if a car were to be pulled out of the initial qualifying line, there would no longer be a guarantee that it would get at least one qualifying attempt.

Over the years, qualifying had changed considerably at Indianapolis. For the longest time, the lead-up to the race took the entire month of May, with the track opening for practice on May 1. As such, there were two weekends of qualifying, four days in total.

One key difference back then was that a car could only qualify once. If a car was bumped from the field by a faster car, it could not be used to try to qualify again. Thus, if owners could afford to do so, they would enter multiple cars per driver—it wasn't uncommon for a driver to have a backup car entered just in case.

Those backup cars often made for interesting storylines in the week leading up to the second weekend of qualifying. If a primary car had been successfully qualified the first weekend and the owner felt comfortably safe in making the field, they had talks with other drivers about qualifying the backup car. Many deals were struck and drivers who hadn't had a car at the beginning of the month suddenly found themselves with a strong opportunity to qualify for the race.

These days, a car could make multiple qualifying attempts, and if a car was bumped from the field and time remained in qualifying, the driver could go out in the same car and give it another try. Many times, drivers would go out and attempt to qualify faster than they did previously, improving their starting position for the race. That, however, came with considerable risk.

Once the initial line of qualifying attempts had been cleared, the Speedway would divide the south end of Pit Lane into two distinct lanes. Lane One would become the priority lane, and if you pushed your car into that line, you could immediately make a qualifying attempt. It came with one big caveat, and it was a big catch at that. As soon as a car was rolled into Lane One, its previous qualifying attempt would be withdrawn.

That meant if something prevented a driver from completing a four-lap qualifying attempt, be it a mechanical failure, a crash, rain, or any other reason, they wouldn't have a qualifying time and wouldn't be in the field come race day.

Lane Two would become the non-priority lane. Any car in that lane could attempt to qualify only if Lane One remained empty. Cars qualifying from Lane Two did not have their previous qualifying runs withdrawn. If they went slower or were otherwise unable to finish another qualifying attempt, the previous speed would hold the car's spot in the field.

Typically, once the initial qualifying runs were completed, there would be a bit of a lull in on-track activity during the heat of the day as teams strategized. Everyone wanted to run as late in the day as possible when air and track temperatures were typically at their most conducive for speed. But, at the same time, they didn't want to be stuck deep in a line in Lane Two and perhaps not get an opportunity to go faster.

At some point in time in the afternoon, there would be a frantic dash to push cars in line. Some would lose out, and if they wanted to make another qualifying attempt, they'd have to consider using Lane One and withdrawing their previous attempt.

The first day of qualifying for the Indianapolis 500 sets the order from positions thirteen through thirty on the starting grid, rows four through ten. It also sets the stage for Sunday, where positions one through twelve and thirty-one through thirty-three would be set.

Today's fastest twelve qualifiers advance to Sunday's Top 12 Qualifying session, where they will get one, four-lap qualifying attempt. The six fastest qualifiers in the Top 12 Qualifying advance to the Firestone Fast Six session, while those seventh through twelfth will be locked into those race day starting positions.

Today's four slowest qualifiers also advance to Sunday, where they'll face off in the Last Chance Qualifying session. That session lasts for exactly one hour, and after each car makes an initial attempt, all four cars can make as many subsequent attempts as time allows. At the end of the hour, the three fastest cars will be locked into positions thirty-one through thirty-three on the last row of the race's starting grid. The slowest car will not make the race.

The last qualifying session on Sunday is the Firestone Fast Six, where the six fastest cars from the Fast 12 Qualifying session shoot it out for the pole. Each car will get one qualifying attempt. The fastest wins the pole position and lines up on the inside of the front row on race day. The others are locked into positions two through six.

In qualifying, drivers push to their cars' absolute limits, but most will do so only to a certain extent. If a driver believes they will rather comfortably make the field and not be the thirty-fourth fastest qualifier for a thirty-three-car grid, they'll use more discretion. Chasing speed at Indy can have dire consequences.

Gaining more than half a mile-an-hour of lap speed from anything other than a very significant setup change is almost impossible at this late stage in preparations. If a driver is on the cusp of breaking into the top twelve, or out of the slowest four, they'll push it just a little more. If they're not on those cusps, they'll likely take what the Speedway is giving their car on the given day. It's much better to survive and get ready for the Indy 500 than collect the pieces of a wrecked race car and go home to watch the race on television.

Qualifying on the pole rewards the driver with a $100,000 prize, which is higher than any single payday a great many drivers have experienced over their entire careers. But, for the race, other than the confidence gained by sitting in the fastest car, the pole position doesn't afford a competitive advantage.

On the grid, the pole position allows for a ten-foot separation from the second-fastest qualifier—*sideways*. At the start of the race, the pole sitter takes responsibility for the start once the pace car enters the pits. They decide when to accelerate to take the green flag, so there's a slight advantage there.

But, at speed, the best line to enter Turn One is on the outside. While it's possible to go side-by-side through Turn One at the slower speed of the race's opening lap, often one of the other two front-row starters find themselves leading when entering Turn Two.

Beyond the front row, however, the qualifying position means an awful lot, particularly on the first lap. Indy 500 history is filled with first-lap accidents, and as all thirty-three cars are packed together on the narrow, fifty-foot-wide front straight, the start of the race is fraught with danger. The biggest fear of drivers is getting caught up in someone else's accident, as high speed and close quarters conspire to limit a driver's ability to react and avoid getting collected in a crash.

A driver can't win the Indy 500 on the first lap, but he or she can certainly lose it.

Another advantage of qualifying high is track position during the race. With the incredibly competitive nature of IndyCar racing, overtaking cars is challenging. Naturally, the fewer cars a driver has to pass, the better.

Newgarden proved last year that a driver doesn't need to start up front to win. Newgarden started in the second half of the field, in the middle of Row Six, in the seventeenth position. Ericsson, who finished second, started tenth. Palou, last year's pole sitter, finished fourth, albeit after racing through the field after an incident in the pits early in the race pushed him far back in the order.

Indianapolis greeted race teams with a glorious late spring day, with only a two-mile-an-hour wind out of the north-northwest. Teams were thankful for the light wind, for it greatly minimized one of their many variables.

One variable that could not be eliminated, however, was the heat. The Indiana sun was pounding on the track, producing 95-degree track temperatures at 11:00 a.m. Crews and drivers resigned themselves to the fact that temperatures would play an important role all day long.

Almost immediately, even before the first car entered the track to attempt to qualify, teams adjusted their qualifying strategies as quickly as they were adjusting their car setups. Qualifying attempts late in the afternoon, particularly those in the final hour, Happy Hour, would benefit substantially from cooler temperatures, likely making them much faster than attempts completed in the heat of the day.

Two leading teams didn't even roll out their cars to the lineup determined by the draw Friday evening. Dixon's Chip Ganassi crew was in the garage putting the finishing touches on replacing the Honda engine in his car. Meanwhile, Arrow McLaren had Rossi's No. 7 car sitting comfortably in its garage. As Rossi held the final draw for an initial attempt, they chose to sit their car in the shade of the garage rather than out in the blazing sun where it would just soak in heat for nearly three hours.

At 11:01 a.m., Kirkwood jumped on the throttle, spinning his rear tires and shooting his car onto the track. For the first and only time this month, he, like the rest of the drivers who would follow him, skipped the warm-up lane and drove directly onto the racing circuit in Turn One. Kirkwood could drive onto the track because qualifying at Indy is a single-car affair. There's no need to be wary of getting in the way of any faster cars approaching.

After completing that first partial lap, Kirkwood, as is the norm on qualifying attempts, continued on another, full warm-up lap, bringing his tires and engine to their optimal operating temperatures.

The warm-up lap is important. Going too hard, too fast, in Turns One and Two might take unnecessary life out of the tires, critical life that might be needed to hold on to a fast fourth and final lap of the attempt. At the same time, high speed exiting Turn Four of the warm-up lap is required to reach maximum terminal velocity entering Turn One on the first timed lap of the attempt.

Dealing with a touch of understeer requiring him to soften his front roll bar, Kirkwood recorded a first lap of 232.964 mph. From there, he remained incredibly consistent, losing less than half a mile an hour in spread from his fastest to slowest lap. First out of the gate, Kirkwood's 232.764-mph four-lap average speed was excellent, and it set the benchmark for the rest of the field.

Next up came the bright yellow No. 3 Pennzoil Chevrolet of McLaughlin, nicknamed "The Yellow Submarine" by his crew and fans. The paint scheme of his car was reminiscent of the long-time livery of cars driven by former Penske driver and four-time Indy 500 winner Rick Mears.

Mears won the Indy 500 twice in yellow Pennzoil cars, in 1984 and 1988. In that 1988 race, Mears qualified on the pole, flanked by his two Team Penske teammates, Danny Sullivan and Al Unser Sr. McLaughlin, who stated after the morning practice session that his car was as good as it had been all month, set out to take the first step in repeating Mears's and Team Penske's 1988 Indy results.

Immediately, McLaughlin showed he was a strong contender for the pole position when he flashed by the start/finish line on his first lap to record a 233.533-mph speed. With his car handling perfectly in the turns, McLaughlin didn't suffer with much fall off on his pace, and his 233.332-mph average speed, over half a mile an hour faster than Kirkwood's impressive time, made him the driver to beat.

After rookie Kyffin Simpson, driving for Ganassi, likely put himself into the field with an attempt at 231.948 mph, Rinus VeeKay drove his green No. 20 askROI Chevrolet onto the track for his qualifying attempt.

VeeKay, still just twenty-three years old, was attempting to qualify for his fifth Indianapolis 500. In his five years racing in the IndyCar Series, VeeKay wasn't a particularly good qualifier, qualifying fastest just twice in his previous sixty-seven IndyCar races. He hadn't been a particularly good qualifier, that is, except at Indianapolis.

In his previous attempts at Indianapolis, VeeKay qualified fourth, third, third, and second. As he drove onto the track, the crowd and his Ed Carpenter Racing crew looked on to see if VeeKay could go just one spot better this year.

Entering Turn Three at 238 mph on his first flying lap, the rear end of VeeKay's car, suffering from oversteer, broke free. VeeKay caught it temporarily but lost it for good a fraction of a second later. His car looped and impacted the outside wall at the left rear, then pivoted and scraped the entire left side of the car down the wall of the short chute, finally coming to a stop along the outside wall of Turn Four.

The left side of VeeKay's car was destroyed. Once his car was delivered back to the team's garage in Gasoline Alley, his team rushed to rebuild the car, quickly deciding to reuse the tub and replace the damaged components. The crew wasted no time in starting the extensive rebuild, as they knew time was extraordinarily tight for them to get the car into a condition to make another qualifying attempt today. If they couldn't repair the car and qualify it today, it would make for a nervous Sunday for the entire team in the Last Chance Qualifier.

VeeKay's crash certainly set back his program, but it also affected almost everyone else. The qualifying session was stopped to clear VeeKay's wrecked racer and the crash debris spread throughout the north end of the track. The delay made the rest of the field wait, but Mother Nature never got the memo—temperatures continued their steady, upward climb.

Once the track was cleared, Grosjean posted an average speed of 231.514 mph, the slowest of the four cars thus far, and Grosjean was heard on the radio saying it wasn't good enough. But even while Grosjean was on his run, all eyes were on Kyle Larson, one of the biggest stories of this year's Indy 500 campaign, and perhaps the single biggest story to hit the Speedway since Danica Patrick's debut in 2005.

Everywhere Larson stepped on the grounds this week, he was thronged by either media, fans, or both. Not a single session went by where he stepped from his car and was not immediately interviewed by NBC Sports, who was broadcasting all on-track sessions on its Peacock streaming platform.

The attention on Larson was warranted, as he was a talented racer and a throwback to the racers of yesteryear, the drivers who would race multiple series of cars over a week. The past Sunday, Larson was racing his NASCAR stock car at Darlington, South Carolina. Monday of this week, the day *before* the first practice for the Indy 500, Larson raced a sprint car on the dirt track at Kokomo Speedway, just north of Indianapolis. His night ended with a crash in his heat race, where he barrel-rolled down the backstretch. Fortunately, he was both unfazed and uninjured from the accident.

With smooth, quiet hands in the car, it appeared Larson's car was handling well on his qualifying attempt, and maybe even set up a bit conservatively with aerodynamic downforce, both in anticipation of a nervous first attempt coupled with a reaction to VeeKay's earlier crash. His first lap speed was a solid, if not spectacular 232.719 mph.

However, on his fourth and final lap, when he downshifted from sixth to fifth while exiting Turn One, Larson's Chevrolet engine abruptly lost power. His team asked him to complete the lap and post a qualifying attempt, but Larson, in his inexperience with IndyCar machinery, had already dropped speed considerably along the backstretch. Entering the warm-up lane inside Turns Three and Four, Larson could be heard working down through the gearbox, signifying that part of the drivetrain was working properly.

Larson's crew rolled his No. 17 back to the garage in Gasoline Alley and quickly set to work on diagnosing the problem. His first qualifying attempt aborted, Larson would have to wait for the long line of cars to work their way onto the track for their runs before he could make another attempt.

After Canapino edged in front of his Juncos Hollinger teammate Grosjean, Ilott took to the track for Arrow McLaren's second attempt. His four-lap average of 231.995 mph placed him comfortably in the field but left the team with the impression they could find more speed, perhaps for Ilott himself, but certainly for O'Ward and Rossi, both of whom would run later.

Will Power then came out and continued to flex the Team Penske muscle. With a track temperature of 103 degrees, ten degrees higher than McLaughlin's earlier run, he peeled off a first-lap speed of 234.030 mph en route to a 233.758 average and the top of the speed chart.

While knowing his speed might still be beaten, his crew also knew it would certainly be fast enough to make the Fast Twelve and take part in Sunday's qualifying session. Satisfied, Team Penske rolled the Power's No. 12 Verizon Business Chevrolet back to the garage to prepare for Sunday. Power disagreed with the decision. He wanted to run again later in the afternoon, in hotter temperatures that would be more reflective of the conditions he would encounter on Sunday.

Power's third teammate, defending champ Newgarden then went out to see where he stood with his No. 2 Shell Chevrolet. His run was consistent, from a first-lap speed of 233.528 mph to a fourth-lap speed of 233.127, and good enough for the third-quickest average speed of 233.293. Still, he climbed out of his cockpit feeling there was more speed to be found from the car.

Rookie Armstrong, the second of the three Ganassi rookies to attempt to qualify, impressed with a 232.183, delivering the team its best result thus far, both in terms of one-lap speed and the drop-off from fastest to slowest lap. As all five Ganassi cars had searched desperately for speed, they'd been dependent on maximizing mechanical grip with the tires. Armstrong's ability to seemingly hold onto the tires over his run on a heating track surface would give his three remaining teammates who had yet to work their way through the qualifying line—Lundqvist, Palou, and Dixon—a little additional, and much-needed, confidence.

Siegel was up next in his backup car and showed he was still not comfortable after yesterday's spectacular crash. He lifted off the throttle briefly on a couple of corners on his first lap, and his 226.900 was a fair indicator of his struggles. But, with no time posted by both VeeKay and Larson, he persevered and finished his run with a 226.621-mph average speed.

Siegel's DCR team had him complete his run for a simple reason. If four or more racers experienced difficulties today that prevented them from qualifying, their speed, despite being relatively slow, would lock them into the thirtieth position for the world's biggest race. If other racers should face calamities today, Siegel might squeeze into the top thirty. If not, Sunday would be the day when Siegel needed to really let it hang out in Last Chance Qualifying.

Under the watchful eye of car owner AJ Foyt, Ferrucci overcame a car suffering a bit too much oversteer to run four consistent laps, with his second lap the quickest, and posted a 232.496-mph average speed, slotting him into fifth. With a solid qualifying run already in the books, the Foyt team would make a slight handling adjustment and get Ferrucci back out for another attempt if necessary to maintain his top-twelve position.

A different story emerged when Lundgaard took to the track, and his first run signaled that Rahal Letterman Lanigan Racing, despite all the hard work done over the past year, was still not out of the woods in safely qualifying for the Indy 500. Lundgaard, who along with his teammate Sato had shown the most speed throughout the week for the team, posted an average speed of just 231.465 mph, placing him eleventh, ahead of only Siegel. Already under pressure to make their cars go faster, the RLL team now had even more to worry about. Observers could almost feel the nervous energy emanating from the RLL crews.

Also at the slow end of the field, Ericsson's difficult week continued, as he and his Andretti crew fought to coax speed out of his backup car. He was slow everywhere on the track, both in straightaway and cornering speeds, and his 230.603-mph average speed was a clear disappointment, particularly for an Andretti Global team that had fast cars under both Kirkwood and Herta.

After four sub-par laps, Ericsson's time slotted him behind Lundgaard, and immediately the spirits in the RLL camp lifted ever so slightly. Ericsson and his crew knew they would almost certainly have to make adjustments and return to the track later in the afternoon.

Ganassi's third rookie, Lundqvist, ran a conservative first attempt with a little understeer dialed into the car and slotted behind Grosjean into eleventh at 231.465 mph. It was the slowest of the three Ganassi cars that had made their attempts, and it continued the team's surprising struggle to find speed.

Owner/driver Ed Carpenter, a three-time pole winner for the Indy 500, posted an average speed of 232.017 mph on a run that featured a significant drop off from the first to fourth lap—over 1.3 mph. Immediately upon receiving the checkered flag at the end of his attempt, Carpenter was on the radio, telling his crew he battled through understeer and his teammate, Rasmussen, would not need as conservative a setup for his run. From a veteran with twenty Indy 500s to draw from experience, his feedback would prove valuable to Rasmussen as he attempted to qualify for his first 500 later in the session.

In her pink No. 51 e.l.f. Honda, Legge pushed up into the gray and brushed the Turn Four wall on her fourth lap, scrubbing just a bit of speed. She kept the throttle wide open and completed her lap at 229.732

mph, finishing with an average speed of 230.244. Ahead of only Siegel on the charts, Legge and her DCR crew now needed to quickly check over her car for any damage from the contact and continue their search to find just a bit more speed to make the grid.

With temperatures soaring and teams learning from watching the qualifying attempts made before their runs, crews busied themselves up and down the remaining line, making setup changes to better fit the track. Arrow McLaren, needing additional time, pushed O'Ward's No. 5 car out of the qualifying line to make their changes. While he was no longer guaranteed a qualifying attempt, with rain not a factor, there was plenty of time in the day to try later.

Despite the heat, Rosenqvist, one of the Honda frontrunners all week, blasted an impressive 232.878 on his first lap on the way to a 232.547 mph average to place him at the preliminary fifth position, just behind the Honda of Kirkwood, who made his run in much more ideal temperature conditions.

As Rosenqvist slowed down on his cool-down lap, eyes were drawn to last year's polesitter, Palou, whose campaign with Ganassi had been surprisingly difficult all week. His first lap of 232.615 mph was good but not great, particularly for a team reliant on mechanical grip from new tires. He managed to hold on as his tires degraded, however, and posted a solid 232.306-mph average, ahead of teammate Armstrong, and the third-quickest Honda-powered entry so far.

Takuma Sato didn't complete a full four-lap qualifying simulation yesterday, as he and his RLL crew fought to get his car handling correctly. He repeatedly aborted attempts and came back to the pits for adjustments, gradually getting the car closer to where he wanted in his experienced hands.

This afternoon, Sato raised the spirits of the entire team when he posted an average four-lap speed of 232.140 mph, by far the strongest performance for the team. He probably locked himself into the field, and in the process, gave his three struggling teammates setup clues to find more speed.

Along with Kirkwood, Colton Herta represented Andretti's best hopes for a top-twelve position and a shot at the pole on Sunday. In the hottest conditions of the day so far and on the edge of control, he impressively laid down four consistent laps to record a 232.236 mph average. Regardless of where Herta ended up qualifying, his performance all week long indicated he should have a great car come race day.

Rookie Rasmussen was next out on the track, and he needed all of Carpenter's earlier feedback as he made his first-ever qualifying attempt at Indianapolis. After a strong first two laps, he made a mistake entering Turn Three, missing his turn-in mark just a bit. He saved his car from sliding into the wall but scrubbed a bunch of speed. Still, he put himself solidly in the middle of the preliminary field.

Graham Rahal then came onto the track, and with the hot conditions, he knew he would need everything to work perfectly to coax enough speed out of the car. Immediately, he and the team knew they didn't have enough, as his first lap was just 230.657 mph.

He predictably lost speed during laps two and three because of tire degradation, and then an additional challenge cropped up. On his fourth lap, he radioed back, "Something just happened with the engine. Felt like the engine was starving there. Like multiple over boosts or something." His final lap speed of 229.729 mph left him with a four-lap average of 230.233 mph. Unfortunately for Rahal, the drama he experienced a year ago looked to be repeating itself.

With O'Ward, Rossi, Hunter-Reay, and Dixon all pulled by their teams out of the qualifying line, Castroneves made the final guaranteed qualifying attempt just after 1:30 p.m. He failed to match the speed of his teammate, Rosenqvist, recording an average 231.871 mph. It was outside the preliminary top twelve but solidly in the field.

⚑⚑

Twenty-seven cars posted qualifying times from the initial draw, leaving only VeeKay, Hunter-Reay, Dixon, and the four Arrow Team McLaren cars of O'Ward, Rossi, Larson, and Ilott on the outside looking in. Illot, who completed a run earlier in the morning, had his time disqualified when a technical inspection showed a wheel offset violation.

With everyone who was ready and wanted to make qualifying attempts already on the board, the Speedway fell into a period of inactivity. With temperatures getting hotter, there was little for teams to gain by making a qualifying attempt. The potential risks far outweighed the potential returns.

For now.

As temperatures finally dropped, cars would eventually be pushed into one of the two lanes at the south end of Pit Lane. Once a couple of cars got pushed into line, other teams would then quickly react to make certain they'd get an opportunity for another qualifying attempt before the session ended.

Team McLaren, still without a qualified car, decided to put Rossi on track to post a time and get him into the field, as well as use the attempt as somewhat of a test session for another attempt or two later in the afternoon. Fast all week and under a well-timed cloud cover, Rossi delivered the goods on his first lap with a 233.493. In the heat, he dropped off on his subsequent laps, but still showed pole-contending pace, recording a 232.962-mph average, good for a provisional fourth-place spot, right behind the Team Penske juggernaut.

Hunter-Reay, having made final adjustments after collecting feedback from his teammate Daly, who qualified earlier, made his first run next. He carefully brought his tires up to operating temperature with a slow 209-mph warm-up lap. That decision rewarded him with a 232.313 first lap, but he scrubbed speed over his last three laps, completing his run with a 231.695, solidly in the midfield for the time being.

Buoyed by Rossi's stout run, Arrow McLaren presented O'Ward in Lane One and sent him off for his first attempt. On his first lap, he experienced a problem with his engine, at precisely the same spot where teammate Larson experienced his earlier in the morning. When O'Ward downshifted, it caused a problem within the plenum, momentarily starving his engine of fuel and, therefore, power.

Desperate to post any qualifying time, O'Ward persevered to complete his run, albeit with three laps in the 230s. His average speed of 229.840

mph was far off his capable pace and left Arrow McLaren shaking their collective heads to get to the root cause of their Chevy engine problems.

Larson was next for the team, and after hitting 240 mph on the backstretch entering Turn Three of his first lap, he recorded a 232.951 first-lap speed. Three impressive laps later, Larson's 232.563 average put him sixth, ideally positioned to make it to tomorrow's shootout for the pole position.

Kirkwood went out next, but through Lane Two, which meant his first qualifying time wasn't withdrawn. It was unlikely he would improve upon his speed considering the temperatures, but it represented a wonderful learning opportunity, as conditions Sunday in qualifying for the pole would likely be similar. However, after three laps below the speed of his first qualifying effort, track officials waved him off the track. It was a surprising move by officials considering well more than three hours remained in the session, but certainly a decision within their rights. With three laps in the bank, Kirkwood and his Andretti team picked up valuable data to improve the car for tomorrow.

Dixon then rolled through Lane One and set off on his first qualifying attempt. With a fresh engine, he started with a 232.347. Using all his experience to make chassis changes with his in-car tools on every lap, he finished at a 231.851 mph average. It was certainly below expectations entering the month but showed a strong step forward from where he and the team were in the morning.

Up next, after having already run through the stress-filled emotional gauntlet of Indy qualifying that morning, Ilott went out to get himself back into the provisional fast twelve. He safely qualified at 231.728 but fell short of the top twelve. It left his Arrow McLaren team with a decision whether to try to improve later in the afternoon.

Ericsson's second attempt was not faster than his posted time earlier, and after experiencing a significant bobble in Turn One of his fourth lap, he aborted his run. Still sitting in the danger zone, his failed attempt only ratcheted up the anxiety of his hard-working team.

Throughout midafternoon, as Rahal's team replaced his Honda engine with a fresh unit and VeeKay's team completed its overall rebuild, drivers worked their way through Lane Two and onto the track to see if they could improve upon their time. Meyer Shank's Blomqvist was the first driver to improve, but only by a couple of positions. Perhaps little reward for a lot of stress and anxiety, but at the end of the day, if it kept him out of the bottom four, it would all be worth it.

Siegel returned to the track with a car he felt comfortable with going full throttle through the turns. However, despite having the throttle pegged and running faster, he wasn't fast enough. His four-lap average of 228.276 mph was still the slowest of the qualifiers but represented a significant step up in the recovery from yesterday's accident. His DCR team had put downforce into Siegel's car to give him confidence in its handling. Now, they'd trim out the aerodynamic drag to gain speed.

Two-time winner Sato, tasked with flying the RLL banner, put down a great 233.275 mph first lap, and he needed every bit of it. A big wiggle in Turn One on his third lap, as well as another scary moment in Turn Three on his fourth lap, conspired to limit those laps to the high 231s. Still, his 232.473 average pushed him up three spots into the provisional ninth position.

As Sato pulled into the pits, VeeKay got out to shakedown his rebuilt car, turning two slow laps to confirm everything was in working order before returning to the pits. The fact he was out there just a few hours after destroying most of his car was a testament to his hard-working ECR crew. Now the fine-tuning to capture the previous setup became the team's top priority.

Arrow McLaren, knowing O'Ward had much more speed than his first attempt showed, rolled him through Lane One and out for his second attempt. O'Ward's job was not to worry about getting into the top twelve, at least not yet. This run was about getting out of the bottom four, and he took care of business. Starting with a 232.459 mph first lap, O'Ward completed his run at 231.833. When temperatures cooled later in the afternoon, he would try again to climb up the charts.

While O'Ward pulled himself out of the bottom four, it meant Legge fell into the bottom four. Dale Coyne Racing now found itself with two cars needing to find speed to avoid a nerve-wracking night and Sunday.

Just after 4:00 p.m., and comfortable with the rebuild of its car, ECR again pushed out VeeKay, this time intending to make a full qualifying effort. His first lap turned was a 231.686, and he finished the attempt with an average speed of 231.166 mph. It placed him twenty-ninth, but, like Siegel, represented a significant forward step in recovering from the effects of his crash.

At 4:15, Rahal, equipped with a brand-new Honda engine, drove onto the track to get into the top thirty and avoid the Last Chance Qualifier session on Sunday. Suffering from understeer in Turn Three on his opening lap, he posted a 230.675, a speed neither he nor the team wanted to see. He wasn't able to improve, but with no other cars in line, officials let him complete his run. His four-lap average of 230.388 mph kept him in the bottom four.

Equally as desperate as Rahal and his team, Legge looked to break herself out of the bottom four. Her first lap of 230.944 seemed deflating, but she improved to 231.063 on the next lap. That speed scrubbed off on her third lap, so she was tasked with pulling a rabbit out of the hat on her final lap. It turned out to be 230.535. Her 230.830 average did not improve her position.

With the clock ticking down, teams started to jockey their cars for positions up and down Pit Lane, ready to pounce into one of the two lanes. O'Ward's crew and the rest of the Arrow McLaren contingent led the charge into the no-risk second lane, and cars jumped into line behind him, knowing they could always pull themselves out of line if they later decided to do so. Simply being in the Lane Two line provided options, provided, of course, Lane One didn't see a lot of action.

Intent on making the top twelve to advance to the shootout on Sunday, O'Ward blasted out with a 233.003 first lap, showing either his car improved tremendously or the track was coming back into drivers' favor. Or, of course, both. Finishing with a 231.956 lap, O'Ward made a huge improvement, posting an average of 232.434, good for the provisional tenth position and an opportunity tomorrow to go for the pole.

Ilott followed his teammate, looking for the same jump in speed. And, like his teammate, he found it, delivering a 233.012 first lap and following it up with a 232.633. Ilott hung on through a wild fourth lap, where deteriorating handling caused him to lift in Turns One and Two. Those brief moments off the throttle left his average speed just 0.006 mph, over four laps and ten miles, shy of Herta's speed to capture the provisional twelfth position.

With no cars in Lane One, Rossi went out again for another attempt from Lane Two, not necessarily looking to go faster than his strong speed of earlier, but to tune his car for the similar weather conditions expected on Sunday afternoon. The fact that he went faster and posted a 233.069 left Arrow McLaren feeling good after their rather rough start to the day. Rossi was still fourth-fastest behind the Penske trio, but he and his crew felt they had a car to compete for the pole on Sunday.

Riding that wave of momentum, the fourth and final Arrow McLaren, that of Larson, came out next to see where he might stack up for tomorrow. Sitting relatively securely in sixth, he aborted his run after a 233.499 first-lap speed. With that, his day likely came to an end.

With Ilott snapping at his heels, Herta went out to climb higher than his twelfth position. In a car that looked better and better every time he went out on track, he started with a 233.039 first lap. Lacking just a bit of top-end velocity, Herta used his cornering speed to keep his overall speed up. His 232.316 edged him up to eleventh, just above Palou, giving himself a bit of breathing room. Still, Palou's Ganassi teammate, Dixon, lurked in line.

Hunter-Reay then came out and surprised everyone with a four-lap average of 232.385 to punch his Dreyer & Reinbold car into the top twelve, raising the stakes for everyone. It served notice that the track was ramping up and getting faster.

With nothing much to lose, Ericsson jumped the long Lane Two queue by going through Lane One. Knowing he'd have to cool the engine after this qualifying run to make another if he wasn't fast enough, he needed to reach down and drag out every bit of speed available in the car—a dangerous proposition at any time at Indy.

His first lap speed of 231.392 mph put him only slightly ahead of Fittipaldi's thirtieth-place speed, and his second lap dropped off to a 230.581. On his fourth lap, officials, knowing Ericsson wasn't tracking to enter the top thirty, waved him off to give those in line a fair chance to get on track.

Seeing the results of his teammate, Hunter-Reay, Daly took off on his second attempt looking to improve upon his qualifying position and possibly break into the Fast Twelve. He was well on his way, too, until a misfire in his Chevrolet conspired to rob him of speed. Cruising down the backstretch after aborting his run, Daly pounded on his steering wheel, knowing he had been fast enough to advance to Sunday but now wouldn't get the chance.

Wanting his turn on the improving track, Rasmussen shot out to a 233 first lap before another Chevrolet engine issue caused his second lap to fall to 229. After clawing back over a full mile per hour on his third lap, officials waved off his run, opening the way for his car owner, Ed Carpenter, to get another opportunity.

Carpenter's second attempt looked eerily familiar to those of both Daly and Rasmussen. Improving slightly on his previous attempt, he recorded two strong laps before his engine encountered a misfire. With three engine issues in rapid succession, it now appeared Chevrolet had a big obstacle to overcome.

Sitting uncharacteristically in twentieth, Dixon drove out to demonstrate his true pace and see if he could squeeze into the Fast Twelve. His first lap of 232.305 mph put him at the very edge, particularly knowing a drop-off was coming. A second lap of 231.629 meant he wasn't going to hit his objective, but he could still improve upon his starting position for the race. He decided against it, pulling offline and hoping to get one more chance as the clock ticked down. With just twenty-nine minutes remaining, it looked like Dixon was done—unless he took a big risk and moved into Lane One.

With twenty-four minutes remaining, Rahal went out once again to lay it all on the line to get himself out of the bottom four. Despite the improving conditions, his struggles to find speed persisted. After a 231.259 mph first lap was followed by laps of 230.623, 230.467, and 230.394, his 230.685 average seemed to doom him to another nervous Sunday Last Chance Qualifier session.

With time running out and the track as fast as it had been all day, Canapino rolled out from the front of Lane Two to take his shot at the Fast Twelve in his No. 78 car. He delivered the goods, too, posting a 233.267

and a 232.975 on his first two laps. Then yet another Chevrolet engine misfire occurred on his third lap, resulting in a slow 221 speed and causing him to abort his attempt.

With ten minutes remaining, Ericsson failed in his last-ditch effort to land into the top thirty and resigned himself to Sunday's Last Chance Qualifier. With two teammates in the provisional Fast Twelve, with Kirkwood sitting fifth, there was potential in his Andretti car. He and his crew now were tasked with eking it out tomorrow.

Legge went out again from Lane One, with VeeKay waiting in the wings while Rahal's team pushed him down Pit Lane to get into the priority line. With those cars in Lane One, it meant Palou, sitting at the front of Lane Two, wouldn't get on track in time to improve upon his thirteenth-place position. The best last year's pole sitter could now do was start this year's race on the inside of Row Four.

VeeKay was safely qualified in the twenty-ninth position, but his ECR team felt comfortable in withdrawing his time for a last-minute attempt under the best temperature conditions of the day. If he didn't qualify well today, they felt their car would be the fastest of any four cars that would need to run in Sunday's Last Chance Qualifier.

Any concerns of not qualifying today eased considerably when VeeKay delivered a 233.448 on his first lap. His laps fell off from there, but his 232.419 average pushed him to eleventh-fastest for the day. It was a remarkable achievement, not just for VeeKay, but for the entire Ed Carpenter Racing crew, who had to rebuild a destroyed car in just a few hours and get it up to speed.

VeeKay's achievement came at the expense of Herta, who, despite having one of the quickest cars all week, now found himself sitting thirteenth and out of the Fast Twelve. There would be no time for him to get on track for another attempt before the gun went off, signally the end of the day's qualifications.

Rahal got in the last attempt, as his car was already on the track as the clock ticked past 6:00 p.m. If he could qualify at a speed to avoid participating in the last-row shootout for the second consecutive year, it would relegate his teammate, Fittipaldi, to the slowest four.

It wasn't to be, however. On his first lap, he radioed back, "It's just not pulling," indicating his new Honda engine wasn't pushing him to top speed. With a speed that wasn't going to qualify, he aborted his attempt. He would join Ericsson, Legge, and Siegel in Sunday's Last Chance Qualifier.

Saturday confirmed the Fast Twelve and the four Last Chance Qualifier session participants, who would be the only cars to run on Sunday. Positions thirteen through thirty for the race were locked in, and those drivers and teams would spend their Sunday debriefing and strategizing on how to best prepare their cars for next week's race.

The margins in qualifying were incredibly tight, indicative of the competitiveness of the IndyCar Series. The difference between Hunter-Reay in twelfth and Herta in thirteenth was just 0.0463 of a second, remarkably close for a ten-mile qualifying attempt.

An even more indicative statistic of the overall competitiveness of the field could be found in the spread between thirteenth and thirtieth. Herta's time over a four-lap, ten-mile attempt was just 0.8152 seconds quicker than Fittipaldi, who qualified thirtieth.

A growing concern spread among the crews of the sixteen Chevrolet-powered cars throughout Saturday afternoon, and it began with Larson's engine misfire suffered between Turns One and Two on the fourth lap of his first qualifying attempt. The issue at hand was a "plenum fire," unless one was a Chevrolet spokesperson, who repeatedly referred to those anomalies as a "plenum event."

Plenum fires are relatively rare but not uncommon, and they don't just happen at Indianapolis, where cars are at terminal velocity at the end of each straightaway. O'Ward, leading late in last year's season opener at St. Petersburg, suffered a plenum fire at the start of that circuit's long straightaway. The momentary loss of power enabled Ericsson to overtake him for the win.

The plenum is an enclosed carbon fiber airbox that sits atop the engine, both on Chevrolets and Hondas. The twin turbochargers of an IndyCar engine send highly compressed air into the sides of the plenum, where it is combined with racing fuel sprayed downward by fuel injectors. That air and fuel mixture is then fed into the engine's six cylinder heads, which are compressed by the pistons and ignited by the spark plugs. The resulting highly controlled explosion creates the engine's power. The burned remnants of the air and fuel mixture are then pushed out through exhaust values, where they travel down the exhaust pipes and exit at the rear of the car.

That controlled explosion happens many times a second per cylinder when, of course, everything works as designed.

A plenum fire is just one of many mechanical problems that can befall an engine. They occur whenever an inlet valve remains open for a fraction of a second while there's still flame in a cylinder. Uncontained because of the open inlet valve, the flame sneaks up and ignites the combustible air and fuel mixture in the plenum, before it gets to a cylinder.

The result of a plenum fire is a sudden loss of power, so much so that the driver is thrown forward in the car, pressed against the safety harness as if the brakes were engaged. It's a momentary hiccup, but the results are immediately felt. In the case of O'Ward last year in St. Petersburg, it was the difference between winning and second place. Today, at the Speedway, it was the difference between a qualifying run at top speed and an aborted attempt.

At least six Chevrolet-powered cars experienced speed-sapping plenum fires on Saturday, seemingly all occurring when drivers downshifted from sixth gear to fifth, seeking to maintain as close to 12,000 engine RPMs as possible for ultimate speed. The day's first plenum fire hit Larson when he downshifted between Turns One and Two.

Larson, being a newcomer to an Indy car, understandably got out of the throttle. For all he knew, the engine was failing completely, and he didn't want to drive into Turn Two where the engine might seize up and chuck him into the wall. Better to save the car and come out and try again, which he did.

Others didn't get another opportunity after their plenum fires. Both Canapino and Daly, whose crews perfectly timed their second attempts later in the afternoon through Lane Two, were on qualifying runs that were tracking toward breaking into the Fast Twelve. Not able to get back on track for a third qualifying attempt, they were now locked into the field, Canapino on the inside of Row 8 and Daly in the middle of Row 10.

Chevrolet's engine woes wouldn't affect Sunday's Last Chance Qualifying session, as those four participants will all run with Honda power. But nine of the cars placed in the Fast Twelve were Chevrolet-powered, and while that was quite a public relations coup for the brand, it would be disastrous if a plenum fire affected the final qualifying order.

In both the Fast Twelve and the Firestone Fast Six, drivers would get only one qualifying run. Overnight, Chevrolet engineers burned the midnight oil to ensure Saturday's malfunctions weren't replicated on Sunday's bigger stage, one with even higher stakes.

SUNDAY, MAY 19, 2024

Dreams and Despair

The final day of qualifications for the 108th running of the Indianapolis 500 afforded two practice sessions, one each for those cars participating in both the Fast Twelve and Last Chance Qualifier sessions. At noon, under bright sunshine, the track opened for an hour of practice for those in the Fast Twelve. It was the hottest day of the month so far, and teams had no experience, from a track testing perspective, on how the new Firestone tires would react.

One of the first cars on track, Hunter-Reay found himself loose in Turn Four. He gathered it up safely, but immediately got off the throttle and headed into the pits to make adjustments. It was a savvy, veteran move. In practice, there's no reward for taking unnecessary risks. Better to prepare for the qualifying session, where risk-taking at least presents a potential reward.

In the first fifteen minutes of practice, Arrow McLaren showed they were ready to fight with Penske for the pole and the front row. O'Ward and Rossi led the charge with speeds of 233.462 and 233.115 mph. Rosenqvist even got into the conversation with Honda, posting a 233.485.

Then Newgarden went out and immediately planted the Team Penske flag with a 234.052 lap. However, his teammate, Power, yesterday's fastest qualifier, encountered problems. His first run wasn't to his liking, and when he went back out for his second run, he suffered a plenum event in his Chevrolet engine.

Power seemed to be going backward from yesterday, and he wasn't happy. After his first qualifying attempt on Saturday, he had wanted to run again in the afternoon to better prepare for the day. His team didn't let him, and Power felt it was a mistake. So far today, it had looked that way.

Like Power, Ferrucci wasn't pleased with his car, either, but it had nothing to do with his Chevrolet engine or taking additional qualifying attempts on Saturday. Rather, Ferrucci wasn't happy with his car's handling and made several trips into the pits to dial in the setup. His sixteen laps turned were second most only to Larson's seventeen.

One driver who was pleased with the session was McLaughlin, driving the third Team Penske entry. His 232.817 was only seventh best, but he told his crew he was good. He was confident in the car he had under him.

Overnight, Chevrolet engineers around the world—literally—went to work investigating the root cause of their "plenum events" of yesterday. Six different cars suffered from the events, each seemingly occurring during downshifts from sixth to fifth gear.

Most cars, notably the Arrow McLarens of O'Ward and Larson, recovered and posted representative qualifying runs. Two others, however, suffered occurrences too late in the day to make an additional run. Both Canapino and Daly, running later under cooler conditions, had early laps that would have made them part of the Fast Twelve. Suddenly though, unexpected drops in horsepower dashed their hopes, and the long Lane Two line prevented them from getting back out.

Today, Chevrolet came to the track with three different software patches to test among their eight runners in the practice session for the Fast Twelve. Ed Carpenter Racing decided to skip the session so its crew could continue working to fine-tune VeeKay's car after the Saturday rebuild from his morning crash.

The Fast Twelve qualifying session would start at 3:05 p.m. and would feature nine cars with Chevrolet engines. Drivers would get just one qualifying attempt in the Fast Twelve, as well as the Firestone Fast Six later in the afternoon. Any plenum event experienced during one of those sessions, like Power experienced in the morning practice session, would eliminate a driver from contention for the pole. During the break, Chevrolet engineers needed to select the best, most reliable software patch for their teams.

At 1:00 p.m., the Fast Twelve gave way to the opposite end of the field, the slowest four, for their dedicated practice session. Waiting for the Fast Twelve to leave the track, the four cars of Siegel, Ericsson, Legge, and Rahal sat in consecutive pit boxes, ready for their session to start.

Siegel, perhaps the most desperate of the four, wasted no time at the top of the hour in leaving his pit box. Compared to yesterday, he found a small increase in speed. Despite needing to breathe the throttle slightly on several turns, he completed an initial four-lap simulation with an average speed of 228.956. Lacking flat-out speed, Siegel's best opportunity to qualify looked to be in stringing together four consistent laps with a minimal drop off in speed.

Rahal went out next, and was a tick faster than Siegel at 229.074, despite continuing to suffer both a lack of straight-line speed and a lack of grip, and therefore a sliding car, in the turns. His RLL team immediately went to work to find incremental improvements.

For her part, Legge proved the best of the three, running four solid laps and posting a 231.011 mph four-lap average. She and her DCR team were confident they had a car fast enough to qualify, so they packed up and prepared for when the runs would count.

Ericsson, however, found himself in unfamiliar territory for both he and Andretti, as he continued to struggle to get his backup car to the place his primary car was before it was destroyed in Thursday's practice crash. Overnight, the team had made extensive changes to the car, adopting much of the setup of the Andretti-affiliated Meyer Shank car of Felix Rosenqvist, who was in the Fast Twelve and turned in a qualifying simulation of 232.848 earlier in the day. Despite the changes, Ericsson could only muster a 230.532 for himself, although he discovered that the rear end of his car was more stable than it had been the last two days.

After making changes along Pit Lane, Rahal went out for another attempt and managed only a 230.038 mph first lap. His speed was relatively good, but handling issues persisted, and he had to lift off the throttle. After feeling an odd sensation in the right rear, Rahal aborted his simulated run and came into the pits. There, he and his team discovered the right rear wheel had not been secured properly. Rahal's experience had saved him from a potentially disastrous crash. But they had to go into the Last Chance Qualifier without knowing exactly what kind of car they had.

As the practice session wound down, Siegel came back out after his DCR team made significant changes to the front end of his car. Still, the car didn't perform. While the car seemed stable in the turns, Siegel was slow down the straights, hitting just 233 mph entering Turn One. Unable to carry what speed he could generate through the turns, Siegel could not improve upon his earlier time. To make the race, his team would have to trim drag off the car, and Siegel would be pressed to take risks with a car with less downforce and grip in the turns.

Drivers in the Fast Twelve session would get one qualifying attempt, and the session would produce two results. First, the top six qualifiers would be set to advance to the Firestone Fast Six to fight it out for the pole and decide the qualifying order for the first two rows. Secondly, those qualifiers in the Fast Twelve that qualified seventh through twelfth would lock themselves into those starting positions on race day.

The qualifying order for the Fast Twelve ran inverse to the twelve drivers' qualifying results of Saturday. Thus, Hunter-Reay was the first to take to the track for his attempt.

Hunter-Reay hit 236 mph entering Turn One, and kept his car in sixth gear, ensuring, at least he hoped, he would escape the threat of another Chevrolet plenum event. After completing a 231.440 first lap, he fell off considerably to a 230.118 on his second lap.

Needing more speed, Hunter-Reay used fifth gear, and he found he could safely do so. His last two laps were both faster than his second, and he finished with a 230.567 mph average speed.

As Hunter-Reay cruised through Turn Two on his cool-down lap, VeeKay drove his No. 21 car onto the track to begin his warm-up. He had skipped the earlier practice session so that his crew could attend to the final details of their comprehensive rebuild of the car over the past twenty-six hours. Concerning how his car would handle, VeeKay wouldn't know for certain until he hit top speed.

True to his character in qualifying at Indianapolis, VeeKay hit top speed right away. His car reached 240 mph at the end of the back straight entering Turn Three, and his first lap was a 233.499. He shifted his Chevrolet engine to fifth in the south end and stayed in fifth at the north end, completing his second lap at 232.777.

On laps three and four, VeeKay worked his in-car tools to stay ahead of the understeer creeping into his car. His speed tailed off a little, but his 232.610 mph average allowed him to jump in front of Hunter-Reay and gave him a good shot at earning a way into the Firestone Fast Six.

Next up was O'Ward, and he was confident he had more speed in his car than was shown on Saturday. His belief was buoyed, in part, by the fact that two of his teammates, both Rossi and Larson, had gone faster.

With Chevrolet power, O'Ward hit 240 miles an hour entering Turn One on his first lap, and he rode that to a 233.196 for the lap, a bit slower than VeeKay's first lap. His speeds slowed incrementally over his run, and his 232.584 average slotted him between VeeKay and Hunter-Reay.

Sato then rolled out in the first Honda-powered entry for his attempt. Unlike his RLL teammates, including Rahal, who would be running in the Last Chance Qualifier session, Sato had found speed in his car and was looking for a place in the top six.

Sato ran four very consistent laps, all in the 232s, and completed his run with a 232.171 mph average speed. His job on track was done, at least for now. Critically, he and his crew debriefed to determine if there was anything learned, from both a car setup and the driver's perspective, that could help Rahal get more speed from his car.

Santino Ferrucci had been challenged with a mishandling car in the earlier practice session, so he and his AJ Foyt crew had spent the lunch break taking an educated guess on a more balanced car setup for the afternoon. Knowing it was put up or shut up time, Ferrucci started off on his attempt.

His first lap was a fast 233.060 mph, and Ferrucci was absolutely committed the rest of the way, keeping the throttle firmly pegged and using every inch of the track. Driving through more than a few nervous moments, Ferrucci completed his four laps with just a little over half-a-mile-an-hour spread, and his 232.723 moved him to the top of the provisional speed chart. With balance back in the car, his Foyt crew now looked to trim aerodynamic drag off the car and take their shot at the pole position later in the day.

Meyer Shank's Rosenqvist had been fast all week, a continuation of the team's strong start to the IndyCar Series season. He ran four consistent laps and posted an average of 232.305 mph. While it wouldn't earn him a spot in the top six, his consistent speed boded well for a potential strong run in the race.

With Rosenqvist finished with his attempt, all eyes turned once again to Larson, who had impressed all week as he rapidly adjusted to both an Indy car and the Speedway. His run only continued to impress onlookers.

Telemetry showed Larson hit 242 mph entering Turn One, and that speed carried over to a first lap of 233.453. Three more strong laps gave him a 232.788 mph average to go to the top of the charts. With his run, the rookie had earned himself a spot in the Firestone Fast Six, and when he exited his car, his crew and the crowd in the grandstands gave him a rousing cheer.

Kirkwood drove out next in his pink No. 27 AutoNation car, his sights set on being both the fastest Honda-powered entry and a participant in the Firestone Fast Six. After starting with a 232.686 lap, he followed up with two more laps in the 232s. He was having to work his in-car tools on each lap, though, as his car's handling rapidly deteriorated.

On his fourth lap, Kirkwood forgot to reset his weight jacker as he entered Turn One. Now with an unexpected understeer, his car slid high in the turn, requiring him to lift considerably out of the throttle. Kirkwood kept his car off the wall, but in doing so, he dropped a lot of speed, and his fourth lap was just a 226.835. His 230.993 placed him ahead of only Hunter-Reay of the qualified cars.

Next up was Rossi, and he wasted no time in showing he was very much in consideration to place his car on the front row, if not the pole position itself. His first lap was a 233.568, and his second lap was over

233 as well. Tailing off only slightly on his last two laps, he recorded a 233.071 to put himself at the top.

That left only the three Team Penske cars, the fastest of the qualifiers from Saturday. Newgarden was the first, and he looked to repeat what he had done in the morning practice, where he had been fastest.

Newgarden used fifth gear at the south end of the track, Turns One and Two, and sixth at the north end, and he completed his first lap with a 233.501 speed—fast but slower than he had been in practice. With his car handling flawlessly, Newgarden followed with three consistent laps, all in the 233s, and even increased his speed on both his third and fourth laps. His 233.286 usurped Rossi at the top, and now Newgarden shifted his attention to the next session and a run for the pole.

McLaughlin was next, and he set a blistering pace with a 233.870 on his first lap, the fastest lap yet recorded in the session. Like Newgarden, he found his car handling well, and he completed his attempt with three strong laps. His 233.492 not only put him at the top and into Firestone Fast Six, but it also relegated O'Ward out of the top six.

Fastest yesterday, Power rolled out of the pits to complete the Fast Twelve session, uncertain exactly what kind of car he had under him after his trying practice session earlier. Receiving instructions from his team on shifting, they recommended using fifth gear through Turns One and Two, and then whatever he felt most comfortable with at the north end.

Power avoided a repeat of his plenum event from practice, and he was fast, although just a tick slower than McLaughlin. He ended up with an average four-lap speed of 233.483 mph, just nine one-thousandths of a mile an hour slower than McLaughlin. The difference amounted to the equivalent of twenty-three inches over a ten-mile qualifying attempt.

And with that, the field for the Firestone Fast Six was set: McLaughlin, Power, Newgarden, Rossi, Larsen, and Ferrucci. Next, attention turned to the Last Chance Qualifier and the building drama of which car and driver would miss out on qualifying for the Indy 500.

The Last Chance Qualifier session to determine the final three cars to make the field for the Indy 500 would have a different format than both sessions to determine the front of the grid. Those battling at the front of the field would be limited to just one qualifying attempt in each of their two sessions. For the Last Chance Qualifier, however, those who were relegated to the final four the day before would be able to make as many attempts as they'd like within the hour allotted for the session.

Like the Fast Twelve, the order of initial attempts was the inverse of how they finished yesterday. As a result, Siegel left the pits first to start the session.

Siegel's run showed the team had made progress in finding speed. His first lap was a 229.808, and he held on for a four-lap average speed of 229.566 mph. It was his best qualifying effort of the weekend. It remained to be seen, though, if it would be good enough to earn a spot in next week's race.

Up next was Ericsson, who immediately went faster, recording a 230.702 on his first lap. Still not fast, particularly relative to where his primary car was before his crash and his three teammates who qualified yesterday, Ericsson was fast enough. After two more laps in the 230s, his crew radioed he was taking the white flag from the scoring stand, signaling one more lap in his run.

Inexplicably, though, Ericsson got out of the throttle as he passed the yard of bricks to start his fourth lap. Despite the radio call from his crew, Ericsson had thought he had completed his run of four laps when, in fact, it had only been three.

Ericsson's mental mistake was indicative of the immense pressure he felt. A former winner of the 500, he moved over to Andretti Global from Chip Ganassi to win races, not struggle to qualify for the year's biggest race. Because of his mistake, his pressure, and that of the entire team, only intensified.

As soon as Ericsson stopped in his pit box, his crew removed the engine cowling to help expedite its cooling. They knew they needed to sap every last degree from the engine before they made another qualifying attempt.

It was Legge's turn next, and her four laps were clearly run on the edge. On her first lap, she had to correct a big wiggle from the rear end in Turn Two. Still, she rode it out for a first lap speed of 230.812 mph. But, as she continued, her rapidly wearing tires made her car even more difficult to handle.

Her second lap was a 230.629, but the back end of her car continued to look nervous as she steered into each turn. After a third lap of 230.091, she entered Turn One on her fourth and final lap, and the back end of her car walked out toward the wall once again.

Legge gathered her car back up, but to keep it off the wall, she had to lift off the throttle considerably. That lost momentum caused her fourth lap to fall to just 228.847. Her four-lap average of 230.092 mph put her ahead of Siegel and provisionally in the race. But she and her crew were far from being comfortable with her speed.

The last of the initial attempts went to Rahal, and he started slower than both Legge and Ericsson, but, importantly, faster than Siegel. He posted a 230.396 first lap and held on to record a four-lap average of 229.974. After taking the checkered flag, Rahal radioed back that his car was "sliding a ton" in the turns, valuable information as he and his team pondered changes to make if Siegel was able to go faster and they would need to respond.

As Rahal stopped in the pits, a momentary lull fell over the Speedway as the crews all worked to cool their cars. Ideally, a team would like thirty minutes to cool down its engine. The challenge for all four teams, of course, was there weren't thirty minutes left in the session.

Legge was in the most comfortable position of all the drivers, but she wasn't comfortable at all. When interviewed by NBC Sports on Pit Lane and asked to describe her run, she commented, "Terrifying. I feel sick and shaky and like I want to cry." Her attempt had been filled with near misses with the wall, and she hoped to not have to go back out and make another desperate attempt to make the Indy 500.

With no cars presenting themselves to qualify, Ericsson's team took a novel approach to cool their Honda engine—they rolled Ericsson out on used tires to make a qualifying attempt. Although, it wasn't *really* an attempt to qualify.

Because of his aborted first attempt, Ericsson did not have a recorded speed. After a slow warm-up lap, Ericsson took the green flag to start his attempt at an equally slow pace. It was clear he wasn't attempting to qualify, as he was nowhere near top speed. Rather, he just wanted to push air through his car's radiator to further facilitate its cooling.

Ericsson ran fast enough to get cooling air into the engine, but slowly enough not to raise its internal temperatures. After taking the checkered flag after four slow laps, he drove back into the pits. His crew had used a masterstroke of strategy. Now, they had one more strategic decision to make, and that was the timing of their true attempt.

If Ericsson's Andretti team left it to the very end of the session before making a serious qualifying attempt, their competitors would not have time to respond. However, that would come with a risk, for if anything happened on that last run that caused them to be slower than Siegel, then they, themselves, wouldn't have time to respond.

Being the slowest car so far, Ericsson and his team felt more pressure than the others. But they also held all the strategic cards. The rules stated that if you left your pit box, you withdrew your previous qualifying time. Therefore, the three teams of Legge, Rahal, and Siegel could do very little more than wait and watch to see what Ericsson and his Andretti team would do.

With each passing minute, tensions rose. Then the clock finally came to a point where it delivered instant relief to Legge and her crew. The fastest of the four cars thus far, there wasn't enough time for three cars to make full qualifying attempts and bump her from the field. She had qualified for her fourth Indianapolis 500.

Finally, with just over seven minutes remaining in the session, Ericsson drove out onto the track. It would be now or never for him and his team. He had spent a good portion of last summer speaking about his desire to be paid as much as his peers. Now it was time to earn his salary and put his beleaguered team into the 500.

Taking the green flag, he barreled down the end of the straightaway and hit 235 mph entering Turn One, a good sign for a team that had fought to find speed for the better part of three days now. Ericsson held on to that speed and posted a 230.672 first lap. Just three more laps to go.

Ericsson drove very high out of the exit of Turn One on his second lap, using every bit of the racetrack to not only keep up his speed but to hold onto a car whose handling was rapidly disintegrating with every turn. His second lap showed a considerable fall off in speed, down to 230.057.

Still, Ericsson fought on, using his in-car tools to get every bit of performance he could muster from his car. Lap three dropped further still, but not as far as the speed had dropped previously, and his 229.737 set him up for his final lap.

On each turn, Ericsson's car looked to be on the verge of snapping out of control. Still, he kept the throttle wide open and wrestled the car through the turns. He was holding on for dear life, and it showed. All would be decided at the north end of the track.

Getting through Turn Three, Ericsson again got close to the wall on exit, then dove down into Turn Four, the scene of his big crash on Thursday. This time, he got through without any trouble, and he raced toward the finish line to complete his attempt. As he crossed, all eyes looked at the time.

Ericsson's final lap had been a 229.644, giving him an average speed of 230.027. It placed him above Rahal and safely into the field, for he was ahead of two cars and time remained for only one more qualifying attempt.

Siegel would take that last attempt to make it into the Indy 500. For the second year in a row, all Rahal could do was climb out of his car and watch. Qualifying for the biggest race of the year was now out of his hands.

On his attempt, Siegel hit 235 mph entering Turn One, as fast as Ericsson had been just moments before. Through Turns One and Two, he carried that speed, and he hit 234 mph entering Turn Three. But, despite the increase in top-line speed for Siegel, his sliding car lost speed in the turns, and his first lap was just 229.288.

Siegel would have to pick up the pace considerably if he was going to bump his way onto the starting grid. That meant keeping his foot in the throttle and taking big chances.

Flying through Turn One, Siegel lost control of his car, brushing the wall with the right rear. With the impact, his car then swung quickly right, where the right front hit the wall. The contact broke his car's suspension, and from that point on, Siegel was a passenger.

As his car shimmied down the track in the short chute, wiggling left to right to back again from the broken suspension, Siegel jumped on the brakes to bleed off speed. In doing so, he lost control of the car for good, spinning and crashing again into the Turn Two wall.

Siegel climbed from his wrecked race car, despondent in knowing that he didn't earn a spot in the Indy 500. Along the grandstands of the front stretch, the crowd gave him a loud round of applause for the gritty and courageous effort put forth by him and his team. It was an ignominious end to Siegel's first Indy 500 campaign, but as a rising star in the INDY NXT series, Siegel would likely be back for another chance. For now, though, his dreams of racing in the Indianapolis 500 were dashed.

⚑✕⚑

With the last row of the starting field determined, attention turned to fixing the first two rows in the Firestone Fast Six Qualifying session. Just like the first session of the day that culled the contenders from twelve to six, this session would have the drivers take their attempts in the inverse order of their previous qualifying speeds.

Ferrucci was the first to go out on the hot, slippery track, driving his stars and stripes liveried No. 14. Pushing his car to its very limits, he recorded a 233.211 on his first lap. Three laps followed in the 232s, and his fourth lap was faster than both his second and third. Getting out of his car after a four-lap average of 232.692 mph, the affable Ferrucci smiled and said, "That was a little sketchy."

Following Ferrucci were the two Arrow McLarens, with Larson up first. His first lap, too, was above 233 mph, but just a touch faster than Ferrucci. Over the next three laps, Larson had to work his weight jacker as his car developed an increasing amount of understeer. He turned in solid, consistent laps, though, and his average speed of 232.846 mph put him above Ferrucci and onto the provisional pole.

Rossi then took to the track, driving with the intention of breaking the stranglehold Team Penske held at the top of the order. When asked by NBC Sports earlier in the day if his crew would be trimming off aerodynamic drag and its subsequent downforce, Rossi had said, "There's always more to trim."

It didn't take long for the results to be seen. When the timing boards showed his first lap speed of 234.062 mph, the crowd erupted in a roar. As the crowd noise was reaching its crescendo, however, Rossi's car, partly due to the aerodynamic trim, got loose in Turn One and nearly hit the wall.

His speed suffered, but Rossi was still fast on his second lap, recording a 233.335. But, just like the lap previous, his third lap started with another big slide toward the wall in Turn One. Clearly, his tires were losing grip. Rossi would need to tap into all his previous Indy experience to hold on over his last two laps.

He did hold on, though he had to lift slightly in a couple of turns. His last two laps fell into the 232s, but he had done enough—his 233.090 placed him above Larson.

Now, attention turned to Team Penske and its three cars, each of which had topped the speed charts over the past three days.

Newgarden went first, and he set a new high mark with his first lap at 234.188 mph. Then his second lap was nearly as fast at 234.004. With his car handling well, he carried high speeds through the turns and onto the straightaways. Closing with two laps in the 233s, his 233.808 mph average placed him on the pole. However, he still had to wait out his two teammates to see if his speed would hold.

On his first lap, Power was the tiniest bit slower than Newgarden, with a 234.128. Then his second lap was also slower at 233.955. It looked like Newgarden's speed would survive.

But Power, with a record seventy poles in Indy car competition, wasn't done yet. He barely tailed off on his last two laps, and his fourth lap was, in fact, faster than his third. His four-lap average of 233.917 made him the driver to beat.

While Power held the record for most IndyCar poles, he had never qualified fastest for the 500. In his previous sixteen Indy 500s. Power had qualified second twice, and third on one occasion, in 2018, when he went on to win the race. He had just four timed laps to wait to see if he had finally won his first Indy 500 pole.

The final qualifier was McLaughlin, and he took away much of the suspense early in his run. His first two laps were faster than anyone, a 234.526 and a 234.371. Seeing those times on the board, Power, resigned to his fate, sighed and began the walk back to his garage.

McLaughlin still had two more laps to go, and he set about his work swiftly. Another lap above 234 and a final lap nearly as good pushed him to a four-lap average of 234.220 mph.

Team Penske had stamped its dominance on qualifying, sweeping the entire front row. The performance of the team replicated what it had achieved in 1988, when Mears, Sullivan, and Unser Sr. had swept the front row for The Captain.

With his car stopped in the pits, McLaughlin emerged from his cockpit and swung both fists in the air, both in celebration and relief. His qualifying speed was the fastest pole-winning run in the history of the Indy 500.

As Roger Penske went over to shake his hand, McLaughlin said, "Next week, next week."

The Captain simply nodded and repeated, "Next week."

MONDAY, MAY 20, 2024

Race Setups

Over the weekend, the starting field was set for the 108th running of the Indianapolis 500, just six days away. The fastest thirty-three drivers and cars had survived the gauntlet that is qualifying for the world's biggest race.

The starting field consisted of eight former winners, led by four-time winner Castroneves and two-time winner Sato. Last year's winner, Newgarden, would attempt to be the first repeat champion since Castroneves achieved the feat in 2001 and 2002.

Six rookies had made the field, with the fastest being Larson. Siegel was the only rookie to fail to qualify.

Showcasing the international scope of the Indy 500, of the thirty-three qualified drivers, just twelve were from the United States. The balance of the grid consisted of twenty-one international drivers from thirteen different countries.

Margins were incredibly tight through the qualifying weekend. On Saturday, the difference between Herta, who qualified twelfth, and Fittipaldi, who qualified thirtieth, was just 0.8615 seconds over a four-lap, sixteen-turn, ten-mile qualifying run. On Sunday, the difference between Rahal, the final driver to qualify, and Siegel was just 0.2778 seconds.

The 108th running of the Indianapolis 500 was shaping up to be a race anyone could win. Now, teams looked to put qualifying behind them and prepare their cars for the race and the 500 miles that awaited them all.

⚐×⚐

There's a considerable difference in car setups for qualifying and racing. In qualifying, it's all about speed over four laps. Everything is set up to maximize the car for those ten miles, and those ten miles only.

The race is, of course, 500 miles, which makes for a much different car.

The first difference to account for in car setup is the power made from the engine. The extra boost added on Friday for qualifications is taken away, and speeds fall to where they were in previous practice sessions. With the power unit taken care of, attention then turns to fuel.

On race day, cars start with full fuel tanks—18.5 gallons of an E85 blend, a mix of ethanol, eighty-five percent, and gasoline, fifteen percent. That full fuel load weighs nearly 122 pounds and would carry drivers about thirty laps in the race. In comparison, a qualifying car setup holds just enough fuel for seven laps—two warm-up laps, four qualifying laps, and a cool-down lap into the pits. Fuel weight alone is an enormous consideration in developing a race-day setup.

With approximately thirty laps of fuel onboard, drivers must make their tires last for thirty laps. In a qualifying setup, teams and drivers depended greatly on the grip generated by fresh, new tires. That dependence, though, causes tires to wear quickly, and their performance degrades along with tire wear.

Over the weekend in qualifications, drivers saw their cars go from well-balanced to incredibly loose with oversteer in just a couple of laps. That would be unsustainable over 200 laps of racing.

When a race engineer or driver describes "tires falling off," they're not referring to the tires literally falling off the car. Rather, they refer to a drop in grip, and that fall-off can have dramatic effects on cornering speed. If a driver struggles with worn tires, multiple positions in the running order can be lost on every lap.

In qualifying, crews trim out their cars by removing aerodynamic drag and downforce. For the race, they add on aerodynamic downforce.

Straight-line speeds will be slower, but more grip from aerodynamics will take a considerable load off the tires in the turns.

Race setups require a driver to hold onto their car's performance and keep from crashing over a full thirty-lap fuel stint. Ordinarily, the first ten laps are relatively easy to control the car. Handling deteriorates from then on, and the last ten laps of a stint can be a handful for even the most experienced racing drivers. Those ten laps at the end of every stint make a huge difference in the competitiveness of a car over the course of the race.

Finally, concerning a car's handling characteristics, a driver looks for a well-balanced, neutral race setup that allows them to be racy for the entire fuel stint. They want a car that works well in traffic, behind another car, providing them the grip to follow closely in the turns and then delivering the straight-line speed to close the distance on the straightaways and complete an overtaking maneuver.

For the two-hour practice session today, as well as the two-hour session later in the week on Friday, teams and drivers would look to dial in their perfect race-day setups. Naturally, one consideration would be the forecasted weather on race day, specifically the air temperature and the forecasted amount of sun, which would affect the track temperature.

One thing the teams couldn't fully account for in their race setups would be the condition of the track itself on Sunday. The race would take about three hours to complete, and over those hours, the track typically changed considerably. Not only would the track temperature fluctuate, but the amount of rubber left on the track from circulating race cars would add grip. Then there's the possibility of wind and its often-dramatic impact on drivability at different parts of the 2.5-mile oval.

So, teams would develop their setups based on driver feedback today and Friday, then supplement it with judgment based on past experience. Then, during the race, they would make any necessary changes at every pit stop to stay abreast with changes in the track, always searching for just a bit more speed relative to their competitors.

For practice sessions last week, teams were assigned pit boxes. Today, and on through the race, they would be at different locations.

At the Indianapolis 500, teams select their pit boxes in the order their cars qualified. This year, Scott McLaughlin's Team Penske crew earned the first selection, and they chose the pit stall at the far south end of Pit Lane, the closest to the entrance of the warm-up lane inside Turn One.

Specific pit boxes were chosen for a variety of reasons. The biggest reason McLaughlin's team chose that pit box was that it makes for an easy exit after a stop. McLaughlin would only have to dump the clutch and take off straight ahead, without any worry of having to navigate around another car and its pit crew.

Ordinarily, multi-car teams liked to have their cars together, facilitating any communication between one car's crew and another. But that was not always the case. Between pit boxes nine and ten is a break, where Gasoline Alley connects to Pit Lane. Pit box nine offers a clean entry into the box; pit box ten offers a clean exit out of the box. Two other empty pit boxes along Pit Lane made for attractive considerations for teams when selecting on one side or another.

Today and Friday, teams would practice out of their respective pit boxes. On Wednesday, in preparation for the race, the Speedway's facilities crew would adorn the pit wall behind each box with a stencil wrap with the driver, car number, and car name, a tradition that went back to the very beginning. Pit box signage would be just another signal that told everyone the race was coming soon.

The sun shone brightly, and the temperature approached 90 degrees as the cars took to the track for the two-hour practice session. Cars jumped out of the pits the moment they could, and for the most part, they stayed on the track for as long as they could.

All thirty-three drivers participated, and together, they ran a total of 2,655 laps. In terms of the number of laps run, the field was led by first-year driver Blomqvist, who turned 106 laps, or more than half of the race distance. It was just what the rookie needed to further acquaint himself with not only running in long lines of traffic but understanding how his car's handling would change throughout a fuel stint and over time on a sunny Indiana afternoon.

One driver who immediately impressed was Herta in his No. 26 Gainbridge Honda. Herta had posted fast times all last week, and he posted two strong qualifying runs in the heat of the day on Saturday. But the qualifying lines conspired to make him miss a Happy Hour run late on Saturday to make the Fast Twelve, and he had to settle for the thirteenth position, on the inside of Row 5.

Today, Herta showed his car was extremely strong in a race setup. Knowing he would need to work his way up the field on Sunday to get to the lead, Herta started practice deep in a pack of cars. Lap after lap, he closed up on cars and passed them, seemingly with ease. Before long, he was at the front of the pack.

After stopping to refuel and get new tires, Herta did the same. In all, he ran ninety-six laps and recorded the second-fastest time of the session, a 226.222 mph lap. So happy he and his Andretti team were with the car, Herta spent the final moments of the session practicing getting into and out of Pit Lane in race-like circumstances.

Out of his car, the laid-back Californian said, "I definitely felt very good. I felt very confident in the car and what I was able to do. The car just felt solid. It was right underneath me. I was happy."

Herta wasn't the only driver to impress. Canapino, in his second Indy 500, ran only sixty-nine laps in the session in his No. 78 car but seemed at ease in traffic. His top lap was a 225.747, and it placed him squarely in the fourth position on the speed chart, his best showing all month.

In his No. 33 car, Rasmussen continued to showcase his capabilities. True to his form in the previous week, the rookie worked his car through traffic and side-by-side with others. In turning an even 100 laps, he was sixth fastest at 225.718 mph.

While Canapino and Rasmussen were somewhat unanticipated at the top of the time sheets, O'Ward, the driver situated between them at fifth fastest, was not. The twenty-five-year-old Mexican was preparing for his fifth 500, and expectations—his own, as well as those of his Arrow McLaren team and his legion of fans—were high.

In O'Ward's first three 500s, he had finished sixth, fourth, and second. Last year, he finished twenty-fourth, but that finishing position didn't tell the story of his race. O'Ward led a race-high thirty-nine laps and was battling Ericsson for second on lap 193 when the two touched entering

Turn Three. O'Ward lost control of his car and clouted the outside wall, ending his race.

O'Ward was back with a vengeance this month, and he had been slowly working to improve his No. 5 car. Today, he was pretty happy with it, knowing they had the foundations of a solid race car. He turned seventy laps, with the fastest being a 225.738.

The fastest driver on the day was Team Penske's Newgarden, in his No. 2 car. He was fast all last week, both in practice and qualifications, and today proved no different. He ran eighty-nine laps and posted the fastest lap of them all, a 226.238.

When Newgarden got out of his car, his eyes were already set on Sunday's race. "The car feels good," the defending champion said. "I've been happy with it since we showed up. I'm excited to go racing. The team has done a great job.

"We're going to see how things shake up. You've just got to be ready for everything. We're going to make a plan, like qualifying, and we might change the plan. You never know with the Indy 500. We're ready for Sunday."

Today's practice session was run with ambient air temperatures nearing 90 degrees and a track temperature of more than 120 degrees. Now, the track would sit silent before the final practice session on Friday.

Friday, the weather forecast called for cooler temperatures and potentially rain. For the race on Sunday, the forecast called for air temperatures in the low 80s with more rain likely.

Those cooler temperatures would affect the performance of the cars, making them handle differently than today. One driver who seemed unconcerned about the possible impact of a change in weather was Herta.

"A lot can change," Herta told the Associated Press in an interview. "We're going to have a little bit cooler temperatures, but I think all that will happen to us is we'll feel even better. I think we feel really nice. There is stuff we can work on, but I think we're there."

Herta's best Indy 500 finish was eighth place in the second of his previous five starts. He'd had good cars before and qualified as high as second in 2021. However, this year seemed different, and there was a quiet confidence in the No. 26 garage as the door closed at the end of the day.

TUESDAY, MAY 21, 2024

Got Milk?

Traditions reign supreme at the Indianapolis Motor Speedway, and with 107 previous runnings of the Indy 500 already in the history books, there are a lot of established traditions. One of the oldest and most endearing traditions is the presentation of a bottle of milk to the winner in Victory Lane.

After Louis Meyer won his third Indy 500 in 1936, he sat atop his car in Victory Lane and asked for a bottle of buttermilk. Once he received the bottle, he held it aloft in his left hand while he raised three fingers on his right hand to signify his third triumph in the race. The next day, that picture was splashed across newspapers and appeared in newsreels around the country. A tradition was born.

Dairy industry executives saw an immediate sponsorship opportunity, and the tradition grew from there—off and on at the beginning but a repeated practice since 1956. Except for 1993, that is.

After Emerson Fittipaldi won his second Indy 500 in 1993, he infamously swigged *orange juice* in Victory Lane. It seemed "Emmo" owned orange groves in his native Brazil, and he simply wanted to promote the citrus industry. It would be an understatement to say the fan reaction was overwhelmingly negative.

Every winning driver since has at least sipped from the bottle of milk. Lately, ever since Dixon poured the milk over his head after winning in

2008, drivers have followed suit with a milk bath. A hot Indiana afternoon and a milk-soaked driver's uniform made for a fragrant post-race celebration.

This year, the tradition was again sponsored by the American Dairy Association of Indiana, which would pay the winning driver a $10,000 award just for celebrating with the cherished bottle of milk. To prepare appropriately, the association polled all the drivers for their preferences to ensure the right bottle would get delivered to Victory Lane.

This year, twenty-six drivers chose whole milk, five selected 2 percent milk, and two picked skim milk. Lundgaard was pragmatic in selecting skim milk, saying it was what he enjoyed every day for breakfast. Legge was more wishful. After selecting skim milk last year, she settled on whole milk this year, and said, "I chose whole milk because it looks the best in pictures."

FRIDAY, MAY 24, 2024

Carb Day

The past three days, the Speedway had been silent, cars tucked away in their garages, with crew members attending to every last detail, over and over again. Like every year, it was a strange feeling for drivers and teams.

At every other stop on the IndyCar Series race calendar, all the action took place in four days, and just three days on the track. Crews unloaded cars and equipment on Thursday, practice took place on Friday, qualifying got sorted on Saturday, and the race ran on Sunday. After the race, the cars and equipment were packed back onto the trucks, and off the teams went to their next destination.

Not so at Indy. The wait since cars came off the track after Monday's brief practice session until their final practice session today was almost as long as a typical race weekend.

Traditions at Indy abound, and today's session is called Carburetion Day, or Carb Day for short. The name is a holdover from years past when the session was the only post-qualifying practice session and once one where the crews would adjust the carburetors on their engines.

Of course, Indy cars haven't used carburetors on their engines since the early 1960s. All the race engines now utilize fuel injectors for greater performance and reliability. That being said, Carb Day certainly had a better ring to it than Injector Day. Thus, the name stuck.

Drivers and teams all pretty much had the same agenda for today. They all wanted to run exploratory laps to better understand how their cars handled in traffic. They'd be searching for a car that was both comfortable and predictable over a full fuel and tire stint, about thirty laps. They'd be looking to set up comfortably handling cars that would allow drivers to battle for position for the 200 laps of Sunday's race.

Some teams, like all three Team Penske entries, expected to race primarily up front all day. But they couldn't assume they'd be racing in relatively clean air. Even leading cars would have to contend with traffic, either from cars on different pit strategies or slower cars being overtaken and put a lap, or more, down on the leaders.

A well-balanced car was the objective: one that was both fast on its own in clean air as well as quick and maneuverable in the dirty air of traffic. However, the threat for drivers and teams was to do too much experimentation in this short, two-hour practice. It was easy to miss on a setup change, and it could quickly spiral out of control, where subsequent changes only made the car worse and worse. If that happened today, it would leave a team with no choice but to take a big, only partially educated guess on a chassis setup over the next forty-eight hours. And if that went wrong, it would make for a long, frustrating day of chasing speed and competitors on race day.

In the morning, the Speedway gathered together twenty-three past 500 winners, from four-time winner AJ Foyt to last year's winner Newgarden, at the famous yard of bricks. There, they stood for a group photo, each proudly wearing new, blue commemorative Winners' Jackets.

In a new tradition mirroring the famed Green Jacket bestowed every year at professional golf's The Masters Tournament at Augusta National, each of the Winners' Jackets had a special lining with personalized photos from that driver's winning race, along with the Indianapolis Motor Speedway logo embroidered on the left chest pocket.

Jackets were produced for all thirty living past Indy 500 winners, as well as IMS's owner, Roger Penske. Fittingly, a commemorative jacket was also presented to the family of 2003 winner Gil de Ferran, who died unexpectedly on December 29, 2023.

The moment wasn't lost on the past champions and was best summed up by 2013 winner Kanaan, who told the *IndyStar*, "This is awesome. When you talk about winning this race and what that means, more and more people will understand it's not about that day. It lasts for an eternity. Look at the group of drivers here today. If you understand a little bit about racing, you feel pretty cool."

After the ceremony, as if they needed any additional motivation, defending champion Newgarden and the seven other former winners participating in this year's race made their way to Gasoline Alley to change into their driver's uniforms for the final practice session ahead of the race. Already the owner of one jacket, each looked to add another to their collection.

In addition to experimenting and fine-tuning setups for the race, drivers would also practice pit stops, especially their own very important roles in a stop.

Over the course of the race's 500 miles, cars would pit six or seven times, and perhaps even more depending on how yellow caution flags fell. Teams prefer pitting under yellow flag conditions when they can because of the relative pace of their competitors on the racing circuit.

The Pit Lane at Indianapolis has a sixty-mile-an-hour speed limit. In comparison, under green flag racing conditions, cars are at speeds above 215 miles per hour, covering more than the distance of a football field in one second. However, under the yellow flag, track speeds are reduced to about eighty miles an hour. For every second a car is stopped on Pit Lane under a caution flag period, it loses less track distance and position to competitors than it would under the green flag.

Monday was the first day when drivers could use the Pit Lane entry off of Turn Four. Before then, all through the first week of practice and qualifying, they entered the warm-up lane on the inside of Turn Three and then drove it all the way around and into the pits along the main straightaway.

Exiting Turn Four at speed and getting into Pit Lane at its speed limit is a learned skill and one that even veterans at Indianapolis must practice. In the 2022 Indy 500, none other than Scott Dixon ran afoul of the Pit Lane speed limit, and it cost him dearly. Having qualified on the pole and led ninety-five laps of the race, Dixon pitted from the lead on lap 175, looking to make his final stop on the way to his second 500 victory.

However, entering the pits, Dixon locked his rear tires, causing him to be just *one* mile per hour over the Pit Lane speed limit. His drive-through penalty, where he had to drive through the entire Pit Lane at the speed limit while his competitors were racing, took him out of contention for the win. He finished the race in twenty-first position.

Today presented the second and last opportunity to practice getting into the pits, and rookies like Larson took advantage and made several practice runs. They practiced coming off Turn Four and veering to their left, all the while slightly warming their brakes by placing just enough pressure on the brake pedal to cause a little friction but not to significantly slow the car. Then, they judged their braking points and determined exactly when they needed to brake, how hard, and for how long.

Braking hard from speed isn't easy, particularly in a car with a chassis setup designed to facilitate fast left-hand turns. Jumping on the brakes can send the car suddenly to the left. It was a lesson learned the hard way by Ericsson in his rookie year of 2019, as a crash on Pit Lane ended his race.

Once in Pit Lane, however, driver learning wasn't over. They needed to find their pit box, and one aid was to look for visual cues, like its proximity to the infield Pagoda or the scoring pylon.

Next, they needed to come to a stop on their marks, already spray painted in their pit box. On pit stops, their crew members would be lined up on those marks, ready to pounce once the car came to a stop. If a driver missed the marks, the entire crew would be required to readjust their positions before they got to work, wasting valuable time while the competition streaked by.

Lastly, the driver had to take off from the pit box once the car had been serviced. A stall would take considerable time from which to recover. Additionally, too fast out of the box could lead to being out of control and causing an accident. Last year, VeeKay lost control leaving his pit, collecting Palou in the process. Both continued the race, but the Pit Lane incident took two potential race-winning cars out of contention.

Crowds thronged the Speedway on the beautiful, sunny Friday afternoon, with air temperatures in the 80s and a track temperature in the low 100s. The fans clogged the walkway behind Pit Lane and packed the grandstands on the inside of the front straightaway. They were there to not only watch practice but also the Pit Stop Challenge later in the afternoon, as well as the concerts in the Snake Pit in the infield, inside of Turn Three.

As the green flag flew to open the session, the cars wasted no time blasting onto the track, getting up to speed right away, then ducking into the pits for a quick leak check. While the drivers all caught a little break, the crews oversaw every last detail. Any potential problem overlooked now would result in missing valuable practice time later in the session.

Larson and his team were keen to make two full-tank fuel runs so he could better learn how his car would handle as it got lighter from less fuel but less stable with worn tires. Dixon and Castroneves had similar plans to one another but for different reasons. Dixon, happy with his Monday practice, wanted to make long runs to seek out incremental improvements in performance. Castroneves, who had missed a large chunk of Monday's practice while his team troubleshooted an issue, wanted to see if changes they had later made to the car would add speed.

Then, of course, there was the ongoing saga of Ericsson and his Andretti car, No. 28. They were still trying to find speed in their backup car, and Monday had been a productive session. Now, they needed to build upon that success to make their car ready for race day, where Ericsson would be looking to charge forward from the last row on the starting grid.

Almost immediately, Herta picked up where he left on Monday, slicing and dicing through traffic seemingly with ease. Trailing teammates Ericsson and Kirkwood in a well-organized Team Andretti practice, Herta raced up behind Kirkwood and made an overtake with relative ease. Running in traffic with a tow, Herta shot to the top of the speed chart with a lap of 226.220 mph, almost a full mile an hour faster than the second-best lap, that of his teammate Ericsson at 225.418. Both of those top speeds didn't last long, however, as Castroneves, perhaps finding validation in the setup change of his No. 06 Cliffs Honda, posted a 226.939.

While the three Andretti cars of Herta, Ericsson, and Kirkwood were running well, the fourth entry, that of Marco Andretti, was proving to be a handful in traffic. After Monday's session, Andretti had commented that it had been his most productive practice session in over a decade. Today, however, he found his No. 98 MAPEI Honda loose with oversteer. His team went back to the proverbial drawing board and started making adjustments by replacing the entire rear wing assembly.

Andretti wasn't the only unhappy driver. After struggling through nine laps with the slowest of all times, a 215.707, Ferrucci came to Pit Lane, where he complained the aero balance of his car was way off on the front end, causing his car to be very loose mid-corner. With wholesale changes looming, his AJ Foyt Racing crew rolled his No. 14 car back to the garage to make changes and get exact measurements on the car's weight distribution.

It was easy for observers to get fixated on the fast cars that had qualified well, as well as those of traditionally strong racers. VeeKay, for example, drew lots of oohs and ahhs from the crowd as he weaved through traffic in his green and black car, eventually trading overtakes with Dixon, both practicing for a time running in clean air at the front of the pack.

Experienced race fans, however, spent the afternoon looking for those sneaky fast cars that flew a bit under the radar in terms of media attention—typically those cars of the midfield, where differences in performance were minute. Just one small change to improve the car, coupled with a little luck, and it was possible for those cars to race into the top ten even if they started from the back of the grid.

Two sneaky fast cars making their cases for race day were the Dreyer Reinbold cars of Daly and Hunter-Reay. Joining them were Canapino and two rookies, Rasmussen and Blomqvist. And, as being the defending season champion, the championship leader so far this season, and the winner of the last race just two weeks earlier would seem to eliminate Palou from consideration as a dark horse candidate for the race, his pace today seemed faster than it had been all month.

It was difficult to get a clear understanding of relative strengths while practicing in the pack, as there were variables to consider, like offsets in fuel loads and tire wear. Still, those six cars looked racy. Hunter-Reay would be the highest starter on Sunday, in twelfth, on the outside of Row Four. The rest would be further back, but their early Carb Day results had them eyeing a strong run in Sunday's 500.

One hour into the two-hour session, with the track evolving as it warmed over ten degrees and rubber was laid down in the turns, there were no signs of practice slowing down. Most drivers were pounding in the laps, completing full, thirty-lap stints. Meyer Shank was running a lot of laps with its three cars driven by Rosenqvist, Blomqvist, and Castroneves.

Ferrucci got back out on track, but not for long. The changes the Foyt crew had made produced a bit of speed, up to 218 mph, but it wasn't nearly enough, and the poor handling kept Ferrucci on edge in every corner. After just eight laps on his second stint, Ferrucci was back in the pits, and his Foyt team towed him back to the garage for more work.

The second hour also saw Lundqvist get some much-needed time on track. Earlier in the session, his Ganassi crew was forced to bring his No. 8 American Legion Honda back to the garage to remedy some technical issues. Now, Lundqvist hurriedly tried to make up for lost time.

Arrow McLaren spent time trying to get Rossi's No. 7 car to "suck up" better behind any car that might be in front. Rossi had been pleased with his car since it rolled onto the track for the first day of practice, telling reporters the team had made just one setup change. Today, however, he found it difficult to pull up behind a leading car and make the overtake before reaching the turn.

Finally, with less than thirty minutes remaining in the session, Ferrucci was back out on track and much more comfortable with his car. By the end of the session, his lap times were in the 223s, and he would finish as the twenty-fourth fastest over a single lap. The Foyt team's chase for speed was over, and now it was time to get the final adjustments made for race day.

With under a minute left in the session, the yellow flag came out, effectively ending the final practice. In total, the thirty-three drivers ran a collective 2,721 laps. Six drivers ran one hundred or more laps, led by Rahal's 106.

Fastest of them all for a single lap was Dixon, at 227.206 mph. Once out of his car, Dixon said, "It was a good day. The car seems pretty fast, pulls up well, pretty consistent."

His plan for race day, though, was to be patient. "I think you have to take the moment as it is," he said with a grin. "You don't want to rush it too much. We've got some positions to make up. Hopefully move up as quick as possible. I'd like to pass all twenty cars (in front of me) on the first lap, but that's probably not going to happen."

Second-fastest on the day was Castroneves, who further fueled discussion of his "Drive for Five" by running 103 laps, with the fastest a 226.939. The four-time winner seemed ready for race day.

O'Ward led the Chevrolet contingent in the session, finishing in third on the speed chart with a 226.666 lap in his No. 5 Arrow McLaren, just in front of Herta. Herta again showed he and his team had his No. 26 car well-prepped for the race. Like Monday, he had knifed through traffic quickly to get to the front of the pack, and he ended the day with the fourth fastest lap, a 226.220.

Sitting at the top of the speed charts after practice was one thing, but it was not the only thing. Team Penske had been dominant, and they would start alongside one another on the front row. But, today, they likely didn't show their full hands. The fastest of them all was McLaughlin—but only twentieth overall, one spot in front of Power. Defending champion Newgarden finished the day in thirty-second, only ahead of Lundqvist.

As much as Arrow McLaren and the other teams, like Dixon's Ganassi team, hoped, no one expected that form to hold on Sunday.

The unsung heroes of every form of auto racing are the crew members. Drivers, and even their owners and strategists, are accustomed to being recognized by the media and, in turn, fans. Whenever Larson, for example, was out of his race car the last two weeks, he seemingly had a camera and microphone in his face, documenting his every move.

Crew members have an equally important role as anyone else in a successful race team. In fact, an argument can be made that they are more important. The best racer in the world can't overcome a poorly prepared car. Still, pit crews, unless they make a very visible mistake in the race, toil almost entirely in anonymity.

Except for today.

Another tradition of the Indy 500 is the Pit Stop Challenge, held ninety minutes after the completion of Carb Day practice, and in this competition, the pit crew members were the stars in the spotlight.

Crowds crammed the grandstand on both sides of the track, and a DJ provided music to lift the entire atmosphere among the fans, who danced in the aisles and basked in the Indiana sunshine.

Select teams were invited to participate in the challenge, based on their pit stop performances in last year's IndyCar Series, last year's Indy 500, and so far this season in the IndyCar Series. Fourteen teams in total participated, two each from Team Penske, Arrow Team McLaren, Chip Ganassi Racing, Andretti Global, Rahal Letterman Lanigan, and Juncos Hollinger. Single-team entries from Dale Coyne Racing and Meyer Shank Racing rounded out the field.

Much more than bragging rights were on the line too. The Pit Stop Challenge purse totaled $145,000, with the winning team awarded $50,000. Plus, there was a prize room for contestants, containing tools, race-worn items autographed by drivers, and more than a little beer.

Befitting the star turn, Alan Bestwick, one of the track announcers at the Indianapolis Motor Speedway, introduced the team members ahead of every round of the Challenge, and NBC Sports put the team members' names on graphics for its live stream of the contest on Peacock.

In the end, the Team Penske crew of Newgarden's No. 2 Shell Chevy came out on top, sweeping the best-of-three finale with the Arrow McLaren crew of its No. 5 car driven by Pato O'Ward. In the contest, which required the driver to launch the car from a dead stop at the start signal, stop in the pit box, get all four tires changed, and then exit the pit box and cross the finish line, Newgarden's team completed all their stops in less than twelve seconds. The last run was a super impressive 10.792 seconds. Their run of form would certainly breed momentum and confidence heading into the Indianapolis 500 on Sunday.

The victory in the Pit Stop Challenge was the nineteenth for Team Penske, matching the nineteenth pole for the organization delivered by McLaughlin last Sunday. And, of course, Newgarden's win in the 2023 Indy 500 was also the nineteenth for The Captain.

Team Penske had been "Penske Perfect" in its leadup to this year's 500, but the biggest prize of them all awaited after Sunday's race. As the other teams pushed their cars back to Gasoline Alley, their attention shifted to fine-tuning their race cars and race strategy to knock Team Penske off its perch.

Pit stops are absolutely essential to having a successful race day. On many occasions, pit stops have won or lost races. A quick pit stop can pull a car up in the running order, freeing the driver from the difficult task of having to overtake a close, competitive field on the track. On the other hand, a slow stop can push a car down in the running order, making it necessary to pass cars on the racing circuit to improve position.

Then, of course, there are the disastrous pit stops that cause a car to retire from the race completely.

Pits stops are incredibly orchestrated events drilled by teams throughout the year. Fractions of seconds saved on a stop can gain a position or two on competitors.

An efficient, effective pit stop begins with the driver hitting the marks, literally spray-painted on the tarmac of each pit box. It's at those marks where the pit crew members have placed both themselves and their equipment.

At Indy, a counterclockwise track, the left side of the car is next to the pit wall. Therefore, on the lap the car is expected into the pits, the left side tire changers, one for each tire, and the right front tire changer will lay their new tires and the air guns necessary to remove the wheel nut out beforehand. To leave room for the car to enter the box safely, the right rear tire changer waits to get into position until the car arrives.

Hitting those predetermined marks is important. The front left tire changer will even be on his or her knees, bravely waiting for the car to stop an arm's length away from a sixty-mile-an-hour approach speed.

During a stop, a maximum of six crew members are allowed over the wall to service the car. When the car comes to a stop, one crew member inserts the airjack hose into a receptacle on the car, activating the airjacks and lifting the car off the ground.

Simultaneously, the refueler inserts the fuel hose and starts to fill the tank. Filling the tank with eighteen and a half gallons of fuel ordinarily takes the longest time during a pit stop. The fuel tank on Pit Lane is not pressurized, so the fuel flows into the car by gravity. Early in the 500, the fuel storage tank is full, and therefore, the flow out of the tank and into the car is faster. As the race progresses and less fuel remains in the storage tank, the fuel flow into the car during a stop takes longer.

While fuel is being delivered to the car, the four tire changers remove the old tires by reversing out the single wheel nut. They place the worn tire off to one side, attach the new tire to the car, and tighten the wheel nut. The front tire changers, once tires have been replaced, sometimes then make adjustments to the front wing if so desired by the driver.

With new tires mounted on the car, the airjack hose is removed from the car, and it falls back to the ground. Once the fuel has been fully delivered, the fueler removes the hose. At that time, a crew member behind the wall squirts water at the car's fuel tank valve, called a buckeye. That water dilutes any fuel that may have spilled so it won't ignite into a fire.

At the final stages of the stop, the driver will look intently at the right front tire changer for directions. As soon as the crew is done working and the right front tire changer determines it's safe to release the car back into Pit Lane, the driver will be told to leave. With smoke billowing from spinning tires, off they'll go to reenter the race.

The entire stop, done well, takes less than eight seconds as the driver sits stationary on Pit Lane. Those who spend the least amount of time on Pit Lane are usually the ones who celebrate most at the end of a race.

Later in the afternoon, much of the crowd along the frontstretch moved over to the Snake Pit, a concert stage set up inside of Turn Three, for performances featuring the Gin Blossoms and George Thorogood. Decades ago, the Snake Pit was a notorious patch of infield between Turns One and Two where a daily encampment of revelers would take up every day the track was open. Construction of the road course appropriated much of the space, and in time, the Snake Pit went away, only to be reborn as a formal, more organized venue at its present location.

Fans enjoyed the concerts, and the beautiful Indiana afternoon was shared by all. But inclement weather was fast becoming a looming story, and Larson, the subject of one of the biggest, if not the single biggest, stories of the month played a central role.

The weather forecast for Sunday called for rain. Larson, of course, was scheduled to race in the Indy 500 from 12:35 p.m. to about 3:30 p.m., then jump into a helicopter in the infield, fly to the Indianapolis airport, and get on a charter flight to Charlotte, North Carolina, in time for NASCAR's Coca-Cola 600, scheduled to start at 6:00 p.m. Under the best of circumstances, the timeline was incredibly tight. Any rain delay at Indianapolis would throw a gigantic wrench into the well-orchestrated plan.

If it rained on Sunday, which race would become the priority for Larson? He had been strong in his No. 17 Arrow McLaren Honda and had the car, if not the experience in it, to contend for the Indy 500 win. At the same time, his full-time job was racing in the NASCAR Series, and he currently led its season championship.

Larson didn't need to make a decision yet. Hopefully, Sunday's weather would be dry and would make the current speculation moot.

SATURDAY, MAY 25, 2024

Eyes on the Sky

Under overcast skies and temperatures in the seventies, an estimated 200,000 people greeted the thirty-three drivers as they participated in the 2024 AES 500 Festival Parade. The U-shaped route through downtown Indianapolis was packed with joyous spectators, and onlookers could feel the excitement building for tomorrow's race.

A few short miles away, crews placed the final touches on race preparations, tending to the smallest of details, from mounting and balancing tires to taping seams of bodywork, from organizing tools and pit box equipment to planning for a variety of race-day scenarios. Once completed, nervous energy would have them repeat the processes, knowing the smallest oversight could make a significant impact on their race.

Amid those preparations were nervous looks at the weather forecast for Sunday. It wasn't good.

At midday on Saturday, the forecast for Sunday called for scattered thunderstorms in the morning, then strong thunderstorms, with the possibility of large hail and strong winds, during the afternoon.

The threat of rain, particularly after the race began, required race teams to set contingent strategies. The race could be declared official after 101 of the scheduled 200 laps were completed. Thus, it was critical to be up front if and when the rain came. A rain-shortened race victory could fall into the hands of the team that planned its pit stops perfectly, allowing their car to cycle to the front of the pack just before the clouds opened.

In the previous 107 runnings of the Indianapolis 500, rain had postponed and/or shortened the race on twelve occasions. The last instance occurred in 2007 when Dario Franchitti won the first of his three 500 victories in a race shortened to 160 laps, just 400 miles.

Rain forced the 1997 Indy 500 to be run over three days. Heavy, persistent rain wiped out the race completely on Sunday and stopped the race after just fifteen laps on Monday. Finally, on Tuesday, the race resumed with lap sixteen, and Arie Luyendyk completed the rest of the race distance for his second 500 victory.

A concern for every team, the weather forecast threw yet an additional wrench into the well-planned and choreographed schedule of Larson and his Arrow McLaren team. Since practice opened, Larson had proven that his attempt at "the double," both the Indianapolis 500 and the Coaca-Cola 600, was more than just a participation objective. He was a legitimate contender to win both races. Inclement weather, however, could ruin it all.

The fastest ever Indy 500 was the 2021 race, when Castroneves won his fourth 500 in two hours, thirty-seven minutes, and nineteen seconds, at an average speed of 190.690 mph. More likely, however, the Indy 500 would take about three hours to complete. If the day proceeded as scheduled and Larson completed the full 500 miles, he could make it to Charlotte Motor Speedway before the 600-miler started.

But any rain delaying the start of the Indy 500, or later, bringing the race to a halt, would complicate matters tremendously.

Importantly for Arrow McLaren, IndyCar rules no longer allowed for teams to have a relief driver step into a car mid-race. If Larson started the 500 but couldn't finish, his No. 17 car would be retired from the race, and the impact on prize money could be substantial.

Earlier in the week, it was speculated that former winner Kanaan, the Arrow McLaren advisor who had been working closely with Larson all month, would take part in a special refresher session on track Thursday to be eligible to race in place of Larson. However, doing so would have required the team to withdraw Larson as the driver of the car, and the team felt it was too early to make such a rash decision.

As a result, that left just one possible driver to take the place of Larson to start the race, that being rookie Nolan Siegel, who was bumped from the field on the final day of qualifying last weekend. If Siegel stepped in and replaced Larson, however, the car would be removed from its qualified position in the middle of the second row and placed at the back of the field, on the outside of Row 11.

After participating in the 500 parade earlier in the day, Larson flew to North Carolina to qualify for the 600, after which he was scheduled to return to Indianapolis where he would spend the night before the Indy 500. How his well-planned schedule, as well as that of his stout Arrow McLaren No. 17 car, played out on Sunday would be, in large part, determined once again by Mother Nature.

SUNDAY, MAY 26, 2024

Race Day

Before the skies lightened, still under the dark of night, fans trekked to the Speedway for the Indianapolis 500, the largest single-day sporting event in the world. For a great many, it's an annual tradition that has been repeated for decades.

Gates to the massive facility opened at 6:00 a.m., and thousands of fans were already in line, having spent the night outside the track, reveling in the world's biggest street party. Once on the grounds, those with infield standing tickets rushed for prime viewing positions on the many berms in the infield.

The anticipation of the race grew as every minute passed. But so did the anxiety of a rainy weather forecast. Rain, and at times heavy rain, seemed an inevitability. The only questions that remained were when it would start and how long would it last. That would determine when the Indy 500 would start, if at all, and how long the race would last.

Still, fans were hopeful, just like the race teams and their drivers, that the race would be held. Determined, they took to their duties. Fans either trudged off to their seats or wandered over to the Snake Pit, where a DJ got festivities moving at 7:00 a.m. In the garages, crews pored over every detail in their extensive race day preparations.

Ordinarily, Race Day at Indianapolis involves a tremendous amount of pageantry. As well over 300,000 spectators file into the grounds and spread out through the facility, bands, including Purdue University's "All American" Marching Band, circle the track, adding to the festival-like ambiance. Vintage race cars, often driven by retired drivers, cruise around, a reminder of the rich history and heritage of the event.

This race day was different. With inclement weather on the horizon, Speedway officials spent the morning making changes to the schedule and issuing updates on every media platform they could, from the track's public address system and video boards to social media platforms like X and Facebook.

Finally, at 11:15 a.m., with a thunderstorm rapidly approaching, the Speedway issued a weather advisory, warning fans to leave the grandstands and seek shelter. Most flocked to the spaces underneath the grandstands. Meanwhile, the thirty-three race cars, normally on the frontstretch in their starting positions at this time, remained safely and securely tucked inside their garages.

The drivers did the best they could to pass the time. Patiently waiting is not something that comes naturally to a great many racers—it's just not the way they're wired.

Some drivers were fully suited, walking anxiously around their cars, chatting from crew member to crew member. Others, like Will Power, hadn't bothered to dress in their uniforms yet. His teammate, polesitter McLaughlin, took the opportunity to get more sleep in his motorhome.

Larson was one driver who was busy, not only with the constant media attention thrown his way but with meetings with his two race teams: his Arrow McLaren team at Indy and his Hendrick Motorsports team in North Carolina. The weather had forced his hand.

All through preparations for both races, Larson insisted his priority was the NASCAR race. But, this morning, he was in Indianapolis, as planned, and not yet in North Carolina. Plus, this Indy 500 campaign had been in the works for well over a year. Larson had been embedded in the Arrow McLaren team for last year's 500, working in the pit stand to gain an understanding of the entire Indy 500 experience.

Additionally, there had been a tremendous amount of investment in Larson's Indy 500 campaign by all involved, including Larson, Arrow

McLaren, and Hendrick Motorsport. Discussions among all the parties drove to a consensus. Larson broke the news to NBC Sports when he told them, "I'm here at Indy, and I'm staying at Indy."

The ramifications of his decision would be dealt with later. NASCAR is a series that has a playoff formula at the end of its season, and it stipulates that a driver must start every scheduled race to be eligible for the playoffs. Larson, currently leading the championship points in the series, would, by the rules, be ineligible for the playoffs.

Larson and his team decided they would cross that bridge when they came to it. For today, he would start as an IndyCar driver and look to take part in his first-ever Indianapolis 500. If, that is, the weather cooperated.

In their updates, Speedway officials said the heavy rain would last for approximately two hours. Wouldn't you know it; they were correct—the rain stopped after two hours.

Immediately, workers began efforts to dry the track. Planning well ahead, the Speedway had rented a fleet of NASCAR's Air Titan drying system trucks. The Air Titan system used onboard compressed air to push water off the racetrack and down onto the track's apron, where vacuum trucks removed the moisture. The Speedway then followed behind with its jet dryers to remove any excess water remaining on the surface.

As track workers continually repeated their drying processes, the Speedway issued an update stating they planned to start the race at 4:45 p.m. It was a last-ditch effort to get the race started and, barring any further rain interruptions, completed.

There are no lights at the Indianapolis Motor Speedway, and sunset would come at 9:03 p.m. More importantly, local law required the Speedway to cease activities at 8:15 to allow for the safe egress of the massive crowd before darkness. Officials hoped to shoehorn the race within those parameters.

Almost every fan had persevered through the storm, and they made their way back to their seats. At 3:00, they gave a rousing cheer as teams rolled their cars out to their spots on the starting grid on the front straight.

The drivers, meanwhile, got back into their pre-race routines. Some had passed the time doing physical exercise, including stretching and reflex testing. Others passed the time in quiet reflection and meditation. Still others took their minds off the race by chatting with team members, sponsors, and others around the garages in Gasoline Alley.

Eventually, the drivers made their way to the green room in the Pagoda along the front straight for the driver introductions. Larson walked alongside his wife, Katelyn, and their oldest son, carrying his youngest on his right hip. The five Ganassi drivers—Dixon, Palou, Armstrong, Lundqvist, and Simpson—posed together for a team picture.

The start of the Indy 500 was drawing near. Would Ganassi Racing be celebrating at the end of the day?

The driver introductions are the sign that the race is imminent, and this year, it took place on the Victory Lane platform. Tradition has the eleven rows introduced, starting with Row 11 and working forward to the front row.

Many drivers enjoyed taking their children up on the platform to share the experience. On this day, starting with Row 11, Rahal walked on, holding the hand of his daughter, and lined up with his fellow final row starters, Ericsson and Legge.

Dixon hadn't previously been familiar with being introduced with the relatively low Row 7 starters, but there he was with his three children, alongside Castroneves and his daughter. Joining them on the podium was Marco Andretti, marking the fifty-second Indy 500 with an Andretti in the field.

More families made the trek up to the platform. Ed Carpenter was introduced with his Row 6 starters, alongside his three children. Hunter-Reay brought his three sons with him for the introduction of Row 4. Lastly, Larson brought his children up when Row 2 took to the platform.

Finally, the front row was introduced, and all three Team Penske drivers took to the platform. McLaughlin looked resplendent in his throwback driver's uniform, a replica of the uniform Rick Mears wore in 1988 when he piloted a Pennzoil-liveried Team Penske car to both the pole position and the race win. In a red uniform with a bold yellow stripe and "Pennzoil" emblazoned across his chest, McLaughlin was dressed for success and looking to celebrate on that very same platform after 500 miles of racing.

Off of the platform, drivers worked their way down to the grid formation on the straightaway, where they tended to the final preparations for the biggest race of the year. Around them, as the sun peeked out from behind the cloud cover, the rest of the pre-race program continued.

The Indy 500 had always been closely tied to Memorial Day weekend, a national holiday dedicated to the American servicemen and women who have given their lives to preserve freedom and liberty, not just for the United States and its citizens, but also for other countries around the world. As such, the military had always played an important role at the Speedway.

After a military color guard paraded onto the Victory Lane platform, the gigantic crowd quieted, joining a moment of silent recognition of the American military personnel who had lost their lives in service to their country.

Following the moment of silence, Archbishop Charles Thompson delivered the invocation. When he was finished, silence stayed over the track while a military rifle company took to the platform, where they performed a twenty-one-gun salute to their fallen comrades. Finally, a bugleman performed "Taps."

After the military traditions, Phillip Phillips sang "God Bless America," accompanying himself with an acoustic guitar. Following him, Jordin Sparks performed a resounding, acapella version of the "Star-Spangled Banner." As she was concluding, a formation of six F-16 Fighting Falcons of the US Air Force Thunderbirds roared down the straightaway.

At that point, drivers were called to their cars, where they hugged and kissed family members, shook hands with their pit crew members, and began their final preparation. They inserted their radio earplugs, donned fire-proof balaclavas, and zipped up their driver's uniforms. Then they pulled on their helmets, strapped them tight, and climbed into their cockpits, where they worked with a crew member to tightly fasten their safety harnesses. Lastly, they put on their gloves and got ready to go to work.

Only two pre-race traditions remained.

First, Jim Cornelison joined the Purdue band at the front of the field to perform "Back Home Again in Indiana," and was joined by a great many spectators in the crowd. Just as his last words of "When I dream about the moonlight on the Wabash, How I long for my Indiana home" rang through the PA, the formation of Thunderbirds returned, this time breaking formation to spiral off in different directions.

With that, the crowd and television cameras turned their attention once again to the Victory Lane platform to await the most famous words in auto racing. In his role as chairman of the Indianapolis Motor Speedway, Roger Penske took to the platform, where he said, "Drivers, start your engines!"

Starters fired the engines, and to the relief of everyone, all thirty-three cars successfully started. Then, led by McLaughlin, the cars slowly drove off and crew members scampered off the track with their equipment. As the drivers drove into Turn One, they got a look for the first time at a changed racetrack.

First, and most notably, the grandstands were packed, which made the already narrow track seem even more narrow than it had all month. For experienced drivers, they were prepared for that sensation. The rookies, however, had to adjust. They would notice it much more when they came off Turn Four and looked down the main straightaway, which at first glance would look like a little black ribbon down the middle of a gigantic canyon of people.

Secondly, the torrential rain of the day had changed the racetrack. Most of the rubber that had been laid down on the track over the countless laps run over the past two weeks was washed off. It was now a "green" racetrack, and it posed yet another challenge for race teams and their crews. They wouldn't understand the impact on their cars' handling, however, until they were at race speed.

As the cars drove into Turn One, drivers aligned themselves into a single file, weaving from side to side to create friction and warm the surface of their tires. Immediately, Ilott discovered a problem with his No. 6 Arrow McLaren car; it wouldn't shift gears.

As the field rounded Turn Four to complete its first of two parade laps, Ilott ducked into the pits. Once there, his crew set out to troubleshoot the cause and swapped out his electronic steering wheel as a precaution. That seemed to solve the problem. As the race hadn't started yet, he hadn't lost a lap to the field. However, by the time he got back on the track, the field was by him to start the pace lap, and he couldn't get back to his original starting position on the outside of Row 5. Instead, he brought up the rear of the field. It wasn't the perfect scenario to start the race, but it was a lot better than being a lap or two down to the field.

After the two parade laps came the pace lap, and the cars formed the eleven rows of three in Turn Two. The honorary driver of the pace car, retired baseball superstar and Hall of Famer Ken Griffey Jr., sped off into the distance to create separation between himself and the field of race cars. At that point, McLaughlin took over the responsibility of pacing the field down the backstretch.

Perfectly aligned through Turns Three and Four, each row about one hundred feet behind the row ahead, and with Griffey safely at the entrance of Pit Lane, McLaughlin raised the speed slightly. When the first half of the field entered the front straightaway, officials, happy with a fair alignment, threw the green flag to start the race. Immediately, teams radioed their drivers, "Green, green, green."

With the race begun, drivers jockeyed their cars for position, going low on the inside of the track to take advantage of drafting off the slipstream of cars ahead of them. At the yard of bricks, they fanned outward to their right, looking to make opportune overtakes through Turn One.

McLaughlin led his teammates, Power and Newgarden, through Turn One, followed by Ferrucci and Rossi, both ahead of a cautious Larson, and roared through the south end and onto the backstretch.

With the entire field almost safely through Turn One, disaster struck at the tail end of the pack. Blomqvist, making his first 500 start, pinched too low into the turn, perhaps feeling squeezed by a car on his right. He drove onto the concrete curbing, and when he experienced the dramatic cross-weight transfer in his car, his cold tires weren't able to help him remain in control. Losing the back end of his racer, Blomqvist spun toward the wall.

Behind him, Ericsson passed Fittipaldi on the outside to gain a position, but once he completed the overtake, he found Blomqvist spinning into his path. Ericsson drove straight into Blomqvist's car, launching the nose of his car into the air and both cars hard into the outside retaining wall.

Trailing the accident and lower on the track, Fittipaldi backed off the throttle to avoid the incident in front of him. But Ilott, who had joined up to the back of the field, couldn't slow down fast enough in reaction. On the inside, Ilott was traveling too fast and bumped into Fittipaldi's left side, causing the RLL driver to spin one and a half loops down the short chute, before backing into the wall.

Although the impact was relatively soft, the damage to Fittipaldi's No. 30 Five Hour Energy Honda car proved terminal. Before the race was a half-lap old, three drivers' dreams of glory had vanished.

During the ensuing caution period, McLaughlin led the pack single file behind the pace car as safety crews cleared the track of debris. After four hours of growing anticipation and all the pageantry and excitement of the pre-race activities, the slow laps allowed drivers and crews to take deep breaths, calm down a little, and plan out their next moves.

Dixon was one driver busily calculating his strategy. He had started twenty-first and took good advantage of his outside position on Row 7 to move up six positions before the yellow flag flew. He now found himself fifteenth in the queue, directly behind his teammate, Palou.

Once the pits were opened by race officials, five cars at the end of the field—Daly and Rahal among them—took advantage of the caution period to change tires and top off their fuel. They were, in effect, free pits stops, for they had very little to lose with respect to track position. They were at the back when they pitted, and once back on track with full fuel loads, they were still at the back. Their advantage, however, was they now had more fuel, and therefore more strategic options going forward that the other twenty-five teams didn't.

Before the race resumed, it lost another competitor. Rookie Marcus Armstrong drove his green No. 11 Ridgeline Lubricants Chip Ganassi Racing car into the pits, smoke billowing from his Honda engine. His first attempt at the Indy 500 lasted just six laps in total, with just a thirtieth-place finish as a return for the team's hard work in the race's lead-up.

Restarts were always going to present a steep learning curve for Larson, as they were about the only thing he couldn't practice ahead of time. Restarts come after caution periods, and since all the cars were bunched up under the yellow caution flag, they afforded the best opportunity to overtake several cars in a short period.

Restarts are dictated by the leader of the pack. Once race officials give notice that they will go green on the next lap, the pace car accelerates off in the distance, leaving control of the speed of the pack to the leader.

When McLaughlin was in Turn Four, he accelerated, and officials, determining procedures had been followed and the restart was fair, flew the green flag, signaling to the drivers they could race for positions. At the same time, radios notified all drivers that the green flag was out.

Larson, however, found himself in the wrong gear at the wave of the green. When he mashed the throttle, he spun his tires and got bogged down. Quickly, cars passed him in droves on the outside of Turn Four and at the start of the front stretch, where, as cars scrambled for position, he bumped his right front wheel alongside Hunter-Reay's left rear wheel. Avoiding a crash, Larson dropped six places on the track, down to twelfth position, before hitting the start/finish line for the start of lap nine.

Meanwhile, Herta discovered his car was handling very much to his liking, and he began to carve his way forward. After losing ground to Palou on the restart, he quickly got back around both him and Hunter-Reay. Then he got around Sato and his teammate, Kirkwood, to settle into ninth place, right behind Rosenqvist. His car handling well in traffic, the only complaint Herta had was a radio message back to his team saying he was hitting the rev limiter entering Turn Three.

At the front, McLaughlin continued to lead comfortably, the first laps he had ever led in the Indy 500. His two Team Penske teammates, Power and Newgarden, were content to follow in his slipstream and conserve fuel, as was Ferrucci.

Deeper in the field, Hunter-Reay was battling a difficult car. After Carb Day practice, he and his Dreyer & Reinbold team opted for an aggressive, low-downforce setup for the race, but it wasn't working on the green racetrack. Confusing to Hunter-Reay, the car was extremely inconsistent, one moment reasonably fine, the next very loose in the mid-corner. Now, with his tires worn, Hunter-Reay found his car exceptionally loose with oversteer, and he fell back.

Rasmussen was the next to take advantage, and on lap eighteen, he overtook Hunter-Reay into sixteenth place to follow behind Dixon. The rookie was now going to school with one of the sport's masters directly in front of him.

On lap twenty-one, Legge's Honda engine started smoking as it ran down the backstretch. She pulled into the pits, and as her DCR crew lifted the cowling to get a look at the engine, she resigned herself to the fact that her fourth Indy 500 was over and climbed from her red and pink car.

Legge's mechanical problem raised an alert for the other Honda runners in the field. Hers was the second Honda to experience problems in the race's early stages, and while the diagnosis of the specific problems was still forthcoming, engineers up and down Pit Row took second and third looks at the real-time telemetry data being returned from their cars.

The caution flag flew to allow track personnel to examine the track to determine if Legge's expiring Honda had dropped any oil on the racing surface. When the pits opened on lap twenty-three, McLaughlin led almost the entire field onto Pit Lane.

As McLaughlin and the others received service from their teams, the cars who had pitted on lap four, minus Legge, cycled to the front. Sting Ray Robb now led the Indy 500 for the first time in his career, followed by Daly and two of the three remaining RLL cars, Lundgaard and Rahal. They were out of sequence with the other twenty-four cars, but they had completely flipped their track position, from the back to the front. Now they hoped for future caution flags to fall their way so they could keep their positions.

McLaughlin got out of the pits in front of both Power and Newgarden, and they were followed in quick succession by Ferrucci, Rossi, and Rosenqvist. Further down the order, the Juncos Hollinger crews got their jobs done well, allowing both Canapino and Grosjean to jump past Hunter-Reay and Andretti. They exited the pits in twenty-second and twenty-third but knowing four cars needed to pit well before they would. Their march forward was going to plan.

When the green flag flew to resume racing on lap twenty-six, Daly pounced to take the lead from Robb in Turn One. Behind them, McLaughlin got around Rahal, and Ferrucci swept past both Newgarden and Power to follow just behind.

Power, who had followed McLaughlin easily during the first stint of the race, soon found himself unable to fight off the cars behind him. In two laps, he fell from sixth to eleventh. It was the first visible chink in the armor of mighty Team Penske all month.

The green flag racing, however, was short-lived. With the cars bunched together on the restart, drivers up and down the order were taking risks ordinarily not seen until the race's latter stages. On lap twenty-eight, the aggressive driving took yet another rookie out of the race.

Barreling down the frontstretch into Turn One, four cars found themselves side by side, at speed. Two cars would have been a challenge. Four cars would almost always be impossible.

Pinched low by the other drivers, Lundqvist entered Turn One too low. Before hitting the apex, he lost control of his car, catching it momentarily as the rear end swung out, but losing it once and for all a fraction of a second later. Out of the groove and with no grip, Lundqvist swung high and hit the wall, first with his right front, then with the entire right side.

Just twenty-seven laps into the Indy 500, three of the six rookies, two of them driving for Chip Ganassi Racing, were out of the race. Only twenty-eight cars remained in contention.

In any auto race, drivers looked to get into a rhythm, and no place more so than at the Indianapolis 500. Two hundred laps around the 2.5-

mile oval made for a long race, and at some point in time, drivers and teams just wanted to put mileage behind them.

They didn't want to lose positions on the track, but they wanted to get through long stints of green flag racing. First, it allowed them to understand the handling characteristics of their cars as the track continued to evolve, both from rubber being laid in the groove and changes in temperature as the day progressed. That understanding led to changes made to the chassis, either through pit stops or inside the car, with the drivers' tools.

Secondly, with the threat of weather removed, it was going to be a long race. They weren't going to win the race at the forty-lap mark, or even the 140-lap mark. A prevailing strategy at the Speedway had been to spend the first 450 miles consistently improving the car and working steadily to improve position by occasional overtakes on track and in the pits. Then, for the final fifty miles, it would be time to take the wraps off and push the car to the limit.

The start-and-stop nature of this year's race had not been particularly beneficial for anyone. All the teams looked to get a sustained run of green flag racing under their belts.

At the restart on lap thirty-three, McLaughlin and Ferrucci fanned out wide and got past both Daly and Robb to resume their battle for the lead. Behind them, somehow the pack got through Turn One, cars nose-to-tail and side-by-side.

Racy in a car that was lighter for its relative lack of fuel, Daly eased back around both Ferrucci and McLaughlin to once again take the lead. This time, the No. 3 and No. 14 cars were keen to duck behind and save fuel for what they hoped was a full stint under green.

Slightly further back, Herta continued his steady rise in the classification, easily cutting his way through traffic and working his way into seventh place by lap thirty-nine. Palou and Dixon were stalled, however, running in tenth and fifteenth positions. Canapino, meanwhile, was eighteenth, battling with Sato right in front of him.

Running out of fuel, Robb finally had to pit his No. 41 Chevrolet-powered car on lap forty-two, with Daly following him in his No.

24 car, also powered by Chevy. Remarkably, the Honda-powered cars of Lundgaard and Rahal were able to stretch their stints to laps forty-five and forty-seven, demonstrating they could achieve better fuel mileage than the Chevys. Teams up and down Pit Lane filed that bit of information away to carefully consider when forming their late-race strategies.

After the pit stops, while the cars raced out on track, strategists were busy crunching numbers in their pit stands. At quarter-distance, they contemplated their end-of-race strategies. They each started by determining a small window, or range, as to which lap they would make their *final* pit stop, using historical data on the timing and duration of caution flags to create multiple scenarios.

With a final pit stop tentatively planned and still very much written in pencil, they then plotted backward. Of the twenty-seven cars still in contention, all but five—the cars of Daly, Robb, Lundgaard, and Rahal, along with the third Ganassi rookie, Simpson, who had made an extra stop on lap thirty-nine—were on essentially the same strategy.

While the strategists worked their calculators, the rest of the crews checked, double-checked, and triple-checked equipment, tire pressures, and anything else they could get their hands on to put their nervous energy to good use.

Pitting under the green put Daly, Robb, Lundgaard, Rahal, and Simpson a lap down to the leader. However, McLaughlin, looking to both control the race pace and conserve fuel, eased off enough on the main straight to allow Daly to overtake him.

While Daly led the line of cars on track, he was at the tail end of McLaughlin's lap, nearly two-and-half miles behind. He looked for another caution flag, where the pace car would pick up the leader of the race, McLaughlin, and allow him to circle the entire track and latch onto the back of the pack.

At the fifty-lap mark, McLaughlin led from Ferrucci, followed by Rossi, Herta, Newgarden, Palou, Rosenqvist, O'Ward, Larson, and Rasmussen. At this point in the race, the front of the field was most interested in ticking away the laps and getting closer to the finish. If overtaking opportunities presented themselves, they would pounce. But, for now, they were content with running with their competitors and learning where their cars worked well and where their cars needed improvement relative to their rivals.

Running in fourth, Herta was pleased with his car. He had shown great pace, particularly in heavy traffic, in the previous week's two practice sessions. That speed had carried over to the race, where he had steadily moved up, overtaking cars all around the speedway.

Larson had regrouped from his error on the first restart and had made up positions to run ninth, where he continued his steep learning curve. On his rear wing was Rasmussen, who had been overtaking cars with flair, picking up six positions in the last ten laps.

Rosenqvist, too, was feeling good running up front. Having started ninth, he was currently running seventh, having traded places back and forth at the bottom half of the top ten as drivers tested themselves and one another.

Unfortunately for Rosenqvist and his Meyer Shank team, that feeling was short-lived. On lap fifty-six, his Honda engine started smoking on the south end of the track. Knowing the engine failure was terminal, Rosenqvist slowed and parked his No. 60 AutoNation/Sirius XM car on the inside of the track by a break in the wall in the backstretch. With Blomqvist out on the first lap, it meant Castroneves, running in fifteenth, was left to fly the Meyer Shank flag alone. Rosenqvist's engine failure was the third suffered by Honda and only further raised concerns among the Honda runners left in the race.

The caution flag was perfectly timed for the leaders, and when the pits were opened by officials, the twenty-one cars on the primary fuel strategy ducked into Pit Lane. This time, Rossi's Arrow McLaren crew got him out ahead of McLaughlin who battled a balking clutch exiting his stall, and he settled into third on the track, behind Daly and Robb. Herta also jumped Newgarden in the pits, placing him fifth on the track, third among the cars on the primary fuel strategy. Further behind, Canapino picked up a handful of places and was now running in thirteenth.

Of course, there couldn't be winners on pit road without losers. While Arrow McLaren got Rossi out first, O'Ward wasn't as fortunate. He lost nine positions on Pit Lane and would now have to fight back from eighteenth. Hunter-Reay, still fruitlessly searching for fixes to his oversteering race car, lost seven places and was twenty-third.

VeeKay, who entered the pits in eleventh, picked up a couple of spots. But, in doing so, race officials noted an unsafe release, where VeeKay had dumped the clutch, spun his rear tires, and blindly shot out of his pit box, bumping his way into the right-most lane. His penalty moved him to the back of the field, where he would start his work all over again. It marked the second year in a row an avoidable Pit Lane mistake sent VeeKay and his very capable ECR car to the back of the pack.

As the caution flag period wound down, four cars at the tail end of the pack came in to top off their fuel, including Lundgaard and Rahal. That put them just three laps to the good of the cars on the primary fuel strategy—not quite a wash but pretty close. In doing so, it was now the teams of Daly and Robb, circling in first and second, respectively, against the rest.

The green flag flew again at the start of lap sixty-four, and the wild racing resumed right where it had dropped off. There's a saying in motorsports: "Cautions breed cautions."

Laps run under the yellow caution flag bunch the pack up, eliminating the margins that had been built under green-flag racing conditions. Bunched together, drivers know restarts afford the easiest and best ways to make an overtake. Of course, all the drivers know that, so they're all searching for any way to get past the driver in front of them.

Two-wide in the turns and three-wide down the straights, somehow the field got through the first couple of laps unscathed and did not cause another immediate caution. Robb led from McLaughlin, the pole sitter happy to follow and save fuel, lifting off the throttle ahead of Turns Three and Four, while Herta and Daly traded third and fourth for a stretch.

Rossi fell to eighth, ahead of the charging Rasmussen, and trailed Palou. Canapino jumped up to twelfth ahead of Dixon, who, being the savvy veteran of twenty-one previous Indy 500s, settled himself in line. The second half of the race would be where he sought to show his hand.

On laps seventy-seven and seventy-nine, Robb and Daly pitted from the front, leaving the point to McLaughlin, followed closely by Herta. On the next lap, the clock clicked past 6:00 p.m., presenting yet another consideration for drivers and teams.

No one had ever driven, much less raced, at Indianapolis at such a late hour. Practice and qualifying sessions always ended at 6:00 p.m. Now, with 300 miles of the race left, drivers would have to cope with the glare and shadows of a setting sun, and, along with their teams, have to adapt to plummeting track temperatures.

Leading up to the race, it might have been predictable that McLaughlin, Herta, and Newgarden would be running first through third at lap eighty. Somewhat of a surprise, however, was Rasmussen running in seventh, hot on the tail of Palou, and ahead of his heralded fellow rookie, Larson. His strong run wasn't a fluke of some far-fetched pit strategy. He had earned his high placement with daring overtakes on track.

Another burgeoning story was that of Canapino, who, coupling great pit stops from his Junco Hollinger team with on-track passes, was now racing in eleventh, up eleven spots from the start. At less than half-distance, he was halfway to the front. But, from there, progress would undoubtedly be more difficult to achieve.

⚑×⚑

On lap eighty-six, the rear of Herta's car bobbled in Turn One, and he could not catch it. Herta, directly in front of Newgarden, spun, looping the car and striking the outside wall with his front wing. Believing his car to be unrepairable, Herta exited his No. 26 and took a seat in one of the safety vehicles. After having a strong two weeks of practice and showing his car was every bit as much the class of the field as any other, his chance for a maiden Indy 500 victory was now over.

Again, the timing of the caution flag was beneficial to McLaughlin and the leaders as he led them into the pits on lap eighty-eight. Robb and Daly, still committed to their alternate strategy, stayed out and were joined, once again, by Lundgaard. VeeKay also stayed out, his crew feeling the need to change strategy to recover from the earlier mistake in the pits and gain track position. In doing so, VeeKay inherited the lead.

In the middle of Pit Lane, problems crept up, first for Ilott and Kirkwood, and, as a result, Carpenter. It started with Ilott, who slowed in the right lane, much to the surprise of Kirkwood, who collided with him, pushing Ilott past his pit box and into Carpenter's, where he stopped.

Kirkwood continued down toward his stall, but Carpenter, following the duo, had no place to go, coming to a stop short of his unexpectedly occupied box. Ilott's Arrow McLaren crew quickly pushed him back into his stall, allowing the ECR crew to push in their stranded driver. But the damage had been done. They would fall to the back of the line.

There, they would be met in four laps time by Kirkwood, who was given a drive-through penalty when the track went green on lap ninety-two, meaning he had to drive through the pits at just sixty miles an hour while the cars on the track accelerated to over 215 mph. It was a tough penalty for Kirkwood and his Andretti team to swallow, for they felt Ilott had caused the chaos by inexplicably slowing in the right lane rather than the left lane to enter his pit box.

Regardless, after working his way from twenty-eighth after his first pit stop to fifteenth entering this last pit stop, Kirkwood had it all to do again, now back down in twenty-fifth.

While the timing of the caution flag benefited the pack, it was also beneficial to Daly and Robb, who had pitted nine and eleven laps earlier. If another yellow flag came out in about twenty laps, they would have an opportunity to join the pit sequence of the pack, and to do so at the front of the field. For drivers who started twenty-ninth and twenty-third, it was a welcomed turn of events.

At the halfway mark, Newgarden, benefitting from a quick pit stop to jump to the front, led, followed by Ferrucci, McLaughlin, Robb, and Daly. Larson sat steady in seventh, just ahead of Rossi in eighth and Castroneves in ninth, the highest the four-time winner had been all day. Rasmussen and Canapino continued to impress in tenth and eleventh.

The No. 5 of O'Ward and the No. 12 of Power ran a surprising twelfth and thirteenth but only about five seconds off the lead. Both had been quiet thus far in the race.

In the first stint, Power seemed to run easily behind McLaughlin in second. However, after the first pit stop, he steadily dropped positions on the racetrack, complaining of being slow out of Turns Two and Four, and therefore, carrying less momentum down the straights, where he found himself trying to defend his position entering Turns One and Three.

O'Ward had started eighth and ran as high as seventh before getting shuffled back a few positions during the first pit stop. Then, his second pit stop was even worse, and he lost nine places, coming back on track in eighteenth on lap fifty-nine. He slowly worked his way up but had spent most of his time bouncing around positions just behind the top ten.

The two cars were not in the positions they expected to be in at the halfway point. Both drivers knew that if they were going to contend for the win, they needed to make their moves now.

Meanwhile, Herta's No. 26 car was back in the Andretti garage in Gasoline Alley, where the team determined the crash damage was minimal. In the accident, the only thing that made contact with the wall was the front wing and nose cone, a very easily replaced assembly. That and new tires were all the car needed to return to the track, so they had Herta prepare himself.

Herta was out of contention for a high finish in the race, but he and his team were eyeing the season championship. Herta would resume racing hoping further attrition in front of him would allow him to creep up a few places in the final classification, earning valuable points that might push him to his first IndyCar Series season title.

On lap 107, Dixon got a strong run on the ill-handling Power coming out of Turn Two and pulled alongside him on the left side at the front of the backstretch. Behind the two, Hunter-Reay got an even stronger run on the two cars exiting the corner.

As Dixon completed his overtake of Power, Hunter-Reay committed himself to overtaking Power and Dixon on the inside of the track, next to the infield. Dixon, however, not being warned over the radio by his spotter perched high above Turn Three, was unaware that Hunter-Reay had closed the distance so quickly and was coming up the inside.

With Dixon overtaking Power, Hunter-Reay thought his long-time rival would drift back higher on the track to prepare to enter Turn Three. Instead, Dixon surprisingly drifted slightly to his left, toward the inside of the track, and right into the path of Hunter-Reay.

At 220 miles per hour, Hunter-Reay found himself pinched at the bottom of the racetrack, between Dixon and the grass. Dixon's left rear tire smacked into the right front tire of Hunter-Reay, breaking Hunter-Reay's right front steering arm on his suspension and sending him into the grass.

On the rain-slicked grass at the edge of the back straight, Hunter-Reay spun clockwise, a full 360-degree spin in front of oncoming traffic, before he miraculously recovered his car in a straight line. He drove immediately into the warm-up lane on the inside of Turn Three and made his way into his pit box. There, his Dreyer & Reinhold crew saw the suspension damage and decided to retire the car.

Interestingly, in tearing down the car after the race, the team found the cause of Hunter-Reay's ill-handling race car. When Larson and Hunter-Reay bumped wheels on the race's first restart, the impact had damaged the left-rear lower wishbone of the suspension, shearing the nut off where it connected to the suspension upright. The bolt that held it all together then backed out, creating an inordinate amount of travel in Hunter-Reay's suspension.

It explained the mysterious handling of Hunter-Reay's car and his drop to the back of the field. Still, the fact that he'd held it together for over one hundred laps and was keeping up, and overtaking both Power and Dixon, said a lot about Hunter-Reay's abilities in a racing car.

With the yellow caution flag out again, race teams had a decision to make: pit or stay out? At the front of the pack, Newgarden, McLaughlin, and Ferrucci drove past the pits as they opened on lap 109. Daly, running fourth, pitted, as did Robb, running in sixth. Among the others who joined them were O'Ward, Dixon, and Kirkwood.

In all, ten cars pitted on lap 109, and fourteen stayed out. There were now two different fuel strategies to get to the end of the race. Left to be determined was which one would be most beneficial.

At the start of lap 114, racing resumed, and McLaughlin squeezed past Newgarden on the inside into Turn One. But, deeper back, Marco Andretti, one of the drivers who had just pitted, wobbled several times, the back end wanting to break free and spin toward the wall. After nearly catching his car several times, Andretti finally lost it, his car spinning lazily, halfway around, until it backed into the SAFER barrier. The hit wasn't hard, but it caused enough damage to end his race and continue the "Andretti Curse."

For the Andretti Global team, a bad day had just gotten worse. Marco's No. 98 was the team's third car to find the wall in the race, and while Herta was still circling at the back of the race many laps in arrears, their lone shot at victory was down to Kirkwood in his No. 27 car, currently in nineteenth position.

With little damage to Andretti's car, the cleanup was brief, and racing continued on lap 118, with the running order at the top being McLaughlin, Newgarden, Ferrucci, Rossi, and Palou. Larson was right in the mix in sixth, followed by Castroneves, in his "Drive for Five," Canapino, Rasmussen, and Rahal rounding out the top ten. Outside the top ten, Power was twelfth, Dixon thirteenth, and O'Ward sixteenth.

As the sun rapidly set under the partly cloudy skies, drivers were very much racing in unknown circumstances. Rookies and veterans alike, none had raced under these conditions.

Shadows swept entirely over the front straight and Turn One. The glare from the sharp angle of the sun left the entry to Turn Two somewhat blind to the drivers, the treacherous curbing on the inside lurking to snare more victims. Then there was the setting sun in the eyes exiting Turn Three and entering Turn Four.

As for the track itself, it had cooled to ninety-four degrees, but the groove had rubbered in on the turns, helping grip. Conditions had moved to favor cars with less downforce. Those cars who had started the race with more downforce, particularly those who anticipated needing to navigate through traffic, were handicapped.

On lap 127, Newgarden got back around McLaughlin and resumed the lead of the race, but he wouldn't hold it for long. Having led when the yellow came out, first for Hunter-Reay and then again for Andretti, he, along with thirteen others, chose not to pit. Now out of fuel, they would all need to come in, this time under the green flag for the first time of the race.

Newgarden peeled off first, pitting on lap 130. If the race went green for the rest of the distance, he would need two more stops to make it to the end.

The very next lap, McLaughlin veered into the pits, bringing Larson and Canapino in tow. It was there where Larson's inexperience reared up and his race began to unravel.

Entering Pit Lane too quickly and with cold brakes, Larson jumped on the binders. He locked up and slid across the timing line, well above the Pit Lane speed limit. He was assessed a drive-through penalty, which when he served on lap 133, dropped him to twenty-second.

Ferrucci and Power were the last of the cars on the pit sequence strategy to come in, doing so on lap 133, leaving Dixon and O'Ward at the front of the race. VeeKay ran third, and Daly found himself right in the mix in fourth, with his strategic running mate most of the afternoon, Robb, just a bit further back in sixth.

Dixon and O'Ward traded the lead for a few laps before O'Ward gave up the point to pit on lap 137 in his Chevy-powered No. 5. Dixon, the master of fuel savings, stretched his run in his Honda-powered No. 9 four more laps, finally pitting on lap 141.

In the lead yet again, Daly went until lap 144 before he ducked into the pits. Both he and Dixon would need only one more stop to make the race distance. O'Ward, however, needed a few laps of caution to make it with just one more stop.

O'Ward didn't have to wait long for that yellow flag.

On lap 147, battling at the tail end of the pack, Power looked to overtake Rasmussen going into Turn One. They entered the corner two-wide, with Power on the outside. Knowing he was too late to make the overtake, Power breathed the throttle, and as a result, the center of gravity of his car shifted forward, off the rear end. Coupled with the dirty air coming off Rasmussen's car, Power lost control, spinning around and heavily impacting the Turn One wall, destroying the left side of his car.

While the caution flag benefited O'Ward and others, it did no favors for either Dixon or Daly, both of whom were on strategies that would still have them pitting once more, but without the need to run lean and save fuel.

During the extended caution period to clear the track of debris, IndyCar officials took advantage of the opportunity to sweep the track, clearing the marbles, tiny pieces of rubber that had scraped off tires. With those marbles cleared, drivers could race more easily side-by-side in the turns. It wouldn't be easy, by any stretch of the imagination, but it would be easier, with much more grip than if the track hadn't been swept.

Also, during the caution, Robb and Rasmussen pitted, among others, and as the green was about to come out again, Larson, already in twenty-first place, ahead of only Rahal, came in to top off his fuel. He'd still have to stop again, but his stop would be later in the race, and shorter in time, as he wouldn't have to wait for as much fuel to be delivered.

While the leader of the pack controls the speed of the cars during a yellow caution period, they don't control when the race resumes. That's done by race officials, and once the green flag waves, drivers receive radio messages of "Green, green, green!"—their cue to accelerate to race speed.

On a restart, the green flag ordinarily waves as the leading cars exit Turn Four, and, with the Speedway's long straightaway, it usually results in the leader being a sitting duck for the following car to ride up behind in the slipstream and then duck out for an overtaking move ahead of Turn One.

On this instance, Dixon led the field to green on this restart, and he was immediately swamped and overtaken by the Arrow McLarens of Rossi, on the outside, and O'Ward, on the inside. At that moment, as Rossi and O'Ward started to pull away, Dixon knew he needed something extra if he was going to beat those two cars to the checkered flag.

Behind the trio, cars fanned out three-wide, and Newgarden seized an opportunity to drift up high at the entrance to Turn One. Having already passed McLaughlin on the run up the straight, Newgarden dispatched Daly, VeeKay, and Palou on the outside before reaching the short chute, positioning himself into fourth. Further back, Ferrucci, Canapino, and Kirkwood resumed a spirited battle for ninth, still only a second and a half off the lead.

The next time around, O'Ward got around Rossi, and over the next dozen laps, they traded the lead several times. Not only were they trading the lead to save a little fuel, but both wanted to learn just exactly when they needed to time their passing maneuvers to complete an overtake by the time they reached the start/finish line. The way this 500 was shaping up, a final lap overtake for the win looked very possible, if not even probable.

Behind them, the rest of the top ten—Dixon, Newgarden, Palou, McLaughlin, VeeKay, Daly, Ferrucci, and Kirkland—were content to run in the slipstream, knowing every car would still need to pit one more time.

Rossi came into the pits first, on lap 169, with Canapino, who was running eleventh, following. Both would be right at the limit of making it to the end if the race stayed under the green flag to the end. Rossi's stop was perfect, and his crew sent him back out to win the race. Canapino's stop, however, was not perfect.

Caught speeding in Pit Lane, Canapino was penalized, requiring him to come back in for a drive-through penalty. Starting twenty-second and benefiting from great pit stops by his Juncos Hollinger crew, Canapino had competed in the top half of the field for almost the entire race. Now a lap down and once again in twenty-second position, all he could do was run out the remaining laps to the finish.

Two laps later, Newgarden, McLaughlin, and Daly came into the pits for their last stops. Newgarden's crew was perfect, and he left Pit Lane ahead of both his teammate and Daly. These three cars would be free to run full-rich fuel settings, which produced maximum power for the engine, until the end of the race, perhaps giving them a slight advantage over Rossi, who was right on the edge of making it to the end.

On the next circuit, Dixon and O'Ward pulled in, and on the track, Rossi squeaked by Newgarden, resuming their running order before the pit stop sequence. Now, the chase was on to see where they stood relative to Dixon and O'Ward, who were leaving the pits and on the warm-up lane.

Dixon's Ganassi crew, consistently one of the best in the business, had conducted their stop flawlessly, and when he merged back onto the track on the backstretch with O'Ward in tow, he was in front of Rossi and Newgarden, accelerating up to full speed.

Rossi flew around Turn Two, and when he exited, O'Ward was just merging onto the backstretch to his left. Riding his momentum out of the turn, Rossi veered to his left, Newgarden shadowing his every move, to get the benefit of following in O'Ward's slipstream. With O'Ward still coming to speed, Rossi and Newgarden quickly got around him and set their sights on Dixon, less than two seconds in front of them.

While Rossi had momentum off Turn Two and the benefit of a slipstream from O'Ward, Newgarden, too, enjoyed a fast exit from Turn Two and had the benefit of a strong slipstream from Rossi. Using that, as Rossi fanned out to the right to pass O'Ward, Newgarden jumped at the opportunity and overtook them both. Heading into Turn Three, the defending champion was on a march forward.

Although he was running twelfth on the leaderboard, Dixon was the front car of those who had pitted, and he and his team knew the eleven cars in front of him still needed to stop for fuel. Only twenty-six laps remained in his quest for a second 500 victory, but did he have enough speed to see it through?

⚑×⚑

Around Turns Three and Four, Newgarden closed the distance on Dixon, and heading down the frontstretch, the crowd roared as Newgarden made his move on the inside, forging his way to the front well before they turned into Turn One. Dixon, however, wasn't done yet.

Dixon returned the favor, overtaking Newgarden while Kirkwood pitted from the lead. Kirkwood had suffered two poor pit stops earlier, one of which resulted in a drive-through penalty. Still, he had persevered in the lone Andretti Global car that hadn't crashed on the day. His Andretti crew delivered on the stop, and he resumed racing in eighth, his dreams for Indy 500 glory still very much alive.

As Kirkwood pitted and then Ilott, the lead fell into the hands of Indianapolis's own Carpenter, and the crowd, growing more and more tense as the laps wound down, roared its approval. After three laps, though, Carpenter, his car needing fuel, relinquished the point and pitted, which left Larson holding the reins in the world's biggest race.

If the crowd was excited with the incredibly competitive racing and popular favorites leading before, they were over the top now. With many fans not knowing Larson still had to pit for fuel to make the finish, the thought he might pull off a victory in the 500 in his first-ever IndyCar race had them on their feet, cheering madly as his car zoomed past.

Behind Larson on the track was fellow rookie Simpson, who also needed to pit, and then the four cars of Newgarden, Dixon, and the two Arrow McLaren teammates, Rossi and O'Ward. Each of those four were perfectly positioned to race for the win.

Trailing those four cars came the cars of Kirkwood, Palou, VeeKay, McLaughlin, Daly, Ferrucci, and Rasmussen. Those drivers knew they were in tougher positions. To race for the win, they needed to improve upon their positions, and they needed to do it quickly. In the seat of his No. 3, polesitter McLaughlin, dominant last weekend in qualifying and leading the race effortlessly early, watched the race slip from his grasp.

Once Simpson pitted on lap 186, the race switched to an all-out run to the finish, reminiscent of the local "trophy dashes" so many of the drivers took up in their early racing years.

Newgarden had complained of front-end vibrations over his last two stints, but while it might have been a bit problematic for driving, it wasn't hampering his speed. He and Rossi looked to have a slight advantage at the front. Dixon and O'Ward were lurking right behind them, calculating their time to pounce.

O'Ward had struggled with his car throughout the day, unable to make an impression on the race for the first half. It was then he decided he needed to take matters into his own hands and push as hard as he could, regardless of the potential consequences. His determination had pulled his car to the front, but his day had been filled with near misses and close calls, particularly in the ever-tricky Turn Two.

Now O'Ward set out to make his final moves. First up was an overtake on Dixon to place him third. Next up was his teammate, Rossi.

Teammates work collaboratively when they can . . . and when it suits them. And racing is very much a team sport. There's the pit crew as part of the team, and multi-car teams also benefit from sharing information, particularly as it relates to chassis setup. But on the racetrack, drivers give no quarter to their rivals, and in the world of auto racing, there are no bigger rivals than your teammates. In cars that should be, at least theoretically, identical, it's important to be better than your teammate.

For six laps, while Newgarden and Rossi swapped the lead every couple of circuits, O'Ward stalked, using the slipstream to edge himself closer and closer. As the laps ticked away, Rossi, the first of the leaders to have pitted, started receiving messages that he needed to drive to a fuel consumption number. He wasn't free to race full rich to the end, not if a caution flag didn't come out.

Having pitted later, Newgarden had less of a fuel worry. The best of them all, of course, was O'Ward, who pitted three laps later than his teammate and one lap later than Newgarden.

At the end of lap 193, approaching the yard of bricks, Newgarden swung toward the inside to overtake Rossi. O'Ward, having patiently waited his time, decided it was time for him to pounce too.

Together the No. 2 and No. 5 cars screamed down the inside of the straightaway, with O'Ward just making it past his teammate as they entered Turn One. With seven laps remaining in the 500, the decisive moves made it feel like it was now a two-race race. By Turn Three, Rossi had fallen back into the grasp of Dixon, still trailing in fourth.

Two laps later, coming off Turn Four on lap 195, O'Ward got a huge run on Newgarden and slipped by on the inside to take the lead. The crowd erupted in support of the immensely popular driver, and fans not already standing were on their feet as O'Ward led Newgarden into Turn One.

Newgarden, however, as befitting a defending champion, wasn't finished. Like O'Ward on the lap before, he capitalized on a big run off Turn Four and rode his momentum past to retake the lead. Only four laps—ten miles and sixteen turns—remained.

Coming off Turn Four on lap 197, Newgarden defended the lead in earnest, weaving left off the turn to break the slipstream for those following, careful all along not to place his tires over the white line that denoted the Pit Lane entry. That move helped him fend off O'Ward entering Turn One.

Three laps to go and the crowd was at a fever pitch, their shouts heard above the roar of the twenty-two cars still circulating. Around the track, spectators stood, straining their necks to see the cars approach and then pass, and then watching the video boards until the cars came back around again in a little more than forty seconds.

Again, Newgarden exited Turn Four and dipped low on the track to complete lap 198. For his part, O'Ward was content to let Newgarden lead and didn't push the issue heading into Turn One. O'Ward lifted gently off the throttle, conceding Turn One to Newgarden, biding his time to make one final overtake to which Newgarden couldn't respond.

O'Ward knifed his way through Turns One and Two, his hands busily correcting his car, and found himself closely rapidly on Newgarden down the backstretch. Still, he felt it was too early to make an overtake on Newgarden as the Penske driver would have too much time, more than a lap, to counter. So O'Ward lifted as the two cars approached the entrance to Turn Three, nose-to-tail.

Just as O'Ward planned, Newgarden led off Turn Four and immediately swung low again to break the draft. O'Ward followed briefly, then changed his tactics from the previous few laps. He veered his car to the right and slipped by Newgarden on the outside to take the white flag, signifying the final lap of the race.

The crowd exploded in cheers. The 108th running of the Indianapolis 500 was now a one-lap shootout for the biggest prize in motorsports.

Newgarden followed closely behind entering Turn One but had to drop back slightly to get better airflow over his car to grip the track. Into Turn Two, O'Ward's lead was two car lengths. Another three separated Newgarden from Rossi. Following behind were the Ganassi teammates of Dixon and Palou.

Exiting Turn Two, O'Ward dove dramatically to the inside of the track, well into the exit of the warm-up lane. Newgarden, needing the benefits of the slipstream, followed suit, and mirrored O'Ward's move up the track and along the outside wall.

With fifteen feet between them at nearly 220 miles per hour, the two hurtled down the backstretch. Halfway down the five-eighths of a mile straight, O'Ward again moved low, near the white line at the edge of the track. He was not going to let Newgarden by him on the inside of Turn Three. If an overtake was going to happen, it would have to be on the high side, the longer and considerably more dangerous side.

Low and on the inside of the racetrack, however, wasn't the preferred entry to the turn. Newgarden, closing rapidly on O'Ward with the benefit of the aerodynamic draft, knew his best chance to overtake presented itself now.

With a slight turn of his steering wheel, Newgarden moved to the outside of the track. O'Ward, seeing Newgarden's move in his mirrors, moved to the right, too, but left some racing room.

Angling their cars into Turn Three, the two cars were side by side. By the apex, though, Newgarden, riding the momentum from the fast run down the back straight, was in front. Exiting Turn Three, both cars moved out toward the wall, ready to race through Turn Four for the final time.

Through Turn Four, Newgarden's advantage grew to four car lengths. Dipping low once again to break the draft and with a glance in his mirrors, Newgarden knew his advantage would carry to the line. Drifting up slightly to the middle of the track, he lifted his right hand off the steering wheel and pumped it, his index finger in the air signifying being first.

He took the checkered flag just in front of O'Ward, and as he drove into Turn One, he screamed into his radio, "Let's go! Let's go!" In his pit stall, as his team jumped in celebration, Newgarden's wife, Ashley, covered her mouth in shock, surprise, and wonderment, shouting, "Oh my God!" and jumped into an embrace.

Last year, Newgarden had won his first Indy 500 on this twelfth attempt. Twelve months later, he had won his second, the first winner of consecutive 500s in twenty-two years.

Like he did the year before, Newgarden drove past the Pit Lane entry and came to a stop at the yard of bricks. There, he was met by his euphoric crew, all of them jumping up and down, raucously celebrating with hugs and high fives.

The packed grandstand cheered, and the mass of standing spectators prepped for what they knew was coming next.

After celebrating with his crew, Newgarden sprinted over to the outside wall, where a break in the retaining fence allowed for a quick escape from the track in case of an emergency. Newgarden used it for a different purpose entirely.

Going through the fence, Newgarden moved into the crowd, celebrating not only his victory but the event itself—350,000 people in attendance and millions watching on television around the world. Newgarden knew the Indy 500 was just as much about the people, the traditions, the history, and the legacy as it was the driver and the race. He had just stamped himself into that history once again, and he was a popular champion.

While Newgarden and his team were celebrating, O'Ward came to a stop in his pit box. Unbuckling his safety harness, he climbed halfway out of his race car before stopping. He rested his helmeted head on the top of his aeroscreen, heartbroken for having come so close yet to have ended up once again in second place—the second time in the past three years. He would have another year to wait, and dream.

⚑✕⚑

After celebrating in and among the crowd on the frontstretch, Newgarden returned to his car, and together they were rolled onto the Victory Lane platform. There, he rode the lift to its elevated position, affording the crowd a better view.

Greeting him was The Captain, Roger Penske, who reached into the cockpit and shook his driver's hand. As the owner of the Indianapolis Motor Speedway, Penske is now present at all celebrations in Victory Lane. But this one, of course, was more special, as he was the car owner too, and now celebrating his twentieth Indy 500 victory.

Next up, Newgarden was bestowed the winner's wreath, which he slung over his head, his left shoulder and arm through the middle. Then came the bottle of milk—whole milk as he had previously chosen.

Through it all, Newgarden beamed. Over the past year, he had experienced all the trappings of being an Indy 500 winner, and while busy and often the focal point of attention from fans and media alike, it had been a positive experience. Then came the push-to-pass controversy and all the negative attention that came from it.

Since the scandal had broken the month before, the lead-up to this year's Indy 500 had a feel of redemption to it, and Newgarden and Team Penske had worked hard to avoid the distractions and focus on the task at hand in defending his victory. In the end, they had succeeded, and Newgarden was effusive in praise for his team, saying, "Unbelievable! I'm so proud of the team. They crushed it. I mean, they crushed it!"

In Pit Lane, Larson climbed from his car, somewhat satisfied with having completed the 500 miles. But, as good as his preparation for the race had been, he was haunted somewhat by his two mistakes that led to just an eighteenth-place finish. However, he didn't have time to stop and reflect.

Already late for the start of the Coca-Cola 600, Larson was quickly escorted to a waiting helicopter at the south end of the infield. There, he hopped in to make the first leg of his commute to Charlotte.

Unfortunately, all the plans for "the double" proved, in the end, to be for naught. By the time Larson got to Charlotte, rain had stopped the running of the Coca-Cola 600. Larson got to the track during the delay and was ready to relieve Justin Allgaier, who had started the race in his absence. The rain persisted, though, and NASCAR officials never restarted the race, instead officially ending it as it stood when the rain had started.

As darkness fell on the Indianapolis Motor Speedway, fans filed out of the grounds, still buzzing about the race. It had been a long day for everyone, and fatigue was right around the corner as the colossal traffic jam of humanity began its journey home. But, for now, there was still the excitement of a thrilling race and, for a great many, thoughts of next year's race were formulated.

The margin of victory between Newgarden and O'Ward was just 0.3417 seconds, and Newgarden's last-lap overtake for the win, while being the second in two years, was just the fourth-ever last-lap pass in the race's history.

In total, there were a record sixteen leaders of the 500, and each one of those leaders finished the entire 200 laps. Between them, they exchanged the lead forty-nine times, the fourth-most lead changes in 500 history.

In addition to action at the front of the field, the competition proved fierce throughout the field. Despite the relatively large amount of attrition—eleven cars fell out of the race—there were 649 overtakes in the race, the most since 2017.

Final Running Order of the 108th Indianapolis 500
1. Josef Newgarden, 200 laps
2. Pato O'Ward, 200 laps
3. Scott Dixon, 200 laps
4. Alexander Rossi, 200 laps
5. Alex Palou, 200 laps
6. Scott McLaughlin, 200 laps
7. Kyle Kirkwood, 200 laps
8. Santino Ferrucci, 200 laps
9. Rinus VeeKay, 200 laps
10. Conor Daly, 200 laps
11. Callum Ilott, 200 laps
12. Christian Rasmussen, 200 laps
13. Christian Lundgaard, 200 laps
14. Takuma Sato, 200 laps
15. Graham Rahal, 200 laps
16. Sting Ray Robb, 200 laps
17. Ed Carpenter, 200 laps
18. Kyle Larson, 200 laps
19. Romain Grosjean, 200 laps
20. Helio Castroneves, 200 laps
21. Kyffin Simpson, 200 laps
22. Agustin Canapino, 199 laps
23. Colton Herta, 170 laps (contact)
24. Will Power, 145 laps (contact)
25. Marco Andretti, 113 laps (contact)

26. Ryan Hunter-Reay, 93 laps (contact)
27. Felix Rosenqvist, Felix, 55 laps (mechanical)
28. Linus Lundqvist, 27 laps (contact)
29. Katherine Legge, 22 laps (mechanical)
30. Marcus Armstrong, 6 laps (mechanical)
31. Tom Blomqvist, 0 laps (contact)
32. Pietro Fittipaldi, 0 laps (contact)
33. Marcus Ericsson, 0 laps (contact)

MONDAY, MAY 27, 2024

Victory Celebration

The 2024 Victory Celebration took place at the JW Marriott in downtown Indianapolis, where drivers, team members, spouses, guests, and fans gathered to recognize the accomplishments of everyone over the month of May.

As per tradition, the prize purse from the Indianapolis 500 was announced during the gala, and, for the third consecutive year, the total purse of $18,456,000 established a new record. Josef Newgarden's $4,288,000 payout, bolstered by the $440,000 rollover prize from BorgWarner for winning in back-to-back years, also established a new record.

The purse for the Indy 500 was composed of awards from both the Indianapolis Motor Speedway and IndyCar, as well as other special awards from sponsors. In addition, it also included a portion of IndyCar's Leader Circle payouts to the twenty-two teams who earned the designation based on last season's overall championship results. Thus, despite not qualifying for the race, Dale Coyne Racing and its driver, Siegel, were awarded $505,500.

Conor Daly, who drove for Dreyer & Reinbold Racing and Cusick Motorsports, was the highest-finishing one-off effort at the race, finishing tenth after leading twenty-two laps. His team earned $159,000.

Ed Carpenter Racing's Christian Rasmussen was the highest-finishing rookie in twelfth place, after running in the top ten for much of the race. Despite his high finish, however, he was not named Rookie of the Year.

That award was almost certainly going to Kyle Larson all along, as he impressed in qualifying sixth and contended for much of the race until incurring his Pit Lane penalty with just seventy laps remaining. Larson's Rookie of the Year bonus of $50,000 boosted his eighteenth-place payout to $178,000.

Closing the evening, Newgarden was gracious in his winner's speech, saying, "I just want to congratulate my competitors; I think that's the first thing I want to say tonight. Everybody in this room that raced in this race, whether it's, you know, crew members or it's the drivers, I think you all deserve to be the winner of this race, just to be there at that track, to put in the effort, and to go the distance is not an easy feat.

"Pato, specifically, my goodness, what a champion you are, my friend. A complete champion. This is not our first race. We have had many duels. And I hope we have many more. And I'm sure the scores will change much more in the future. We're going to find out together. But you are a great competitor, one of the best in the world. We're lucky to have you in IndyCar.

"The race that we had at the end; I don't think anyone knew how it was going to unfold. It just happened to work out for us, the timing and all that, but you also deserved to win that race."

At the end of the evening, the crowd dispersed in different directions. For those competing in the IndyCar Series, it was the end of a physically and emotionally exhausting two-and-a-half weeks. However, there wasn't much time to rest.

Crews and cars were already on the way to Detroit, the next round in the IndyCar Series season. Practice for that race, run on the streets of downtown Detroit, would begin in just four days.

While there might not be time to rest, there was still time to dream about next year's Indianapolis 500. Preparations for "The Greatest Spectacle in Racing" never really stop, not for the Indianapolis Motor Speedway, the race teams, or race fans. They all hoped to be back to chase those dreams next May, with the 109th running of the Indianapolis 500 just 363 days away.

Payouts for the 108th Running of the Indianapolis 500
1. Josef Newgarden, $4,288,000
2. Pato O'Ward, $1,050,500
3. Scott Dixon, $835,000
4. Alexander Rossi, $688,000
5. Alex Palou, $614,000
6. Scott McLaughlin, $781,500
7. Kyle Kirkwood, $568,000
8. Santino Ferrucci, $568,500
9. Rinus VeeKay, $563,500
10. Conor Daly, $159,000
11. Callum Ilott, $538,500
12. Christian Rasmussen, $128,000
13. Christian Lundgaard, $537,000
14. Takuma Sato, $119,500
15. Graham Rahal, $537,000
16. Sting Ray Robb, $228,300
17. Ed Carpenter, $510,500
18. Kyle Larson, $178,000
19. Romain Grosjean, $517,500
20. Helio Castroneves, $102,000
21. Kyffin Simpson, $158,300
22. Agustín Canapino, $511,000
23. Colton Herta, $513,000
24. Will Power, $543,000
25. Marco Andretti, $102,000
26. Ryan Hunter-Reay, $102,000
27. Felix Rosenqvist, $514,000
28. Linus Lundqvist, $508,500
29. Katherine Legge, $158,800
30. Marcus Armstrong, $156,300
31. Tom Blomqvist, $156,300

32. Pietro Fittipaldi, $507,500
33. Marcus Ericsson, $507,500

Nolan Siegel and Dale Coyne Racing with HMD, $505,500

ACKNOWLEDGMENTS

First and foremost, I would like to thank my wife of thirty years, Lori. She's always been on "Team Ray," even on those occasions when I behave like maybe I shouldn't. Over our more than thirty years together, she's been my biggest fan and steadiest advocate, blessing me with unconditional love and empathetic compassion at every step and turn in our journey together. She gives me strength daily, and I'm forever grateful.

Thank you, too, to our children, Olivia and Raymond. It's been the greatest honor of my life watching them grow to be the people they are and will be, and they inspire me daily.

A big "THANKS" also goes out to my extended family, including my father, Ray, my mother Helen, and Ruth, Tom, Colleen, Noah, Audrey, Eli, and Sophie. Also, I want to add those who are no longer with us but never forgotten, including my mother, Irene, and Lori's mother, Alice.

I owe a continued debt of gratitude to Fran Carpentier, the "Godmother," who has ushered me through the entanglement of book publishing and promotion like only a renowned expert as she can.

Importantly, thank you to my editor, Cortney Donelson, whose feedback makes me a better writer while not crushing my fragile writer's ego, as well as the entire team over at Morgan James Publishing, including David Hancock, Jim Howard, and Gayle West. Without you all, this book never happens.

Most of all, I would like to thank you, the reader. I hope you enjoyed the book, and I encourage you to leave your authentic review at any bookseller's site. Thank you for spending your time with me, this book, and my story of the 2024 Indianapolis 500. I'm grateful.

#PunchTodayInTheFace

ABOUT THE AUTHOR

Ray Hartjen is a writer and musician who lives in Mission Viejo, California, with his wife, Lori, and their goldendoodle, Quinn.

In a professional career that has spanned parts of five decades, Ray has pivoted on many occasions, from investment banking to pharmaceuticals, from consumer electronics to SaaS software. The constant throughout his career path, however, has been storytelling.

In the past, Ray has been a frequent source for quotes from the national media on both the consumer electronics and retail industries. Additionally, as a contributor to several online outlets and platforms, including his rayhartjen.com site, he has spun his fair share of yarn on topics as far-ranging as sports—primarily football, hockey, and auto racing—and business, particularly revenue team functions, like sales and marketing. Ray's previous works include being the coauthor of *Immaculate: How the Steelers Saved Pittsburgh* and the author *Me, Myself & My Multiple Myeloma*, both published by Morgan James Publishing and available wherever books are sold.

Diagnosed with multiple myeloma in March 2019, Ray is a cancer fighter every day of the week that ends in a *y*. And with the soundtrack of life playing continuously in his head, Ray also performs and records with his two-piece acoustic band, the Chronic Padres. A native of Texas, Ray holds an undergraduate degree from Eastern Kentucky University and an MBA from the University of Washington.

One to always welcome an opportunity to chat with others, please feel free to connect with Ray at www.rayhartjen.com, on X @RayHartjen, on TikTok at @rayhartjen5, or via email at rayhartjen@gmail.com.

A free ebook edition is available with the purchase of this book.

To claim your free ebook edition:

1. Visit MorganJamesBOGO.com
2. Sign your name CLEARLY in the space
3. Complete the form and submit a photo of the entire copyright page
4. You or your friend can download the ebook to your preferred device

Print & Digital Together Forever.

Snap a photo   Free ebook   Read anywhere

www.ingramcontent.com/pod-product-compliance
Lightning Source LLC
Jackson TN
JSHW020905310325
81701JS00001B/2